One Man's Education

An Autobiographical Scrap-book

by

Allan Bradley

The cover design Two-way pattern *symbolises the thought that educating others and continually being educated are interlocking processes.*

© Copyright Allan Bradley 1987

ISBN 1 85072 024 X

Facsimile printed by
William Sessions Limited
The Ebor Press
York, England

ONE MAN'S EDUCATION

CONTENTS

List of Illustrations

Photo no.1 by A.F.Dobson; no.21 by M.J.Wardell.

Diagrams

All photographs (other than nos.1,2! and, possibly, 26) and all drawings
and diagrams, including the idea for the cover design, by A.B.

iii

Acknowledgements

The suggestion that there should be a book about Kamusinga, and that I should write it, came first, in 1980, from Henry Owuor Anyumba, to whom I am grateful for the stimulus. The original version was undertaken in 1981, but had many defects. Between 1981 and 1985 I was subjected to further stimuli, though too busy to do any writing, while participating in the affairs of the Northamptonshire Education Committee, and in particular in a working party on "The Curriculum". I am grateful to all those fellow-members, officers and inspectors who kept me thinking and learning as well as talking. I also came to reflect on the early days of Kingswood School, where the experience of collaboration with a new group of colleagues gave me further cause for gratitude.

I wish to thank Dr. Eric Ogilvie, Director of Nene College, Northampton, for his painstaking and detailed critique of the original version, and Mr. Michael Henley, until recently County Education Officer for Northamptonshire, for his equally generous reading of the penultimate draft. Each of them has helped me to improve the final text. An earlier draft of the Kamusinga section has also been read by a number of former students, (now middle-aged gentlemen of some consequence,) whose encouragement has been very rewarding.

The quotations from E.B.Castle's "Growing up in East Africa" (1966) are made with the permission of Mrs. Ann Castle and the Oxford University Press. In Chapter 2. Part 1. (Preliminary) I have drawn quite extensively on the Binns Report, published in 1953 by the Nuffield Foundation on behalf of the then Colonial Office. I am indebted to the Library of the Institute of Education of London University for the loan of a copy, which I have found most helpful. I wish to thank the Friends United Meeting, of Richmond, Indiana, for providing me with a copy of the Elliott-Lampman Report, fom which I have also quoted extensively.

Finally, and most of all, I thank my wife, Mary, who not only sustained me in many a stressful situation, especially in Kamusinga days, but has also shown great forbearance in tolerating my more recent pre-occupation with the process of writing. Without her Kamusinga would have been a lesser place, - and its early history would not, at any rate by me, have been recorded.

A.B.
Rothwell, Northamptonshire
February, 1987.

FORE-WORD.

One day, as we sat waiting for a committee meeting to begin, my neighbour, (a consultant surgeon,) remarked to me: "I think if you had a transverse section cut through any portion of your anatomy, it would lay bare the word 'Education'." Rather like a bit of Blackpool rock, I suppose.

It is true that I have been involved, from my earliest years, and still am, as a beneficiary of education in many forms and in many places. And for much of my life I have also found myself with responsibilities for the education of others, first as a teacher, then as a Head, (in which capacity I helped to found two new schools, one in Kenya and one in England,) and more recently as an elected member of a Local Education Authority. The exercise of those responsibilities has at the same time laid me open to further personal education.

So this book is about the education I have received and the education I have helped to provide: in a nut-shell, about what I like to call my "two-way-education".

1. – A.B., 1921

2. – A.B. and M.B., 1942

3. – A.B., 1982

1. My basic education. Phase 1.

My formal basic education began just over a month after the outbreak of the First World War. I was 4¾. I went with my friend Alan Dobson and his cousin Joan to "Miss Crane's School" at the end of the road where we lived in Deal. It was, and still is, (though with some other function,) a large red brick building. I have only a vague recollection of what we did. There was a large folding board, which, when it was opened out, had a lot of letters on it, either on hooks or in slots, and the letters were made to congregate in small clusters, using imaginary transport such as aeroplanes, cars, etc. to make up words like cat, sat and mat. I don't remember that reading ever presented difficulties to me, but I cannot remember more of the learning process than that folding board. I must have performed reasonably well, I suppose, since I still have in my possession a book prize entitled "Eric, a Golden Heart", by Cecilia Selby Lowndes, which was awarded to Allan Bradley as a Prize for General Improvement in Kindergarten Class. It is signed by M. S. Crane, of Wellington School, Deal, and dated, Dec. 21st 1915. I do remember, rather hazily, one very patriotic occasion, when all the little boys were dressed in red crepe paper uniforms lined with newspaper, and formed into a marching band. I was much the fattest and rosiest and least musically gifted, as far as instruments went, so I marched at the rear beating a little drum, to the accompaniment of frivolous adult comments to the effect that I was really Lloyd George. I hope we were not a part of Kitchener's drive for volunteers, particularly since, when conscription came along, my Father, Howard, and his two youngest brothers, David and Ronald, were all conscientious objectors.

By mid 1916 the three brothers had all been before tribunals. My uncles served with the Friends Ambulance Unit in France, while my Father was seconded from the F.A.U. to the Y.M.C.A., and we moved from Deal to Southsea to be near his unit. But it was not long before he was sent overseas to Malta, and subsequently, after a short leave, to Salonika. So my Mother, Meg, was left in Southsea, with a "companion help" and 3 children, – myself, my sister Margaret, 2 years younger, and brother Newton, who was born in November, 1914.

My formal education continued in the junior classes of Portsmouth High School for Girls, where I remained for two years, and appear to have continued to make good academic progress. I even started Latin and was known in class as Marcus. There were, of course, a number of other small boys in those junior classes. I still have some of my reports from those days. Evidently I had one very irritating habit. My eye tended to wander from the teacher, and gaze inattentively away through the window. Teacher would pounce upon me with a request to know what she had just been saying - and I always knew, apparently. It seems that my daughter inherited this tendency, because she not infrequently brought home school reports which duplicated my own. But I had to work quite hard, and I remember having to struggle on Saturdays to write compositions with a pen and ink, and it was a real problem to avoid blotting both myself and my copy-book. The smell of an ink-bottle still sometimes reminds me of those days.

We spent summer and autumn terms of 1918 in Ventnor, where we had passed the long summer holidays of 1917. The reason for the move I do not know, but I suspect that it had something to do with the apartment situation in Southsea. I was sent as a weekly boarder to a local private school, the name of which I shall not mention, since it was not a very fine establishment. The principal shall also remain anonymous, as he did not have much use for me, and I seem to have been a bit of a nuisance. I do not remember any of the lessons, except chanting tables and trying to copy, with much frustration, a printed bell-shape, which was the sum of the artistic education offered.

As my Father was still away, although the Armistice had been signed, his eldest brother, Wilfred, sought the advice of a very worthy Quaker as to what had better be done with me. I still have the letter in which it was suggested that I be sent to Stramongate School, Kendal, the oldest of all the Quaker Schools, having been founded in the 17th century. So my Mother took me on the seven hour journey from Euston to Kendal and left me there as a boarder. Stramongate School was at the lower end of the street of that name, not far from the bridge. Half of the older boys were housed there, at School House. The younger boys, including me, were in Eddington House, not far away, and close to the River Kent. Eddington House was named after the famous scientist, who was a former student of the school. The remainder of the older boys were boarded further away. alongside the headmaster, at Dalton House, named after a still more famous scientist former pupil. On Sunday afternoons we were able to exchange houses on an individual basis and go and have high tea at School or Dalton Houses, which we much appreciated.

I am afraid I was still something of a nuisance, and was always getting into scrapes. Legend had it that I held one unenviable record. The housemaster was an enormous sixteen stone man, who was an accomplished goal-keeper and wicket-keeper, as a result of which he had very horny hands. He also wore a signet ring bearing his initials. One evening I was found misbehaving in the dormitory, whereupon the housemaster laid me across his knee in my pyjamas and imprinted his initials with much enthusiasm, 44 times, upon my bottom, while I yelled the place down.

4

But Stramongate left marks of quite a different kind on me, and
I have reason to think kindly about my two years there, despite
various vicissitudes.   Academically I did well enough, as is
evidenced by the reports which I still have.   But the two
experiences which have meant most to me were in a different
mode.   The first of these was my introduction to a Quaker
Meeting, and the second was my introduction to the Lake
District and mountains.

I must not give the impression that the impact of Quakerism was
a religious one.   In fact, it was rather bizarre.   On Sundays
we wore eton suits, (bum-freezers), with hard eton collars and
elusive studs, and mortar boards with blue and white tassels.
I seem to remember sitting, very bored, in meeting, and
plaiting together the strands of the tassels.   The important
thing was not the impact, but the contact, which had much to do
with the subsequent course of my education and of my
professional career.

Stramongate School had no Sixth Form, so a good many of the
boys went on from there to other Quaker schools, including
Bootham School at York.   Such transfers often took place at
the age of about 13.   It was my Mother, I feel sure, who
determined that I should eventually go to Bootham, and the
seeds of that determination must have been laid in my early
days at Stramongate.   And to Bootham I went, though not direct
from Stramongate.   And it was at Bootham that seminal elements
of my education were sown.

But to return to Stramongate.   In days before the war the
custom had been for the whole school to go forth on a three day
expedition into the near-by Lake District.   But by 1919
economy dictated something more modest.   However we did all
set off early one morning for a day-trip, it must have been in
the summer of that year.   So I made my first acquaintance with
the Lakes, - from the top of a horse-drawn brake, - the "char-
à-bancs" of those days.   We began by visiting Skelwith Force,
and then continued over Dunmail Rise to Wythburn, beside
Thirlmere.   Here we took to our feet, and climbed to the top
of Helvellyn, to admire the memorial to the faithful hound who
watched beside the body of his master for three weeks after the
master died.   We gazed   down to the Red Tarn in the awesome
amphitheatre below.   It staggers me now to think that we then
scrambled along Striding Edge and down into Grisedale, - a
swarm of boys, many of us no older than 9.   It was not a
bright day, in fact it was a bit dismal;   but I remember
standing in a damp shirt in Grisedale Tarn, - because having a
bathe was the thing to do.   Afterwards we trudged down the
dale and along to a hotel in Grasmere, where we had a sumptuous
high tea.   I guess it must have been dark by the time we got
back to Kendal.   It was many years after I left Stramongate

before I went to the Lakes again, but none of my later visits could compare with that first unforgettable outing.

My time at Stramongate ended in unfortunate fashion. When I arrived home for Christmas in 1920 it was remarked that I was suffering from an unpleasant skin complaint, which had evidently not been noticed by the school. So I was never sent back, and some time in the spring I was entered as a day boy in the Junior School of Dover College, where I remained until the end of the summer term, 1923.

Dover College was just celebrating its golden jubilee, having been founded in 1871, when it had 15 pupils, including my grandfather and his brother. A third brother, and the sons of all three, as of a sister, were all pupils in the school. A cousin of my Father's was still in the Senior School when I entered the Junior School, but when I left in 1923, without going up to the College, the school was for the first time without a Bradley. I cannot say that the Junior School did a lot for me educationally, although I made good academic progress, being good at Mathematics, Latin and French. I got the form prize for the top form, which gave me a bit of a swelled head. But the most significant thing about those 2½ years was that I lived at home, and went to school each day on the top of a Dover tram, together with my friend Douglas. I really became a Dovorian, like my forebears and my numerous cousins. Family played a large part in my life, and still does. In 1984 we enjoyed a heart-warming re-union with all those cousins, together with their partners and offspring and grandchildren. But it has to be recognized that the link with Dover has almost disappeared.

In September, 1923 I entered Bootham School, York. When I left, four years later, I was still a very callow, immature and ill-shapen youth. Yet those four years were a major determining factor in the whole of my subsequent experience. Not by the operation of the old-school-tie principle, although that was sometimes very helpful, but by my immersion in the very unusual ethos and philosophy of the school. It is therefore important that I should try to describe some of that ethos and philosophy.

But let me dispose at once of three opportunities which came my way largely because I had been at Bootham. The first was getting a place at Caius College, Cambridge without being interviewed by the College; this was because of the rapport which the school had with the college. The second was getting my first job as a teacher; this was because the Head of Leighton Park School asked the Head of Bootham if he could suggest a young teacher with a degree in German and French.

And the third was my second teaching job, in a school in the public sector where the Head was himself a former Bootham pupil and had gone to his Headship from a post at Leighton Park, so that my application probably attracted his notice a little more than some of the other scores which, in those sad days of the 'thirties, he received. Having admitted these three instances, I hope that in most respects my educational progress owes more to what I learned, than to where I learned it.

Bootham had just celebrated its centenary, and for the past 24 years it had been led by a remarkable Headmaster, Arthur Rowntree, who had also been on the staff of the school for 7 years before he became Head. The first impression he gave, especially to young boys, was of austerity and of moral rectitude. In the main corridor of the school there was an extremely accurate clock. Often, at break-times, he would be standing silently beside it, keenly watching us as we made our way to class. At 7.15.00 each morning it was the duty of a reeve, (prefect), to start ringing a ship's bell which hung beside the clock. 120 seconds later, no more, no less, the doors of the John Bright Library would be closed, if necessary by main force, and anybody still outside would be officially late, and excluded from "Silence", namely the daily assembly which began the day. And on the platform, in silent and impassive meditation, sat the Headmaster, while we puffed and panted to regain our breath after the mad scamper to beat the clock. Sometimes one had not had time even to complete one's dressing. I can remember an occasion when I had only succeeded in getting one arm into my waistcoat, and after we had been dis-missed was putting the matter to rights in the classroom, when in walked the Head, took a look at me, and said, rather sardonically I think : "Count late, Bradley," which. of course, meant the appropriate punishment. This could amount to anything from one to six. "One to six of the best ?" I hear you ask. No, one to six columns, according to how many times I had been late that term. "Columns?" Yes, columns of words copied in my best hand-writing in my "work-book" (provided for the purpose,) from the dictionary, beginning with the letter prescribed for the term. That meant about 20 words, the column(s) to be completed before next morning and submitted to form master for approval. If I was unfortunate to be late as many as 6 times in a term I would appear before the Head and get an hour's detention on Saturday afternoon. The same would happen if my cumulative score of columns reached 20 in a week. There was a sort of tariff for various standard offences, such as "7 beds" for misbehaviour in bedrooms. The surprising thing about all this, as well as the rest of the system of punishments in the schoool, is the contrast between the austerity of the regime and the virtual insignificance of the burden of punishments in use.

The moral effect was very considerable. I might add that the deterrent effect of the punishments was re-inforced by a sort of corporate responsibility in each class. Each week the number of columns against the members of a class was totted up, and if it came below a particular figure everyone in the class got a bonus of 3 columns, which simply meant that the first three columns of any punishment were excused. The bonus earned could be cumulative, so that it exceeded likely punishments ! Woe to any members of the class who went on the rampage and raised the weekly total so high as to cause the whole class to forfeit the bonus ! On the other hand, I remember that one term there were three classes whose bonuses had risen to over 30, - so they all had an extra half-holiday awarded. I have already indicated that we had "reeves", or prefects, who were also armed with sanctions. These consisted in requiring a miscreant to do so many "rounds". The miscreant had to make a certain number of circuits about the school playground. He did not have to run, and he was not supervised. He simply had to report that he had carried out the assignment. For more serious offences the punishment might be 10 or 15 rounds. But if the reeve wanted to be perverse he would require the miscreant to do one round, but having changed into games clothes.

The system thus stimulated a sense of responsibility, not only at personal, but also at corporate level. However, it was not the punishment system, or even the austerity, which did most to foster this sense of responsibility. When problems of real importance occurred they were dealt with on the basis of conversations between members of staff and individuals, and punishments were irrelevant. It was not the prospect of punishment which gave a boy butterflies in the stomach, but the prospect of what in school slang was called a "juice meeting", "juice" hinting at tears. From this circumstance it can be understood that the boy population of the school did not consist of a band of angels, or even prigs; they were no different from boys in any other school in the matter of mischief and other misdemeanours. However, it is a fact that I only remember one occasion when a boy, recently entered from another school, hinted at a dirty story; we were blessedly free from such, as from obscene graffiti.

One other example of Bootham austerity is perhaps worth mentioning. It was the accepted practice that every morning began with a plunge into a cold bath, no matter what the season, and the weekly routine bath-night was also automatically rounded off by a similar plunge. I do not think the system was ever enforced, but it was certainly practised. There might occasionally be some snide remarks between boys, if someone was suspected of dodging the "cold". I remember an occasion in mid-winter when one rather plump and timorous youth was alleged to have emerged from the bath with a little belt of ice crystals about his middle. At a less rigorous level we were all expected to make our own beds, turning the matress each day, and we had to clean our own shoes, and have them passed as acceptably clean by an overseeing house-reeve.

But I have dwelt on these aspects of the school, not to emphasise the effectiveness of the discipline, but in order to set off the notably liberal aspects which characterised the school. And these emanated, of course, from the staff and their relationship with their students. There was nothing namby-pamby about this, and masters almost always addressed boys by their sur-names, and boys always addressed masters as "Sir".

There were twelve members of the teaching staff apart from the Head, and in September 1923 there were 144 boys, whose names were arranged each term in order of age, regardless of which class they might be in. I believe I started as 129 and finished up in 1927 as about 9. There were 5 classes leading up to General Certificate and they all had unusual names:- Middle Schoolroom at the bottom, then Upper Schoolroom, followed by Lower Senior, Middle Senior and Upper Senior. The last two both took the School Certificate exam. Above the Upper Senior was the College class, which was, of course, actually a Sixth Form. I found myself in the Lower Senior, though I used to go to Maths in the Middle Senior, because the subject was setted across the three Senior classes. The great thing about the Lower Senior classroom was that it had an unrivalled view, from the first floor, of the North West aspect of York Minster, a view which nobody who was in that class can ever forget. Except where setting was in operation , or p.e. or science subjects were on the time-table, teaching was done in the form base, which was where we also did our "prep" in the evenings. The Minster and its bells, in the ever changing light, formed a permanent backdrop to that year.

The curriculum of class-room teaching was conventional and, by modern standards, limited. There was no art or music on the time-table at Lower Senior level, nor any sort of craft subject. At Dover College Junior School I had never done any Science, so that I was out of my depth when Chemistry and Physics were on the time-table. In the Upper Senior, the following year, I was able to satisfy the London G.S.C. regulations, which required entry on the basis of a group of subjects, by taking maths and Latin, as well as French, instead of a Science. It was not until, in 1941, I was drafted into a class of trainee Naval radio mechanics, that I applied my mind seriously to Ohm's Law and six months of intensive instruction in further electrical mysteries. So one might fairly assume that I emerged from Bootham with a warped mental outlook.

I like to think, however, that this is not so, despite my almost complete lack of academic scientific qualifications, a claim which I must now explain and justify. And to do so I must mention an important Bootham institution and a remarkable man who worked at the heart of it. The institution was the Bootham School Natural History, Literary and Polytechnic Society, the earliest minute book of which is dated 1834, giving it a fair claim to be the oldest Society of its kind in England. And the man was John A. Dell, who, for most people, personified the Society. Meetings took place each week, on Tuesday evenings, I fancy. Anybody could attend, and at each meeting there might be anything from one to four papers presented, mostly by boys, but on special occasions by masters or even visitors. The range of subjects was great, including botany, zoology, astronomy, geology, conchology, entomology, chemistry, physics, photography and so on. And since the Society was so wide in its scope, we also had many talks on archaeology, brass-rubbing, and the like.

This very varied programme was one of the fruits of a policy which was often referred to by Arthur Rowntree, namely, the encouragement of the full and constructive use of leisure, (which A.R. always pronounced as though the first syllable were "lee"). Indeed. each of the talks at the weekly meetings was the result of work done by people in their free time. And most of them were illustrated by carefully prepared demonstrations or illustrations. I still have some lantern slides which I made to illustrate a talk on ecclesiastical costume in monumental brasses. Encouragement to take up one of these interests was very deliberately pursued, especially for new and younger boys, at the beginning of each school year. There was a so-called "exhortation meeting", at which the "curators" of each of these departments, discoursed upon the attractions of their activities and invited new recruits to join them. It has to be mentioned that most of these pursuits involved excursions on half-holiday afternoons, to woodlands, ponds, bogs, rivers, churches, ruined abbeys, archaeological excavations, and so on. As far as archaeology was concerned there was a further attraction. Excursions led by a very weighty Friend and former member of staff, namely A. Neave Brayshaw, usually ended with tea in some cafe. I have to admit that I joined the archaeology group. This eventually led to an interest in brasses, and I used much paper, heel-ball and elbow grease, both in term time and in the holidays, in collecting rubbings. Incidentally, in Neave Brayshaw I met the weighty Friend who had advised my uncle that I should be sent to Stramongate in 1919.

I must say that my own efforts in connection with the N.H. Society were very amateurish and immature. But I heard talks by fellow pupils whose knowledge was deep and scholarly, and whose leisure interest led, in fact, to their life work. I have already referred to the long history of the Society, which was the cradle for so many future scientists. At the time when I was at school, and the numbers were higher than ever before, there were 6 living Fellows of the Royal Society who started their scientific careers at Bootham, - and before the days when the school had anything like a Sixth Form.

So it was, that despite the lack of science in my own academic programme I acquired some acquaintance with science, and understanding of what it is all about. This was enhanced by a series of lectures given by John Dell as part of a so-called "post-matric" programme which was arranged to fill up the time between the end of the London exams and the publication of results, which normally arrived almost on the last day of term, at the end of July. This was a course on the history of the idea of evolution and covered the work of scientists from Buffon to Darwin.

Other flourishing leisure activities in which I took part were the Debating Society and the Essay Society, which met on alternate Thursday evenings. Of these the more significant was the Essay Society. A.R. almost always presided, and meetings began with the reading of the minutes and a reading, chosen by A.R., but read by one of the committee. There followed three or four essays written and read by members. After each reading verbal comments could be made by anybody, and the secretary subsequently had to write a sort of review for the aforementioned minutes. The essays had to be written on a particular kind of paper, and in due course they were bound and preserved in a series of volumes entitled "The Observer". So the habit of literary criticism was a regular experience, quite apart from the class-room.

Meetings for worship in the Quaker style were, of course, routine. We all walked through the city on Sunday mornings, (wearing bowler hats !) to the Friends' meeting at Clifford Street, where we occupied most of one side of the meeting, while the girls from the Mount, our sister school, occupied the other side. I cannot claim to remember much about any spiritual uplift I got from the meetings, but I daresay I was not the only one given to fantasising about the adjacent but oh, so distant, maidens. Indeed, one didn't know any of them. And this was one of the short-comings of Bootham, - that we were almost entirely without feminine society. I always maintain that, far from preserving us from distraction, many of us, myself included, probably spent more time and energy thinking, in total ignorance, about girls, than if we had all been schoolfellows. Bootham, like other boys' schools with which I have had to do, never seemed to me a good argument for single-sex education. The distance was not only emphasised on

Sunday mornings, but we sometimes went to another meeting in the evening, usually with a speaker, and again on Wednesday mornings, when the meeting was essentially for the two schools. From a religious point of view the most that could be said, as far as I personally was concerned is that I became accustomed to silent gatherings. But I cannot say that I used the silence very well; much less was I moved to be a Quaker.

Another shortfall in the experience provided by Bootham was that, as in other independent, particularly boarding, schools, there was no social mix. Indeed, this experience did not really come my way until I found myself on the lower deck in the Navy during the war. As to academic experience, almost any modern comprehensive school includes in its curriculum more art, craft and music than was available at Bootham while I was there. Once again, it was leisure provision which catered for these aspects of education, and not everybody took part in them. On the other hand, there was no lack of experience in literacy and literature, both in the classroom and in leisure activities.

But the most abiding experience of the school was the impact of the staff. Within the peculiarly austere framework which I have mentioned there was a notable atmosphere of expectation, encouragement and trust. The concept of obedience played virtually no role in the discipline of the school. One never heard a teacher say: "Who do you think you are?" or "Because I say so". This applied even to the Headmaster. There is an interesting story told by A. J. P. Taylor*, (who was the senior boy in my house when I first arrived,) about how he out-argued the Head so as to achieve liberty to explore York on games afternoons, instead of playing football. I am still conscious of the moral impact of many of the staff, which owed nothing to coercion, and which, in my better moments, stood me in good stead very many years later. We were encouraged, not to learn to obey so that we should be qualified to command, but to be responsible at all times.

On the day when our School Certificate and Matric results arrived I said to my friend, John Hume: "Let's do languages in the College and become schoolmasters." So that is what happened. I tried doing advanced maths, but found it was not my scene. I began German, continued French and Latin, and did a rush job on subsidiary English in order to take Oxford and Cambridge Higher Certificate in 1927. Both John and I tried for entry to Oxford, but were unsuccessful. When, after a walking tour in the Pyrenees, we began a year abroad, learning German, neither of us knew where we should be in autumn, 1928.

* A.J.P.Tayor, nowadays doyen of historians, and a well-known TV personality.

It is not my purpose in writing to attempt a full account of Bootham School. I have confined myself to mentioning and explaining those parts of my experience in the school to which I look back with a sense that they led to particular experiences and modes of thought, some of which became significant as much as decades later.

My year abroad was arranged on the basis of an exchange between me and an Austrian student, home to home. I lived with his parents for 6 months, and then had a room in a neighbouring household in Innsbruck. I registered as a student at the university, where the Professor of English advised me on a suitable selection of lectures. As I have a good ear for language I picked up a good academic vocabulary, although I did not, in fact, while at Innsbruck, put it into written practice. When the autumn term was well under way I embarked upon activity of quite a different kind, namely attending a course in ball-room dancing, organized by one of the senior classes of the boys' Realgymnasium, with the participation of a bevy of girls invited by them. Such classes were a very regular institution in those days. They were very formal, and took place under the watchful eyes of the girls' mothers. The class met once a week. We started with the Viennese waltz, and progressed to fox-trots, polkas and tangos, as well as valetas. The emotional effect of this course was strong. To hold a girl's hand, and actually to clasp her to one's breast in the dance was, of course, intensely exciting. I fell in love, naturally, but it was all so innocent and formal. It was a long time before we progressed beyond the "Herr Bradley" and "Fräulein So-und-so" stage and used first names. As for using the familiar 2nd person singular, I only got to that stage by correspondence, long after I had left Innsbruck. But it was a huge improvement on sitting in meeting on Sundays, eyeing the girls at the Mount from afar, and my social education advanced considerably. But I was on very close terms with some of the boys, who accepted me into their group. We sometimes had parties, and in the summer we also had excursions together, sometimes with the girls, (accompanied, of course, by their mamas) and from an academic point of view I benefited greatly from the lively conversation of a group of young people, – a nice counterbalance to the more heavily academic language of the university. The consequence of these two parallel experiences was that I acquired great facility with German, even if I had a bit of a Tyrolean accent and used all sorts of ungrammatical endings. The linguistic part of my German studies at Cambridge thus presented me with no problems, and I had no difficulty in getting good results. I even acquired some facility in using the now out-dated old Gothic-style script.

Being in Innsbruck for the academic year 1927-28 I was not really available for interview in England. As I have already mentioned, it was the relationship between Bootham and Caius College which persuaded the college to accept me on the school's recommendation, without interview. I was also accepted by the "Training College for Schoolmasters", which at that time was the nearest approach Cambridge had to an Education Faculty. I had to commit myself to entering the teaching profession after taking my degree and my Certificate of Education, and in return my fees for the four years were covered by government grant. I was also awarded £30 a year for 3 years from the school's own scholarship fund. My Father found a further £150 a year to see me through. I got a good enough degree in German and French in the first three years, and scraped a third class certificate in my fourth, during which I cannot claim to have been very industrious. I spent the first term of that year doing "teaching practice" at Shrewsbury School and returned to Cambridge in the second term, to devote most of my energies to training and athletic competition, culminating in the Sports against Oxford in March, when I was second string in the three miles.

I thus emerged from Cambridge with adequate qualifications for a career as a teacher. But education is about thinking, not qualifications, and on reflection I cannot claim to have derived from Cambridge anything like as much education as I did from my last school or from my first teaching post. This was not a short-coming of Cambridge, but an indication of a lack of maturity in myself. I took part in various societies, particularly the German Society. I joined the Union and regularly attended debates, though I never spoke. I heard many distinguished speakers, both contemporaries and visitors. One of my exact college contemporaries, whom I knew quite well at the time, became President, and in more recent years has been the occupant of the Woolsack. I have still quite vivid pictures in my mind of people like Lord Hugh Cecil and George Lansbury. I used to go regularly to the Festival Theatre, a repertory theatre where I saw many performances by Flora Robson and Robert Donat, and productions by Tyrone Guthrie. The programmes of occasional productions of the Marlowe Society did not name performers, but one nevertheless got to know that Prince Hal, in "Henry IV", and "King Lear" were both played by a young actor called Michael Redgrave. At another level of social activity, I helped to run a Sunday afternoon boys' club in Barnwell. This was a joint venture by a number of students at Trinity Hall and Caius, and we even took the boys for a week's camping in the summer vacation. Yet another sphere which I touched tangentially was the religious one. When I went up the school had sent my name automatically to the Friends' Meeting at Cambridge, so I went there sometimes. My family were Baptists, so my Father had sent my name to the

Minister of St. Andrew's Baptist Church, and I went there
sometimes too.   In my fourth year, largely through my Father,
I became interested in Toc H, and this, in turn, led to an
interest in the Church of England.   I was actually confirmed
in Canterbury Cathedral in the summer of 1932.   But even this
turned out to be, as I have put it, a tangential experience,
which was superceded by a more long-lasting one three years
later.

I have already mentioned that my first teaching appointment was
the result of an enquiry by the Head of Leighton Park School,
Reading, to the Head of Bootham, (who by this time was Donald
Gray, formerly Geography teacher in the school, Arthur Rowntree
having retired in 1927.)   I was invited to visit Leighton Park
in December, 1931, on my way home to Dover from Shrewsbury.
In February I was sent for again, and the Headmaster, Edgar B.
Castle, offered me the post of resident assistant housemaster
of Reckitt House and teacher of German and French.   I
accepted, and took up my post in September, 1932.   One of my
colleagues was my own former French teacher at Bootham, Victor
Alexander, now housemaster of School House, and in the next
year or two there were six members of the Leighton Park staff
who had been pupils or teachers at Bootham.   Leighton Park,
like Bootham, was, (and is), a Quaker boys' boarding school.
There were many differences between the schools, but the Quaker
cast of thought was the most vital component of both.   The
staff was a lively, stimulating and vigorous one, by no means
all of them Quakers, but all in sympathy with the objects of
the school.   For the first time I found myself a full member
of an educational team, free, and indeed also bound, to   make
my own contribution in a mature and responsible way.   I may
say that my growing up was also violently accelerated that
October, when my younger brother died, very suddenly and
unexpectedly. I must point out that in what I have to record
about the 4½ years I spent at Reading it is not my purpose to
give a rounded description of Leighton Park School, any more
than I have attempted a full description of Bootham during my
school days.   What I shall try to do is to analyse the effect
on my own educational development of my experiences, both in
school and out of school, during that period.

There was nothing unusual about my first steps as a fledgling
teacher.   Nor was there really anything new about my life as a
resident member of staff, although it was very nice, of course,
to have a sitting room and a bed-room and bathroom of my own.
Again, as a young and active member of staff I became fully
involved with athletics and other games duties, and took part
in a staff play and in a couple of Gilbert & Sullivan operas.
(Should   I regard starring as Katisha, falsetto, in "The
Mikado" as a formative educational experience ?)   And at
Easter, in 1935 I took a small group of boys, including one

Old Boy, on a Youth Hostel visit to Hitler's Germany, in the course of which we met some of the Quakers working in Berlin.

Outside school there were two very important components in my life. One of these was my participation in the activities of the Reading Branch of Toc H. I deliberately involved myself in this way because I felt it most important to spend some of my life quite apart from the school. Toc H, still a relatively young movement in those days, provided a considerably wider social mix than the pretty sheltered scholastic and home environment in which I had lived until then. Apart from this, the ideas and ideals of Toc H were congenial, and provided a stimulus to much lively discussion and healthy motivation.

The other out of school component in my life is still with me to-day, after more than 50 years, and is still furthering my essential education. As soon as I received my first salary cheque, at the end of my first term of teaching, I took Mary Harris, of Dowlais, South Wales, to a jeweller's, and we obtained an engagement ring. We had met at a party in my home in Dover during the Easter vacation of my first year at Cambridge, and during my last year we agreed to "go steady", as they say nowadays, with the intention of getting engaged when I could get that ring with my own earned money. For the time being I was committed to remaining resident in the school, and it was not until June of 1934 that the Head was able to release me from that part of my duties, with effect at the end of term. So we made hasty arrangements, and were married in August at the Toc H Church, All Hallows, Barking, on Tower Hill, by Pat Leonard, a Toc H padre, who later on became Bishop of Nottingham. For the next two years we lived in a flat about a mile from the school.

As I have stated, the staff of Leighton Park was lively, stimulating and vigorous. School policies were thrashed out at long staff meetings as well as in frequent arguments and discussions. Everybody took part, and occasionally we had visitors to introduce a topic. The consideration of disciplinary difficulties and the writing of reports were on-going concerns. We could always depend upon one colleague, Bill Brown, to puncture pomposity, platitudes and complacency, and there was never any shortage of riposte, often very witty. E. B. Castle, the Head, was a man of ideas, which he both gathered and propounded. But such a staff was not always an easy one to lead, and I remember remarking, at one stage, that if there was one thing I never wanted to be, it was a Headmaster. But Bill Brown prophesied that I should become Head of a country Grammar School. He was actually right !

But it would be true to say that the most significant enduring formative influence upon me during those years, though I did not fully realize it at the time, was the Head himself, Edgar Castle, who came to be, especially from the late fifties until his death in the early seventies, one of our closest friends. As I remarked, he both gathered and promoted ideas. When he gave an address on a Sunday evening he would lay several books on the table before him, and read marked quotations from them. I particularly remember that he was enthusiastic about John Macmurray, who was a very popular broadcaster on religion and philosophy at that time. He invited well-known people to speak on Sunday evenings, and afterwards he and his wife would entertain them to supper in their home. He and his family lived in a house which was structurally a part of Reckitt House, and the housemaster, the matron and I had our evening meal with the Castles in their dining room. So on those Sundays when guests were present we also met them. I particularly remember meeting F. S. Smythe, the Everest climber and writer, and Vera Brittain. It was strange meeting with a person whose intimate "Testament of Youth" one had so recently read. But the opportunity to meet with interesting individuals was less significant than the atmosphere of persistent intellectual activity, with emphasis on thinking about many aspects of education.

Indeed, a year or two after the war Edgar Castle left Leighton Park, to become Professor of Education in the University of Hull, where he remained until 1961. From being a compulsive reader he became a compulsive writer, mostly on educational themes, but also on Quakerism. We had the opportunity, in later years, to consider education together, and he continued to take an interest in my own activities. For over 3 years he was one of my Governors. He even referred briefly, later on, in two of his books, to what I had been trying to do in particular circumstances, (though he named no names).

My stay at Leighton Park lasted until the end of 1936. When I was appointed there was a clear understanding between us that it would be right, both from the school's point of view and my own, for me to move on after 4 or 5 years. I felt a need to get into the public sector of education, and applied for a post as language teacher at King Edward VII School, Sheffield. As I have already indicated, I was fortunate in that the Head there had formerly been on the staff at Leighton Park, so that his eye would be caught by an application from a base which he knew. So I was one of two successful candidates, and we moved to Sheffield at the end of the year.

Since what I am writing about is my own educational development
I should at this point interpolate that during our last year at
Reading Mary and I reached a joint decision about our religious
affiliation.   Whereas I had, as mentioned, become an Anglican,
Mary, brought up a Baptist, felt no inclination to follow me in
that direction.   So with the background of experience at
Leighton Park, and regular attendance at the Friends' Meeting
in Reading, we were accepted as members of the Society, and
remained active in it for some 35 years thereafter.   In
Sheffield we became thoroughly involved, though with no
parallel school association.   It was at Sheffield Meeting that
my new Head, Richard B. Graham, (himself a Quaker), introduced
us to another life-long friend, Bernard de Bunsen.   B. de B.
was not himself a Friend, but had been a pupil at Leighton Park
and was now an H.M.I. of Schools, first in West Riding, and
then in Sheffield.   We saw him often when he was Principal of
Makerere College, Kampala, Uganda, and later, as Sir Bernard de
Bunsen, Vice-Chancellor of the University of East Africa.

At King Edward VII School I learned what it means to have to
work really hard at my classroom teaching and all that went
with it.   The numbers with which I had to deal at Leighton
Park were quite small, and the levels at which I taught quite
modest.   The burden of preparation and marking was really
pretty light.   Not so at K.E.S.   I found myself with an Upper
Sixth Form German class with 19 students in it, several of them
in their third sixth form year.   They did a piece of German
prose writing every week.   The average time for marking each
script was approaching 10 minutes.   I had continual surprises.
One week I found that a certain student had translated a German
poem in verse in the style of Walt Whitman, - just for fun !
In fact, this was my introduction to that poet.   At fifth form
level I had both German and French classes, each of them quite
large, and doing two pieces of written work for me each week.
In the fourth year I had a class of beginners in German, who
were supposed to reach School Certificate standard in two
years, with a deplorably out of date text book.

I also had a "Remove" class of less gifted and somewhat
eccentric pupils, who were being allowed 3 years instead of 2
for their School Certificate course.   I do not remember what
other classes I had in that first year, but I do remember that
I only had 4 "free" periods, and that in at least one of these
I was first in line to replace any colleague who might be
absent, and some of the other 3 were quite often at risk.   So
marking had to be lugged home most nights, and back to school
in the morning.   At exam time one was usually assigned the
marking of a particular paper right across a year group, which
consisted of 4 parallel classes.   One had to set the paper and
get it approved by the head of the department, who belonged
very much to the old school.   And on the evening after the exam

had been taken one had to collect the papers, take them home, and
return them next morning, fully marked, with lists attached.   I
can remember that I once found myself taking home the Third Form
French scripts together with the Lower Sixth (so-called Transitus)
German Literature papers.   Mary lifted my nose off the last of
the Transitus scripts at about 6 o'clock the following morning.
In the afternoon, if I remember aright, I freshened up by
supervising the annual inter-house cross-country race.But it was
not only in the matter of my teaching duties that K.E.S. gave me
new kinds of experience.   Nowadays it is a co-educational
comprehensive school, but in those days it was the crack boys'
Grammar School of the City, with a first class academic reputation
right across the conventional curriculum.   The staff was of high
calibre, and membership of it provided a springboard for many a
promotion to headships, administration, the inspectorate and
university posts.   And at the same time there was a core of
veterans, mostly, like my departmental head, of the old school, but
others whose interests lay in other directions than promotion.
Such a one, for instance, was E.F.Watling, whose translations of
the Greek dramatists are still valued Penguins.   He wrote plays
himself, and was a very accomplished actor, a king-pin in the
Sheffield Playgoers Society.   Of course, he produced the school's
plays and operas.   Both Mary and I had much pleasure and profit
from taking part with him, both in school and in the Playgoers.
Other colleagues had musical and artistic talents, and the staff
could usually raise a full football or cricket team to play
against the school.   I well remember taking unexpected catches in
the "gully" and getting ribs broken while keeping goal.

The disciplinary regime at K.E.S. was totally different from
anything in my previous experience.   Richard Graham, the Head,
was a Quaker and a pacifist.   But he was very tough, physically,
morally and intellectually.   An accomplished rock-climber, he was
considered for a place on an Everest expedition, but it is said
that his tendency to be contentious kept him out of a party which
needed to be socially uncomplicated.   Perhaps the most surprising
thing is that he was a beating headmaster.   There was nothing
occasional about his use of the cane.   Many offences reported to
him carried automatic corporal punishment by him as their
consequence.   There was sometimes a queue of offenders.   But any
member of staff was entitled to use the cane, within clear
regulations.   A cane had to be sent for to the school office: a
colleague had to witness the punishment, which took place in the
corridor outside the classroom: and a report had to be recorded
in the office.   The maximum number of strokes was four.   Most
members of the staff did use the cane, some rarely and some more
often.   But there were some who managed to avoid doing so, and
who found the practice unacceptable.   I was once or twice called
upon to witness a punishment, but I never used the cane myself.

(What I could manage at K.E.S. proved more of a problem later, as I shall have to relate.)   Apart from the Head, the most dominant personality in the school was the Senior Master.   His influence can be illustrated by mentioning the daily routine at morning assembly.   The school, numbering about 700, would be in the school hall, which was a sort of amphitheatrical Methodist chapel, chatting, when suddenly every sound would cease.   This was because, two classrooms away from the entrance to the hall, and unseen by anybody inside, the door of the staff common room had opened and the senior master had emerged into the corridor. It was uncanny.   He would then stride into the hall and take his place to one side of the platform, and a signal would reach the Head, who would then make his entrance, with swishing gown and tasselled mortar-board.   Arrived at his place, the Head removed his "square" and a conventional assembly followed, the end signalled by the Head when he donned his square again.

At the end of 1938 Richard Graham left, to become Head of Bradford Grammar School, where he remained until his retirement. The new Head of K.E.S. was Dr. A. W. Barton, and he took up his post at the start of the summer term, 1939.   He came from Repton School, where he had been Senior Physics master, and was well known for his text-book on "Light".   He had also been a soccer referee at the Olympic Games in 1936.   He was an amiable person, very tall and impressive in appearance, but, as it turned out, sometimes rather unimaginative, so that the effect of some of his pronouncements fell rather flat.   But he had no easy task, with the outbreak of war when he had only been in the school a term, and the requirement of the Director of Education, Dr. (later Lord) Alexander, that all schools should be sub-divided into sub-schools, and dispersed in small groups of a dozen boys, mostly in private houses.   And when this scheme had been abandoned he had to cope with staff changes as men's deferment from call-up came to an end.   To add to his difficulties, on 12th and 15th December, 1940, Sheffield suffered two "Blitzes" and the school became, overnight, a refuge for about 300 people from devastated homes.   His task, from then until things settled down again, well after the war, was far from enviable.

But I suppose it was reaction to these two Heads, and the stimulus of the lively staff, which first made me think of being a Head myself.

There was a good deal more than school to add to my significant experience at Sheffield.   There was the opportunity to go to Halle concerts and the Repertory Theatre, for instance.   I have already referred to our participation in the Playgoers Society. But the most important element in this out-of-school experience was the Friends' Meeting at Hartshead, and the friendships we made and the related activities in which we took part.   We made our contribution to the Sunday meetings, and we were drawn into a group of forward-looking, but seasoned Friends, who carried much of the responsibility of the meeting. It was here that our understanding of the Society was grounded and commitments were undertaken. What I absorbed at this time was most valuable to me two decades later, when I had some ticklish responsibilities to exercise.

Amongst the related activities to which I have referred was the Peace Movement, which, in those days, had most to do with the Peace Pledge Union and the issue, when conscription was introduced, of conscientious objection. I became one of the leading group in the Sheffield organisation, and when the time came for me to register for national service I registered as a conscientious objector. This was in the autumn of 1940. In January, while the Blitz was at its height, Mary and I went for interview in Essex, arising from a rather misguided application for a community job, the exact nature of which I no longer remember. On the way home I became ill, and took to my bed with what was diagnosed as scarlet fever. This meant six weeks off school and confined to the house. I read a good deal and examined my conscience afresh. The upshot was, that since I could in no way feel impartial in the matter of the war, it seemed to me wrong to stand aside from the conflict in order to salve my personal conscience. At first I thought I would ask to be sent into the Fire Service. But it did not particularly appeal to me, and in any case, if one abandoned the absolute pacifist position, it did not seem to me that there was any moral difference between the Services. I therefore withdrew my conscientious objection, and asked to be accepted in the Navy. In September I was in fact called up, and joined H.M.S.Royal Arthur, (which was Butlin's Holiday Camp at Skegness,) for training.

My action naturally caused some dismay amongst Friends and conscientious objector associates, and some thought I should resign from the Society because of its traditional peace testimony. Others, including some particularly staunch pacifists, thought differently, and were most sympathetic in their attitude towards me. I did not resign, and all the friendships I had made remained intact. During my national service Mary and I maintained our attendance at meetings whenever we could, and afterwards returned to full participation in the meeting.

From an educational point of view the Royal Navy affected me in two important respects. The Navy gave me a wider social experience than I had ever had before, and it gave me the opportunity to gain what nowadays would be called some "hands-on" experience of science and technology. Soon after arrival at Royal Arthur new recruits were sorted out for training in trades after the initial basic "square-bashing". I found myself assigned to a group of future radio mechanics. When I tentatively mentioned that I had absolutely no knowledge of

physics the reply was: "You've got a degree, haven't you ?"
"Yes, sir." "Right ! Two paces, step backwards, march !" So
as a radio mechanic I was trained.

At the end of October, 1941, I was the oldest of a class of
ratings sent to the Rugby College of Technology, to undergo
training. I was 31; there was a 27-year-old insurance clerk,
with a number of bank clerks and other young men in similar
occupations, all about 21. We had 4 hours of instruction in the
mornings, Monday to Saturday, and another 4 hours in the
afternoons, Monday to Friday. We had P.T. twice a week and I
actually succeeded in touching my toes with straight knees. The
mornings were usually lectures and class-room work, and the
afternoons we spent in workshops or in laboratories, testing
theories. We had stringent written tests almost every week, and
to survive intellectually one had to be able to score 90% or so
each time, otherwise one fell hopelessly behind. Writing up
notes and making sure one was ready for the next lesson occupied
at least a couple of hours each evening.We started at the very
beginning, both in theory and practice. I learned Ohm's Law for
the first time. I learned a bit about filing metal to specified
thickness and smoothness. And I learned how to use a soldering
iron. From D.C. (3 weeks, taught, most appropriately, by an
instructor whose normal occupation was teaching educationally
sub-normal children,) through basic A.C. to simple and then ever
more complicated radio circuits, and then making acquaintance with
the magical Cathode Ray Tube. Finally aerials and their
directional properties. I found the course very demanding, but
stimulating and satisfying, because it let me into a world which,
despite John Dell, I had never trodden. It lasted 4 months and
I enjoyed it immensely. I was often able to get home to
Sheffield for the week-end, and sometimes Mary came to Rugby to
stay in my billet. My host was a real craftsman of the old
school, a charge-hand at British Thompson Houston in the town,
and his wife fed me most copiously. Mr. and Mrs Hancox, of
Caldecott Street, near the College, could not have made me more
welcome and comfortable. I might add, since I am writing about
my educational development, that I even managed to make some
study of elementary calculus as bed-side reading ! I alternated
it with such works as "Silas Marner" and "The Mill on the Floss".

From Rugby, after a week's leave, we proceeded as a class to
H.M.S.Valkyrie, which was actually a row of hotels on the sea-front
at Douglas, I.O.M. Here we were to study the application of our
knowledge to the very latest kind of radio, namely R.D.F., (Radio
Direction Finding). Each day we marched up to Douglas Head,
where we found ourselves before working sets, including the very
latest 10 centimeter wave-length ones. These were the sets
which, on completion of our training, it would be our duty to
maintain and repair. We were in Douglas for 6 weeks, which
included a very pleasant Easter, and for four of the weeks Mary

was able to be in Douglas.   I had "shore-leave" on alternate
nights, so that we enjoyed that spring, particularly since I had
no homework such as had been essential at Rugby.

The final stage of training was at the Royal Naval Signal School,
where we were to spend 2½ weeks learning about standard naval
radio apparatus.   Signal School was actually situated in Leydene
House, which belonged to Beatrice Lillie, the actress.   It was
early summer, and I spent part of my last night at Leydene on
sentry-go, supposedly guarding some equipment which was kept in
tents in the woods.   I had the middle watch, (midnight to 4 a.m.)
and as I did my little march up and down there was a whole bevy
of nightingales singing their hearts out all about me.   About me,
did I say ?   Well, perhaps so: I was now a Leading Radio
Mechanic !

But the next day was less romantic.   We went down to Royal Naval
Barracks, Portsmouth, to be freshly kitted out and to await
drafting to our ships.   Until that time we had been dressed in
traditional sailor's uniform, with bell-bottomed trousers, "square
rig", as it is known in the Service.   But at this point we
changed to "fore-and-aft rig" - peaked cap and jacket and ordinary
trousers, also referred to, rudely, as "taxi-driver" rig.   But as a
newly qualified Leading Hand one was entitled to wear an anchor,
or killick, on one's left arm.   On one's right arm one wore the
badge of one's trade, which was that of a telegraphist.   A
Leading Hand, whatever his trade, was normally referred to as a
Killick, this being the old name for a stone anchor.

I did not have very long to wait for my draft, and early in June I
was on my way to Devonport, to join H.M.S. Vansittart.   This was
a first world war 1100-ton destroyer, retrieved from retirement,
with torpedo tubes removed and enlarged fuel tanks fitted, to act
as an escort vessel for convoys.   She was completing a partial
re-fit, after a two-year commission based at Freetown, Sierra
Leone.   I soon learned that the crew expected to spend the
coming commission in the same area.

I was assigned to the Petty Officers' mess, which had room for a
couple of Leading Hands, although the rest of my mess-mates were
Petty Officers.   There were 2 Upper Deck, or executive, P.O.'s.
There was the P.O.Tel, in charge of the radio.   The Yeoman of
Signals was responsible for all visual signalling.   "Torps"
(P.O.Torpedo Man) was actually the chief electrician, since we had,
as I have mentioned, no torpedos.   We also had the P.O.Cook,
whose galley was close to the entrance to our mess.   One entered
the mess through a hatch and down a perpendicular companion
ladder.   So it was quite a tight little space.   And it was here,
more than anywhere else, that my social education was advanced.
All these Petty Officers, as well as the three or four Chief P.O.'s
in the adjacent mess, were "Active Service", not "Hostilities Only"

ratings. The Navy had been their life, in most cases, since they
joined as boys. It is therefore not surprising that the Service
dominated much of their conversation. One other topic played a
major and regular role in the rest of conversation; but I need not
go into detail.

Most men came from the west country, but we also had men from
Liverpool and from the north-east, and the cook came from
Northern Ireland. Anyone with an accent like mine was an
oddity in such company. However, I was accepted with good
humour, and I learned much from my companions. There was, first,
the professional competence they all had, which was worthy of
every respect, - a competence quite different from my own, - and
indeed, so very superior to any competence I had in my new trade.
Then there was the understanding they gave me of the life they
led. There was a whole new vocabulary which intrigued me as a
linguist, and I still have a little dictionary which I compiled
while I was a member of the ship's company. I need hardly add
that there was another vocabulary in common use, which added
considerably to my comprehension, if not to the way I expressed
myself - though I must admit that our merry Yeoman once remarked,
with a grin, that "Mr. Bradley has improved quite a lot !" I
regret to say that since those days there are not many examples
of coarse humour that are beyond my comprehension. But I like
to think that, as the Yeoman's remark implies, my 8 months in
that company had a humanising effect upon me.

I did, of course, improve my geographical education, since we
travelled a good many sea-miles during my 8 months. Within 12
hours of leaving Devonport at the start of our commission we
found ourselves sent to pick up survivors from a sister ship
which had been dive-bombed about 200 miles south-west of Land's
End, and take them to Milford Haven. After a brief stop at
Londonderry we joined a southward convoy, keeping company with it
as far as the Azores, but there we left them to go and spend
about 6 weeks with Force H at Gibraltar. This involved a couple
of "Club Runs", escorting an aircraft carrier which was flying off
Spitfires to Malta, and joining the escort of the last great
Malta Convoy of August, 1942. We then went south to Bathurst, in
the Gambia, and Freetown, but after less than a month found
ourselves ordered back to Liverpool, calling at Gibraltar on the
way. After a brief further re-fit we sailed to Londonderry
again, and then out into the Atlantic, where we joined an enormous
fleet, and in November stood off-shore, watching the landings in
North Africa. Sent back to Liverpool we next found ourselves
joining a slow-moving convoy bound for Argentia in Newfoundland.
Steaming from Argentia to Halifax, Nova Scotia we collected 200
tons of ice on the upper deck, and took 3 days for a journey
which should have taken 20 hours. We lost our Asdic dome on the
way, so we had to be in dry dock over Christmas and New Year.
We had some kind hospitality ashore, but I spent Christmas

24

evening, 1942, sitting on a torpedo at a party in a British submarine lying alongside us and a Russian sub. We sailed eventually to St. John's, Newfoundland, where we picked up a convoy which was to cross the Atlantic at 5 knots, a prey to any U-boats in the vicinity. Delivering most of the ships at Londonderry, we then sailed round the north of Scotland to Middlesbrough, where I left the ship.

I should explain that in the course of these long voyages there had been pretty little for me to do, and I began to get a little bored. The only way to escape was to see whether the Captain was prepared to send me back to Signal School with a view to being considered for training as a Special Branch, (later Radar), Officer. I suspect he thought this might be a way to get a new Radio Mech. who wouldn't have so many things go wrong, so he sent me off. After some leave I began quite a long wait, sitting in Royal Naval Barracks, Portsmouth. Eventually I was accepted and joined the Officers' long Radar Course, which lasted some 13 weeks. (In fact, the name Radar only replaced R.D.F., to align with U.S. terminology, in late 1943 or early 1944.)

Once again, therefore, I found myself a student in the classroom, this time trying to master material more advanced than I had coped with before. It was very hard work, and by the time the course was over I said that I hoped that from that time until I returned to Civvy Street I should have nothing more to do with examinations, either sitting or setting them. So I was amazed to find myself the first member of the class, in which I had not distinguished myself, drafted to the same teaching staff. The thinking was, I am sure, that Sub.Lieut.Bradley could be entrusted more confidently with care of a blackboard than a ship's radar, even if his knowledge was pretty shaky. Anyhow, I found myself as assistant to Lieut. Ronald Brown, who, in Civvy Street, was Senior Physics Master at the Leys School, Cambridge. As it turned out, this was a most valuable experience for me, because from Ron Brown I learned how an active scientist thinks and pursues his enquiries. I worked and learned under him for two years.

I was on the staff of the Radar School, or H.M.S. Collingwood, as it was called after installation in new premises at Fareham, for two years. Mary was able to join me, and we lived in Portsmouth during that time. In July, 1944 a new phase and aspect of education began for both of us, when our son Peter arrived on the scene; forty years later he is still educating us, sometimes more like a benevolent uncle than a son. Before he could walk he could move about, and exercised his already enquiring mind by unscrewing the U-bend of the wash-basin in the bathroom. He continues to be our technical adviser.

My instructional duties did leave me a reasonable amount of leisure, because I could not, of course, bring any work home with me, as it was mostly secret. So apart from enjoying some social life with colleagues and their families I also joined the local branch of Toc H. And it was my contribution to the discussions that took place, to study and expound the significance of the new Education Bill which was on its way to becoming the Butler Act of 1944. As the possibility of an end to the war began to appear, one was beginning also to think about the return to civilian life. But I cannot pretend that I thought, at that time, beyond the tri-partite scheme for secondary schools, or had the slightest notion of comprehensive education. One only became aware of such a development when comprehensive schools were introduced into the reconstruction programme of the city of Coventry. But the idea was beginning to emerge that I might apply for Grammar School headships. In fact I had made one application even before being called up, but it was most premature and produced no response at all.

Then something unexpected happened in August, 1945. I was on a course at the Army College of Science, at Bury, when a signal arrived, summoning me back to Collingwood immediately. I caught a crowded night train from Manchester, and when it stopped at Stoke-on-Trent we heard the announcement that the Japanese had surrendered. It was VJ Day, an ironical circumstance in view of what lay before me. A new Head of Radar School had been appointed. His predecessor was another physics teacher by profession, who evidently had a poor view of my technical prowess, since I was passed over for promotion to Lieutenant. The new man, to whom I reported on arrival, took a fresh view. "You are a graduate in German, aren't you ? So you will be drafted to become Radar Officer to the Flag Officer, Western Germany, with a long overdue promotion to Lieutenant." So at last, my expertise in German was to be noticed by the Navy ! So off I went, reporting first to Minden, and then at Buxtehude, not far from Hamburg. Apart from a week's leave in the middle, that was where I remained until the time came for my demobilisation in mid-December. The job was something of a sinecure, since the work of dis-arming the German fleet of its radar had already been done by my predecessor. But I was able to visit bases like Cuxhaven and Wilhelmshaven, as well as Heligoland, so recently blitzed almost out of existence, Bremen, and, of course the utterly devastated city of Hamburg. In the naval barracks where we were housed there was an effort made to provide opportunities for Further Education, and I joined the carpentry class. But I also took a beginners' class in German, a parallel one being conducted by the Medical Officer. Both of us happened to be rather better at German than the interpreters. In the course of my travelling about I was able to make contact with German Quakers in Hamburg, and had serious conversations with one of them, in particular, named Katerina Petersen. She had been Head of an international

Quaker school at Ommen, in Holland, before the war. We had met at conferences of the Friends' Guild of Teachers.There was no heating in her small apartment, and we huddled together under a rug to keep warm while we talked. She was a splendid, courageous person, and became the highly respected Director of Education for the area around Hannover. We kept in touch for many years afterwards.

I have already mentioned that I was beginning to think of applying for headships, and now I was about to act. I took the Times Educational Supplement and scanned the advertisements. At this stage I had a piece of real good fortune. The Director of Education for Hertfordshire. Mr. (later Sir) John Newsom, was touring naval establishments in Europe, to enquire into educational provisions being made for personnel. I met him at Buxtehude, and was asked to ferry him to his next port of call, Wilhelmshaven. On the way we had plenty of conversation, and I ventured to take the opportunity to ask him what authorities were looking for when they received applications for headships. He told me that the first thing was to be clear in one's own mind why one was applying for a particular post, and secondly to convince the appointing authority, both in written application and at interview, that one thought highly of the post itself. This was excellent advice, which I found of value, not only when I was myself applying for posts, but also a long while later, when I was sitting on the other side of the table. I sent off my first two applications, which had to be in by the end of October. One was to Derbyshire and one to Somerset. I was back in the classroom at King Edward's before I heard from either of them.

The first response came from Derbyshire. In February I was called for interview at Staveley, near Chesterfield, where the sitting Head, an old Cambridge friend of mine, was leaving for another headship. The Chairman of the Governors was Sir Osbert Sitwell, who, however, handed over the meat of the interview to Mr. Briggs, the Director of Education for Derbyshire, - which is what I had been told to expect. He was a person of rather forbidding aspect, and intense and direct in his questioning. The first question was: "Why have you applied for this particular post ?" So I was ready for him. At the end of the afternoon the Governors decided to re-advertise, but to allow one of the other candidates and myself to remain in contention. I heard later that they did not feel the competition had been hot enough.

The second response came from Somerset, and on 12th March I appeared for interview for the headship of Elmhurst Grammar School, Street. The opening gambit was much as it had been at Staveley, though not so forbidding. For one thing, candidates had all met the Chairman of the Governors and her husband the previous evening, so that the atmosphere was a little more

relaxed.   What I did not know beforehand was that I happened to
have picked on two referees, Bernard de Bunsen and Edgar Castle,
who were known to some of the Governors.   In addition, when I
appeared before them it was encouraging to see the benign and
familiar face of Ellen C. Waller, who had been Head of the Mount
in York in my day and for a long while afterwards.   I was given
the post, and later heard from the Chairman that the motivation I
described was a telling factor;   one of my competitors had ruled
himself out by saying merely that his reason for applying was
that he wanted promotion.   I remember going home in the bus
across the Mendips, and then in the train from Bristol   to
Sheffield, smiting my breast, as it were, and asking   myself
repeatedly, with dawning trepidation: "What have I done ?   What
have I done ?"   I had six more months to think about it.

1. My basic education - Phase 2.

The reason for the title of this chapter is that although I was still involved henceforth in my own basic education, the words "my education" now had an additional meaning. I was no longer merely being educated, but the education offered in the school of which I was Head was, to a degree, dependent upon me, in that I played a major role in determining policy and practice. This second aspect of my education needed to be revised as and when the first aspect seemed to achieve increased enlightenment.

Elmhurst Grammar School was, of course, precisely the kind of country Grammar School of which Bill Brown had said I should be Head. It served Street and Glastonbury and the villages in the surrounding countryside, with children coming in daily by bus. The retiring Head had, in fact, opened it 26 years earlier. There were about 300 boys and girls, but the numbers were to fall off considerably during the next few years. Indeed, we had to boost them by admitting boys and girls from the growing north of Somerset, underprovided with schools, and arranging for a couple of dozen children to be billeted locally, on a weekly basis, in private homes .

The school had not had an easy time during the war. For one thing, for much of the period it had had to share its premises and facilities with evacuees from the South-East Essex Technical College, and in fact the last of these pupils had only just left. The Head had a heavy burden, and was sometimes ill. I believe he had stayed on beyond normal retirement age. He was held in the greatest respect by everybody, and was a most conscientious and meticulous person in everything he did. Staffing had not been easy during the war. The Physics master, for instance, an excellent teacher, had been in the Navy and had not yet returned. He never did, in fact, but got a post elsewhere. This was not really surprising, since we knew one another. He had been one of my senior officers at Collingwood, two ranks higher up than I ! We were very good friends, and he eventually became Head of Dartmouth Grammar School. There had been a number of changes, and there were gaps in the provision of cover for the curriculum. On my behalf my predecessor came to an arrangement whereby, from the autumn term, when I was to take over, we should share a P.E. mistress with the Blue School, Wells. The art teacher and the D.S. teacher were also part-timers. But the establishment did not allow for even half a P.E. master. This circumstance led to a further broadening of my education, because the Education Committee agreed to pay for me to go to the Loughborough College Summer School, so that I might have 3 weeks of training in how to conduct P.E. So my main teaching responsibility during that first term lay in the gym. When a message was brought over to the gym by my wife, to say that an H.M.I. had arrived, I had hastily to don my gown over my shorts and sit behind my desk with my lower frame concealed. (Gowns were held to be de rigueur in those days, and the H.M.I. was, after all, Lady Helen Asquith !) My campaign to increase the staff establishment was successful, and since other staff changes made some flexibility possible we were able to appoint a full time teacher, to divide his time between P.E. and Biology. So my physical exertions only lasted the one term.

My training in the profession of headmaster was much shorter than the training to teach physical education. In fact, I had none. In those days one learned on the job, and in my case I had not even carried responsibility for a department or held a post of special responsibility of any kind; they had not yet been invented ! This is one strong reason why it was essential to meet with one's colleagues in other schools, to compare notes, and perhaps to learn from one another. I regularly attended meetings of the Headmasters' Association in the area. More importantly, there was a termly meeting of the Heads of Somerset Grammar Schools, both men and women. This was a professional gathering, which enabled us to have a corporate relationship with the educational administration. I was Secretary for two or three years.

Being so green, I of course made mistakes, and I was often faced with problems. Fortunately I had a very warm relationship with the Chairman of my Governors, Sarah Clark, the doyenne of the shoe-making Clark family which is so closely identified with Street. She was American by birth, but had lived her life in Street, and had a large family, by then well into the third generation. (I had her eldest grandson in my first-year P.E. class that first term at Elmhurst.) She was refreshing, sagacious ever accessible and supportive. She was, of course, a Quaker, and her husband, Roger Clark, had been the Presiding Clerk of the London Yearly Meeting of Friends. We were often guests in their home. Apart from Sarah Clark, one of my most valuable governors, by reason of both her experience and her personality, was Ellen Waller, whose counsel I often sought, and who helped me with a number of crucial appointments.

I do not remember that I had any unusual educational ideas while at Elmhurst. But I certainly approved of the impending introduction of the new General Certificate of Education, which was to replace the Old School Certificate and Higher School Certificate. Several of my pupils had suffered most unfairly by reason of the group principle of the School Certificate, which meant, for instance, that a candidate might gain half a dozen Credits, but be denied a School Certificate because of a failure in English Language.

But I can claim to have broken new ground as far as relations with parents were concerned. A school with a catchment area like Elmhurst's cannot expect parents to come inconvenient distances to meetings in school. So, with the assistance of Primary School Heads, I arranged a series of meetings in a number of different places and took a colleague or two with me to meet parents on their own ground. The response was very good, and everybody benefited accordingly, the parents, the pupils, the Primary Schools, and those of us at Elmhurst.

In this connection I must mention another activity of those days. When we arrived at Street, C.E.M.A. (the war-time Council for the Encouragement of Music and the Arts,) was giving up its activities in the area. During the war there had been a good many concerts of all kinds, which had been much appreciated. They took place in the Elmhurst Hall. So the local enthusiasts formed themselves into the Street Society of Arts, and as host to the Society I found myself Chairman of its committee. This involved helping to organize a whole series of activities, engaging artists and their accommodation and getting reviews written for the local weekly press. The Secretary and I sometimes went to Arts Council events to be introduced to up and coming artists.

It occurred to me that during their school days in the middle of Somerset few of my pupils would have the chance to go to performances such as were available to people living in cities and large towns. Nor could they very well come in to Elmhurst from their villages to attend evening concerts. On the other hand, we were going to have artists on the spot: it was too good an opportunity to miss. So I used to write to the artists and ask whether they were willing, for a modest additional fee, to come in time for an afternoon concert, or to stay overnight, and perform next morning, - in either case, of course, for the school. I managed to get the majority of the parents to subscribe modestly to a fund to finance this. This often involved us in giving meals, or even accommodation, to the artists, because we lived "over the shop", in the upper storeys of the large, stone, former manor house around which the school had grown. So it was, for instance, that we entertained in our home Joseph Cooper, Owen Brannigan, Jan van der Gucht, Dobson and Young, Arthur Jordan, (first singer of the Fairy Song in the original production of Rutland Boughton's "Immortal Hour" at Glastonbury), and Suzanne Rozsa the violinist, (now married to Martin Lovett, the cellist in the Amadeus String Quartet.) We also had visits from "Ballet for Two", "Intimate Opera" and a progressive theatre group.

There was also plenty of "do it yourself" culture and entertainment going on, in which we were involved. At school we managed to produce, in alternate years, a Gilbert and Sullivan Opera. The latter opened new windows for fifth form boys, whose main interests were sport. We managed to recruit most of the football team into the chorus, and after that they were leading enthusiasts. As to drama, we had more than one modest one-act

31

play festival, with contributions from all ages. In Street itself there was a well established amateur dramatic group, "The Street Players", of which the father figure was the playwright, Lawrence Housman, who lived in the village. There were regular play readings, in which Mary joined, and then she took part in a performance of Lawrence Housman's cycle of plays about Queen Victoria. She also took an important part in "Ladies in Retirement", which was performed in the school hall.

We were also fully involved with the large local Friends' Meeting. I was even made an Elder, which meant that I was one of the people responsible for caring for the quality of the Meetings for Worship and of contributions to them. I can remember being so bold as to "elder" Lawrence Housman, who attended regularly, because he talked rubbish about the working of radios in a supposed parable in which they featured ! He was getting rather old, - in fact Mary made a cake for a large party to celebrate his ninetieth birthday.

Another family event caused us further learning, namely the arrival, in October, 1947, of our second son, Paul. He succeeded, in spite of the fact that he was unwilling to speak before he was three, in making himself well understood, which put us on our mettle. Furthermore, since, as I have mentioned, we lived above the school, and had access to the garden by an outside staircase, Paul used to find his way downstairs, and go to see the classrooms, which had ceiling to floor windows. On one occasion an amused girl appeared upstairs with Paul, with a message from the rather solemn history master: Please would Mrs. Bradley keep Paul upstairs, since he would stand outside the class-room watching proceedings, with his nose pressed against the window, which was proving distracting. The upshot of this was that an approach had to be made to the Head of the local Infants' School, to see whether she would admit Paul as a pupil. She agreed, and he began school roughly on his third birthday. This is the only instance of which I am aware, of a pupil being relegated from a Grammar School to an Infants School.

One other educational experience which I had at Street was in some ways the most memorable of all. The system used in Somerset for selecting pupils for admission to Grammar Schools involved, first, the usual 11+ examination. But Somerset was a fair-minded county, and after the clear cases had been listed a procedure was followed for considering the "border-line" cases. A small panel was established, consisting of an Education Officer, a Psychologist, a Primary Head, a Secondary Modern Head and a Grammar School Head. This team spent several weeks visiting different areas of the county to review these border-line children. They were given some further tests of a novel kind, to try to establish how they thought, not merely what they knew. They also did some relaxed P.E. together, and each was interviewed

by two of the panel members, on a one to one basis.   At the end
of the session the panel reviewed each case in the light of all
the information, and a decision was reached.   The first year I
was the Grammar School representative. The particular experience
which I have never forgotten occurred during one of these little
interviews.   I sat on a low wall with a charming little 11-year-
old girl, and we chatted away.   As usual, the time came when I
asked her what she would like to be when she left school.   "A
teacher," she said, without hesitation.   "And what would you like
to teach ?" went on the benign Grammar School Head, purring
gently.   "Why, children !" she said.

My secretary and I had to spend an enormous amount of our time
and energy in making arrangements for those pupils from North
Somerset whom I have mentioned.   But as the local numbers were
falling there was no other way open to me for trying to keep the
school of viable size.   I began to look for a new post in a
place where this sort of problem did not play such an important
role.   In the autumn I applied for the headship of a school in
Oldham which was about to move into new buildings and, hopefully,
to take on a new lease of life.   I was again fortunate, in that
one of my referees was the former Deputy Director of Education
for Somerset, now Director in Cumberland, by name Gordon Bessey,
and he was highly regarded in Oldham.   At the beginning of
December I went to Oldham for the first round of interviews, and
was then invited, with one other candidate, to return for a final
interview on 11th December.   On Sunday, 10th, when I was
preparing to depart we had a domestic crisis; a new member of
our family decided that this was the moment to be born.   So Mary
was packed off in an ambulance to hospital in Taunton, while I
handed over the two boys to the care of very dear friends on a
near-by farm.   (These friends were always our welcoming refuge
when we needed a break from education and much else.)   Too
excited to sit in a train I set off by car, to spend a night at
Sheffield before returning to Oldham.   On the way I stopped at
Broadway, and was actually able to speak on the phone to Mary,
who had only just given birth to a girl, to be named Joan.   At
the interview next day I was offered the job of Head of Counthill
Grammar School, Oldham,   with effect on 1st May, though the
school, still known as the Oldham Municipal High School, was not
due to move into the new building and take its new name until
September.   So I was to have the summer term to prepare for the
move, while the retiring Head remained in post until the school
year ended.

The Municipal High School at Oldham had been promised a new
building before the war, and construction of the building had, in
fact, been begun.   But for the duration of the war and for
several years afterwards it was left as an empty shell.   A
strong and long established Headmaster had retired just before the
war began, and because it was thought that it would be a good

thing for the appointment of a substantive Head to co-incide with the opening of the new building, the Senior Master was asked to hold the fort in the interim. He was left holding it until 1951. Amongst his colleagues were some particularly keen teachers, who had been on the staff for between twenty and thirty years. A new Head, arriving on the scene, might have expected to find a hide-bound, tired, suspicious group of people. This was far from so, and I found the Senior Mistress, the Senior Master, and three or four other long-established women teachers who were all straining at the leash, looking forward to a fresh and exciting start in the new school. They had all had some years of frustration, partly because of the poor facilities, and partly because of an absence of effective leadership from my predecessor, amiable person though he was. It was thus my first task to get to know my new colleagues, and to consult with them about the way in which we would organize and use the new school, and to consider what changes were necessary, and a very enjoyable and stimulating experience it was.

I do not remember that we had any particularly radical views about the curriculum itself; in this area the main advance simply consisted of the vastly improved facilities, particularly in specialist areas like laboratories, physical education, workshops and domestic science rooms. All departments were well led and competent, - as is indicated by the fact that a number of staff left on promotion of one kind or another.

But after Elmhurst, which was thoroughly co-educational, one thing bothered me. The school had what nowadays is called a four-form entry, but the boys and girls were segregated into separate classes. I felt that this was the worst of all possible arrangements, so it was agreed that we would have mixed classes in the first year, and extend the principle in succeeding years, as it might seem right to do. There were some mixed classes also, for reasons of economy, in the fifth year, and the Sixth Form was mixed.

When we moved in at Counthill, and the new regime was in operation, with myself having responsibility in the day-to-day running of the school, I introduced one other important change. In all Oldham schools the instrument of summary discipline was the strap. It could be used by any teacher. At Counthill it was decided that the power of corporal punishment should be confined to the Head and the Senior Master and Senior Mistress. This placed me in a different position from the one I had at Sheffield, since I had to be seen to support colleagues, and one had also to take into account the ambience of Oldham schools to which I have referred. There were, therefore some occasions, not many, when I did cane a boy, always with the Senior Master as a witness. The school flourished and gained in standing as the activities stimulated by my enthusiastic colleagues were extended. We had first-rate dramatic productions and we had good music.   Sport ranged through soccer, rugger, rugby league, cricket, hockey, netball, tennis and athletics.

We had meetings for parents, though we did not have an Association.   In those days I used to say that I believed in association rather than Associations.   Now I would say that one needs both !   There was one problem in particular which concerned parents, and I found myself involved, on their behalf, in a thorough-going dispute with the Education Committee.   It concerned awards to students proceeding, or wishing to proceed, to higher education.   At that time there were still state scholarships and county scholarships, bursaries and grants.   But county awards were far from automatic.   It was up to each Local Authority to decide the level and number of awards it would make, and the qualification required.   So a would-be student who was offered a place in a university could not necessarily count on getting a grant.   And this was the position of two of my sixth-formers in 1954, including my Head Boy.   Unfortunately there was no possibility of enlisting the support of my Board of Governors, because it never met as such.   In fact, my Governors were the Secondary Committee of the Education Committee, and they governed all the secondary schools in the town.   If and when they ever met they would see heads one by one.   So when this problem of the grants came up I called a meeting of parents, which was very well attended, and invited the Chairman of the Education Committee, with one of the Oldham M.P.'s to take the chair.   I felt it necessary, when the subject came up, to express my fullest support for parents who had raised it, and to challenge the Education Committee Chairman's claim that the Authority was actually generous.

That was not the end of the matter, as all the teachers' organisations were highly critical.   I belonged to the "Joint Four" (the four associations of heads and assistants in secondary schools) as well as the NUT, which I had joined in Somerset, and both supported me.   It so happened that in January, 1955 it was my turn to be President of the Oldham Association of the NUT, and I was encouraged by my colleagues on the Executive Committee to publicise the matter in my presidential address, which would be reported verbatim in the local press.   This I did, in no uncertain terms, creating a good furore in the Authority.   But I never learned how long it took Oldham to recognize that students offered university places should be entitled to grants, because by the autumn I was 4,000 miles away, and otherwise pre-occupied.

There were some Authorities which accepted the responsibility of entitlement, and others which tried to steer a middle course. One of these was Cumberland, and one year, I think it was in 1953, I was drawn by the Director, Gordon Bessey, into their procedures. They had a panel, consisting of the Director, the Education

Committee Chairman, Professor Brian Stanley, of Durham, representing universities, and myself, a Grammar School Head from outside the county. We spent several days interviewing students who had not automatically qualified, by exam results, for grants, and then decided whether a grant should be awarded, and at what level. It was a careful attempt to be fair, within the parameters of resources supposed to be available, which is why I agreed to take part, though I made it clear to Gordon Bessey that I was rather reluctant to accept the principle involved.

My escape from educational selection procedures still lay over a decade in the future. We had the usual 11+ problem in Oldham, where it was dealt with by a group of very conscientious Heads of local schools, using quite sophisticated statistical methods, including profiles of exam results and reports from primary school heads. If selection had to be, this was as fair a way as any. Incidentally, Counthill and its sister school, Greenhill, which was established in about 1952, "suffered" before this procedure even began, because many of the most gifted pupils had already been "creamed off" by Direct Grant Schools like Manchester Grammar School and the two Hulme Grammar Schools in Oldham. This was, of course, very frustrating when we were trying to raise the status of our Sixth Forms.

But Comprehensive Education was very much in the air, and it is to the credit of Oldham that the intention to "go comprehensive" had already been approved, though the means were not yet available. In the Head Masters' Association the recently declared policy of the Labour Party had raised hackles. The Branch to which I belonged covered Lancashire and Cheshire, and included such formidable personalities as Dr. Eric James, of Manchester G.S., (later Lord James, Vice-Chancellor of York University,) and F. R. Poskitt, of Bolton School. Each year in the autumn it was the custom to have a week-end conference at the Heaves Hotel, near Kendal, and to invite distinguished guests to share it with us. I believe it was in 1954 that our guests were Hugh Gaitskell and his two aspiring spokesmen on education, Michael Stewart and Alice Bacon. Also in attendance were the editors of the Times Educational Supplement and "The Teacher". I do not remember details of the very lively debates, to which Gaitskell paid the most careful attention, but I do remember feeling that Eric James, in his ivory tower, was not a true representative of Grammar Schools, since he was only dealing with the supposed "cream" and had no involvement with pupils soldiering on in the lower reaches of ordinary Grammar Schools, let alone the people in the Secondary Modern Schools who felt deprived.

Moving to Oldham, where no school house was provided, (or wished for !) we embarked for the first time on the purchase of a house. We found a former farm-house, stone-built, in Grotton, just over the county border, in the little bit of Yorkshire which intruded into Lancashire. This was the time when my personal education involved me in the domestic arts of decoration and construction, with some rather pathetic attempts at gardening. (It took 2 years to grow a carrot.) I became virtually a compulsive painter and paper-hanger, and also converted an old greenhouse into a garage. The family were growing up, and at the end of November in that first year Mary gave birth to another daughter, Ruth. We were fortunate to have a French "Au pair", Geneviève, who was well integrated into the family, and very capable. She shared with us the great sadness which befell us in the New Year. We knew that Joan was a "hole-in-the-heart" baby, but we hoped to care for her successfully until she was old enough to have an operation. However, when she was only 13 months old she died suddenly early one Sunday morning. Her ashes were buried in the Quaker burial ground at Rochdale, a yard or two from the grave of John Bright.

We kept up our participation in Quaker meetings, though the tiny meeting at Oldham was very different from those at Sheffield and Street. I was also, for a few years, Treasurer of the Friends Guild of Teachers, which held interesting conferences, usually in a Friends' school or college, just after Christmas each year. And we were regular readers of the weekly journal, "The Friend". Although I imagined myself settling down at Counthill for 10 years or so, and was not seeking to move, this did not stop me from looking at advertisements which appeared from time to time in "The Friend". And in the late autumn of 1954 I noticed a repetition of one particular advertisement.

The Friends' Service Council was the committee responsible for the relief and missionary work of the Society outside the United Kingdom. (Nowadays it is sub-sumed into the department of "Quaker Peace & Service"). F.S.C. had been asked, by the American Friends' Board of Missions, the missionary wing of "Five Years Meeting", based in Richmond, Indiana, to recruit a British Head for a new boys' secondary school in Kenya, under the aegis of the Friends Africa Mission, (F.A.M.), based at Kaimosi, some 30 miles from Lake Victoria. The advertisement which I have mentioned arose from this request. As I mentioned, it was being repeated. Mary and I talked about it. I was a Friend and a Headmaster. Why was it necessary to repeat such an advertisement ? Perhaps we should find out. So I wrote to the Secretary of the Friends Education Council, a former headmistress, whom we knew well, and asked if she could find out discreetly what the situation was, without mentioning my name, though she was free to indicate my status. The answer came back, that the personnel department were in difficulty because they had had no response. The Americans were in even greater difficulty, because they had been told that if they did not find a suitable head by the end of the year, the government funds which were available for building the new school would be allocated to the Catholics in the area instead of to the Friends. In the circumstances we felt that the least

we could do was to offer to come to London to learn further
details.   This we did, making it quite clear that we were not
making an application.   We met with a group of senior Friends in
Friends House, and at the conclusion they told us that if we
agreed they would with great relief commend us to the Americans.
We returned home with our minds and spirits in turmoil.   Just
before Christmas we travelled to Coventry to talk with Walter
Chinn, Director of Education there, and a Friend himself, who had
visited the Friends schools in Kenya, (there were about 300 !) in
1953.   He was able to give us more first-hand information, and
clearly gave us encouragement to decide to go.   Another
circumstance which added to the persuasion was that another
English Friend, Kenneth Goom, and his wife, whom we knew well,
were about to go to Kaimosi in response to another request to
English Friends, to supply a Supervisor for all the Friends'
primary schools.   By New Year's Day, 1955 we had decided to
accept, but not before a breakfast-time family conclave.   Would
the children agree to our going to Africa ?   Ruth, 3 years and 1
month old, agreed - 'if she could have lots of bananas".   Paul, 4
years older, agreed 'if he could have a bush baby'; - we had all
been watching the TV programmes of Armand and Michaela Dennis.
Peter, now 10½, agreed because he was keen to go to Africa anyway.

So it was, that together with the rest of the family, I looked
forward to a new adventure, - my African education.

In fact, there had been various nudges long before 1954.   Even
before the war Bernard de Bunsen had asked whether I wouldn't
like to go and join the staff of Makerere College, in Uganda,
which was a school at that time.   While I was at Leighton Park
Edgar Castle had wondered whether I wouldn't like to go to the
Friends' school at Antananarivo, in Madagascar.   At one of the
conferences of the Friends Guild of Teachers Helen Neatby, at that
time an Education Officer in Uganda, told us directly that we
ought to go to Africa.   And in 1952 I attended an international
Friends' education conference at Woodbrooke College, Birmingham,
where I met 3 Kenya Africans.   Their names were Joeli Litu,
Hezekiah Ngoya and Fred Kamidi.   Little did I know that one day
the sons of each would be my pupils.

2. My African Education.   1. Preliminary.

At no stage did the two aspects of my education interlock more
closely than in the years 1955-1964.   Before I could begin to
make a contribution of any value I had an enormous amount to
learn.

The first need was to learn about the educational scene in Kenya
at the time, in order to set in context the particular scene in
which I should be operating.   In writing the account which here
follows I have drawn heavily on information contained in three
important documents.   These are:- The Kenya Government's Ten Year
Plan for the Development of African Education, 1948, (which I will
refer to as the Plan);   the Beecher Report, 1949 (Beecher); and
the Binns Report on Education in East and Central Africa, 1952,
(Binns).   I had a copy of the last-named, which was a report
presented to a Conference in Cambridge on African Education in
West, as well as East and Central Africa.   Mr. A. L. (later Sir
Arthur) Binns, Director of Education for Lancashire, was leader of
a small group of educationists who had visited and studied the
East and Central section; they produced some illuminating
statistics and some important recommendations.   I was fortunate
enough, during the summer, to spend an evening with Sir Arthur,
who commented further and gave me much encouragement.

From Binns the following emerges :-

In 1950 the population of Kenya was about 5,400,000, of whom
rather more than five million were Africans.

The Government's revenue was £13,244,019, or £2.9s. per head of
population.

Government expenditure on African Education was £630,000, or 4%
of income.

Schools   were   of   three   grades:-   Primary,   Intermediate   and
Secondary, each catering for 4 years of education.

> 31.2% of each age-group completed Primary schooling,
>   having entered at 7 years of age or more !
> 3.7% of each age-group completed Intermediate
>   schooling; and
> 0.08% of each age-group completed Secondary
>   schooling, (i.e. they completed a Cambridge
>   Overseas School Certificate course.)

It is clear from these figures that the selectivity involved was
draconian.   I have often said that compared with an African
Secondary School at that time, Manchester Grammar School looked
like an all-embracing comprehensive !

The Government's 10-year Plan of 1948 gave further details of contemporary secondary provision, but clearly accepted the need for expansion. The classes in secondary schools at that time were known as Forms 3 to 6.

The Plan reveals that in the whole of Kenya, in African Secondary Schools, there were:

        in 1946   179 pupils in Form 3,
                       145 pupils in Form 4,
                        34 pupils in Form 5,
                        37 pupils in Form 6.
               (Forms 5 and 6 were both in the one school).
So there was obviously yet another stage of selection between Forms 4 and 5, operating under the Kenya African Secondary Schools Examination. (KASSE)

The Plan suggested that there should be:

        in 1957   800 each in Forms 3 and 4, and
                       400 each in Forms 5 and 6,
still, obviously, retaining selection between Forms 4 and 5.

The Beecher Report was the work of a committee set up by Government under the chairmanship of the Venerable Archdeacon L. J. Beecher, (later to become, successively, Bishop of Mombasa and Archbishop of East Africa,) to :-

"examine and report on the scope, content and methods of the African educational system, as well as a whole series of financial aspects of the same."

It may be thought surprising that Government should entrust such responsibility to a Churchman. But it has to be remembered that the first African schools in Kenya were all the result of missionary initiative. There was no government Department of Education until 1911, whereas in Nyanza Province, for instance, the missionaries had arrived at Lake Victoria with the new railway in 1902, and lost little time in establishing schools alongside their churches. It was not until 1934 that District Education Boards were set up, to manage secular primary schools. So, as Binns indicated, 5 out of 6 schools in Kenya were under the management of voluntary bodies, (i.e. missions), but funded by government, in recognition of the vital service they were rendering. Binns, (an entirely secular body, be it noted,) actually recommended:-

"that eventually all grant-aided schools should become at the same time State schools and religious schools, with governing bodies representative of the African local authorities and the African Church or Churches . . . "

Beecher demanded a greater expansion than was proposed in the Plan. It recognized this as essential if a greater number of educated Africans were to become available for administration, the teaching service, commercial and industrial life and, of course, the churches. It recommended the following revised figures :-

| 1950 | Forms 3 and 4 | 330 | Forms 5 and 6 | 120 |
| 1957 | Forms 3 and 4 | 960 | Forms 5 and 6 | 480 |

This was a modest improvement, but selection still remained between Forms 4 and 5. (KASSE again).

The report also referred, incidentally, to provision beyond Form 6. At that time the most successful Cambridge Overseas School Certificate (C.O.S.C.) candidates could be considered for places at Makerere University College, Kampala, in Uganda, which served the three East African territories, Kenya, Uganda and Tanganyika. Of course, this involved still more stringent selection. After two years on the equivalent of a Sixth Form course, or of the old Intermediate exam, which paralleled the Higher Certificate in my school days, students suffered the final selection procedure. If they were thought to have done sufficiently well they could then begin a degree course, various faculties, including medicine, being open to them. Short of that, there was a 2-year training course for secondary teachers. Beecher thought that Makerere ought to be relieved of the need to admit students straight from C.O.S.C. (This actually happened 12 years later, as I shall relate. Curiously enough I learned, in the autumn of 1985, from the most reliable of sources, that Sixth Forms are being phased out again with effect from 1986.)

In fact, development took place more quickly than either the Plan or Beecher envisaged. This was because the Colonial Development and Welfare Fund of the United Kingdom Government undertook to augment the pathetically inadequate capital provision that had been postulated. Accordingly, at the beginning of 1952, (in Kenya the school year runs with the calendar,) about 15 Intermediate Schools all over the colony began the process of up-grading to secondary status, by what one might call "growing out at the top". This meant that by the end of 1955 there ought to be almost 20 schools taking C.O.S.C., instead of the 4 which were doing so before that.

Amongst the Intermediate Schools to be up-graded was the Boys' School at the Friends' Africa Mission, (F.A.M.), Kaimosi, in what was then called North Nyanza. With the up-grading would go the provision of up to £80,000 for the building of a new school. But all was not to be plain sailing.

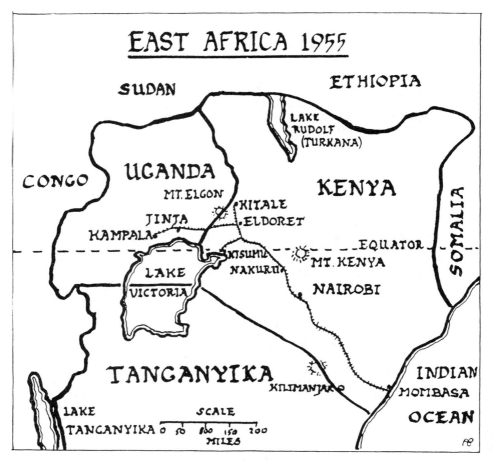

1. – Map of East Africa, 1955

I have described how I learned, while still in England, as much as
I could about the historical background.   But at the end of July
the time came for the family to set sail for Kenya.   Even on the
three weeks voyage from Tilbury to Mombasa we began to encounter
the actualities of life in Kenya.   Most of the passengers were
white public servants, missionaries or settlers in business or
farming, returning after 'home leave', or, like us, approaching
Africa for the first time.   We got to know quite a number.   But
there were also two Africans, returning to educational duties
after graduating in England.   We became very friendly with them.
Seth Odhiambo was returning to the Teacher Training College at
Kericho, while Ishmael Omondi was to rejoin the staff of the
Alliance High School at Kikuyu.   (This was the school which had
all the Form 5 and Form 6 pupils of Kenya in 1946.)   One
evening, in the latter part of the voyage, there was a dance on
the upper deck.   Mary and Ishmael danced together, - very well,
in fact, since Ishmael, as it turned out, was a champion dancer.
Relations with lady settlers, hitherto normal and friendly,
suddenly became frosty.   One lady went so far as to rebuke Mary,
telling her she had let the side down.   "Would you dance with
your cook ?" she asked.   "Do you realize," asked Mary, rather
high-horse, "that these are university graduates, probably more
highly qualified than most other passengers, and coming back to
Kenya to very responsible positions ?"   And as an afterthought -
"Anyhow, I expect you're actually rather jealous because I had such
a good dancer for a partner."   (Our fellow-passenger had, alas,
no crystal ball, or she might have seen us, in 1980, talking in
his office with the Director of Basic Education in Kenya, the same
Ishmael Omondi.)

I may add that there was quite a good library on board, and two
books, in particular, were of considerable interest to me.   One
was R. O. Hennings' "African Morning", a sensitive account of the
early experiences of a cadet District Officer in the Elgeyo
Marakwet District of the Rift Valley.   I now have a copy of my
own, which still gives me much pleasure.   The other was Elspeth
Huxley's "A Thing to Love", which made an impact of a more
immediate kind.   The Kenya Emergency, as we were soon able to
observe for ourselves, was an all-pervading reality.   Her
representation of it, published in 1954, inevitably leaned in
sympathy towards the whites and the 'loyal' Kikuyus, but also
showed understanding of the 'rebel' point of view.

When we reached Mombasa our inexperience landed us in an
embarrassing situation; or rather, it literally didn't land us.
We had not been warned that we needed an official permit to enter
Kenya.   Fortunately the retired missionaries with whom we were
to stay a few nights were able to help, by lending money for the
permit to land as visitors.   But I learned the lesson, and after

we got to Kaimosi I was able to persuade the mission to take out
a bond, which made it unnecessary for new arrivals to pay for
their permits, which we could obtain for them before they set off
from home.

We then began to learn about transport in Kenya.   All places on
the train to Nairobi were booked for quite a long time ahead, so
we had to get seats on a bus, for which we did not need to wait
so long.   The journey of over 300 miles took all day.   We had
our first sight and feel of the pot-holes and our first sight and
smell of the all-pervading dust which rose from the murram
(laterite) road.   And we had our first fascinated view of the
African Bush. When, after dark, we reached Nairobi, we were met by
members of the English Friends' team working in Nairobi and Embu.
They installed us in the Norfolk Hotel.   Now we saw direct
evidence of the Emergency which had been in force since 1952.
Many people wore holsters, and notices were on display, warning
people to keep their guns safe and not leave them in rooms.

A day or two later we visited the Friends' Centre on the Ofafa
housing estate, and attended out first African Friends' Meeting, -
so different from meetings with which we were familiar.   Our
contribution to the meeting was unusual.   Most of the Friends were
from North Nyanza, and the meeting was conducted in their
language, Luragoli.   The hymn-book was in Swahili.   We
understood neither language.   But the Friends did not know the
tune of one of the hymns.   Since we did, we led the singing, and
the Lord must have been quite intrigued to receive this unusual
musical tribute.

But it was on our first morning in Nairobi that I was plunged
into a particularly important learning situation.   While one of
the younger Friends took Mary and the children on their first
visit to the National Game Park, I began to attend to my duties -
and had a big surprise.   Our acceptance for service by the
American Friends Board of Missions, (A.F.B.M.), on the
recommendation of the Friends we had seen in London, had taken
place in January.   This, as I have explained, cleared the way for
the Mission to be awarded the government funds for building the
school.   I hoped I had not arrived too late to be able to play
some part in planning the physical development.   So I went to
see the private architects entrusted with the design.   In his
office I met Mr. McCullough, one of the partners in the firm, and
introduced myself.   "I'm so glad to meet you," he said.   "Now
please tell me, what is it you want me to design ?"   I had
clearly not missed the beginning !

It was difficult to reply because, for one thing, I had not yet
been to Nyanza province, much less seen the proposed site.   For
another, I had not yet seen any African school, and had little
idea of what might be appropriate.   I think we agreed that the

architects would sketch out some classrooms, labs, dormitories and a dining-hall, as well as some staff houses.   In due course, after I had been to the site, we would meet again.

On 27th August we left Nairobi, again by bus, arriving just after dark at Kisumu, on Lake Victoria, to be met by a posse of Friends from the Mission, who transported us about 30 miles and up about 2000 feet, to Kaimosi, where we were glad to go to bed in the house normally occupied by Kenneth and Helen Goom and their family, who were away on holiday.

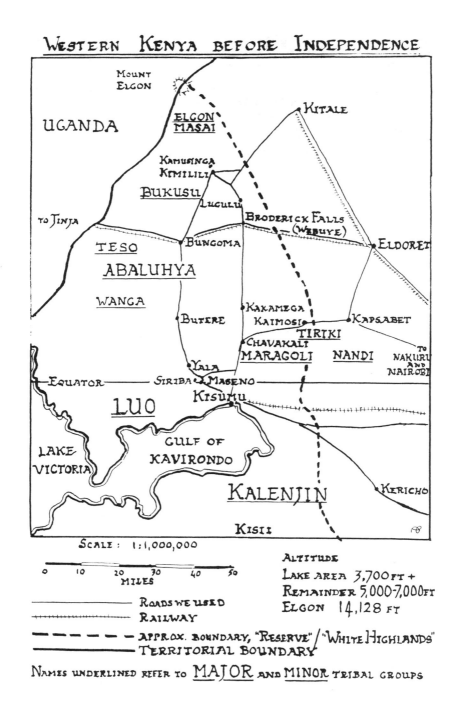

2. – Map of Western Kenya before Independence

The following morning we had our first view of Kaimosi.   The
various institutions and dwellings were set in grassy clearings,
with brightly coloured gardens.   Everywhere there were splendid
trees, survivors from the clearing of the forest which surrounded
the mission.   The spathodia, or "Nandi flames", were alight with
their large scarlet blossoms.   (Nandi is the name of the tribe
whose home lies just to the east of Kaimosi.)   Kaimosi lies at an
altitude of over 5000 feet and the climate, as we soon discovered,
is delightful.   Mornings are almost invariably bright and fresh.
In the rainy season the clouds build up, and in the afternoon or
evening there may be an enormous tropical thunderstorm, sometimes
with hailstones as large as table-tennis balls.   The older,
larger houses were mostly built of wood, but more recent ones of
cement blocks.   All had corrugated iron roofs.

A main road, rutted and corrugated by the erosion of the rain, ran
through the centre from east to west and there was constant
coming and going.   Local buses, called taxis, passed by, grossly
overloaded with passengers and goods of all descriptions, and
stirring up the dust.   There were always people on their way to
or from the hospital.   Women carrying live chickens, eggs,
vegetables or fruit, or with 30-pound bunches of bananas on their
heads, went from house to house, offering their wares.   In the
various gardens, or yards, as the Americans called them, African
men languidly attacked the grass plots with 'slashers', to make
sure there was no hiding place for snakes near the houses.   (A
slasher is a piece of metal, about an inch wide and a yard long;
the bottom of it is curved like a hockey stick and the edges are
filed sharp, so that they shave the grass as the slasher is swung.
-    Mowing machines would not have been the best way of dealing
with creeping couch-grass.)

Exotic birds, such as hornbills, flew between the trees and a
couple of sedate golden-crested cranes stalked the compounds,
sometimes stopping to admire their own reflections in the chrome-
work of a motor car.   At the edge of the forest you could often
see handsome white colobus monkeys swinging between the branches,
and sometimes little green monkeys could be seen raiding the
vegetable gardens or the plots of growing maize.

During the next few weeks we were acclimatising ourselves, not
only to the weather and the roads, but also to the company of
missionaries in which we found ourselves.   There was much that
was strange to us, because the practice, even the beliefs, of
Middle West Friends differ so widely from those of English
Friends.   Our reception was cordial and sociable in every way.
At Kaimosi every new arrival or departure was an occasion for an
open-air party, with what was called a "pitch-in supper" (or
"pigeon supper", as Ruth called it.)   But some of the underlying

differences did lead to difficulties before long, and these are a
part of the history of the new school and of my own learning, as
I shall tell.

Kaimosi was quiet at the time when we arrived, because term had
not yet begun and a number of people were on holiday, like the
Gooms.   So we had the opportunity to become familiar with the
lay-out, and to learn what institutions did, in fact, exist.   At
that time there were the Bible School, the Hospital, the Girls'
(Intermediate boarding) School, the Teacher Training College and
the Boys' Secondary School.   There was also a small Primary
School. The Industrial Department was responsible for water
supply, the electric generator, the timber-yard and the posho-mill,
(for grinding meal from maize,) as well as automobile servicing
and building repairs and construction.   The evangelical
department was not a physical structure, but an on-going activity.

There was a tiny office in which the daily business affairs of the
Mission were conducted.   The general direction of the Mission
took place from the large house occupied by the Executive
Secretary of the Mission, Fred Reeve, and his wife, Inez.   He was
also Education Secretary of the Mission, an arrangement dating,
like his appointment, from 1954.

Based at the Mission was the management of all its schools, which
were spread over the whole area where Friends were to be found.
(This covered a part of what was then North Nyanza, perhaps 30
miles from east to west and 80 miles from south to north.)
There was a small office, adjacent to the financial office of the
Mission, but for most of the time Kenneth Goom himself was
visiting schools throughout the area, or consulting with
government authorities and his counterparts in other Missions,
both Protestant and Catholic.

The corporate character of life at Kaimosi was very real, although
often difficult, even tense.   A deliberate effort was made to
make sure that we were all at least acquainted with one another.
For the first week or ten days after their arrival newcomers only
had breakfast in their own houses, because a programme was
arranged for them, so that they had their main meals with each of
the various households in turn.   This was very welcome and
helpful, and so it was that we began our social acclimatisation.
The children were occasionally non-plussed.   In one home we sat
down at a festive table, and at each place found a small card
bearing an uplifting Bible text.   Paul, accustomed as he had
become to the lengthy printed menus at every meal on the ship,
whispered anxiously, as he looked at his card : "Is this all we're
going to get ?"   It must be said that these social courtesies
considerably mitigated later tensions, even when they could not
remove them.

There was a regular programme of services, or "worship-meetings".
Every Sunday morning in term-time there was a large service in
the Mission Church for all the students in the Mission.   This
was normally conducted by a member of one of the staffs, and the
speaker might be a visitor or a member of staff or one of the
other missionaries.   There were hymns, readings and prayers,
much as in any Non-conformist chapel in England.   We were quite
accustomed to attendance at such services, because, as I have
mentioned, we were both brought up in Baptist families, but we did
find the hymns embarrassing.   Apart from some rather curious,
sometimes even painful, local deviations from familiar tunes we
found few hymns in the available hymn-book which we would have
thought appropriate for young people.   To us there seemed to be
overmuch   preoccupation with sin and its remedy, and a shortage
of opportunities for praise and rejoicing.

On Sunday evenings there was a Mission service in the Mission
room, a pleasant detached building which doubled during the week
as a nursery school.   This was a distinctly ex-patriate occasion,
although African staff were invited, and a few were usually
present.   The worship was led, in turn, by various members of the
Mission and the messages were very various in character.
(Curiously enough, I myself once expatiated on the Seven Deadly
Sins !)   Another purely Mission occasion was on Friday evenings,
- a Prayer Meeting which was held, in turn, in the houses of those
who regularly attended.   Here too leadership circulated.

By the time we arrived in Kaimosi a number of missionaries were
working   there   who   came   from   a   European   style   of   Quaker
background, based on the practice of silent worship.   These were
Dr. Rothe, of the Hospital, and his wife, from Germany, Onni Rauha,
Head   of   the   Boys'   School,   and   his   wife,   from   Finland,   and   the
Gooms.   Several of the American missionaries also found an
unprogrammed meeting helpful.   So these Friends had begun, during
1955, to hold a small "silent meeting" in   the Church, beginning
an hour or so before the service for students.   This had come to
be an acceptable innovation, even to people who did not wish to
attend.   Its significance as an innovation may be gauged by the
fact that when it was first mooted the leading evangelist in the
Mission declared that if anybody tried to start a silent meeting
he would get him thrown out of the Mission.   This was a legacy
of the Hicksite controversy in America early in the 19th century,
which had resulted in dividing American Friends into two main
groups of Yearly Meetings.   It was naturally the evangelical
group, incorporated in due course as "Five Years Meeting", which
set up the American Friends Board of Missions and engaged in
missionary   work   of   a   traditional   character,   founding   Friends
Africa Mission in 1902.   So the accession of personnel from the
other tradition inevitably caused concern.   At the same time
African   Friends,   who   had   their   own   Yearly   Meeting,   (with
considerably   more   members   than   the   20,000   of   London   Yearly

Meeting,) had begun to move about in the Quaker world community, and to experience aspects of Quakerism which were new to them. Hence the sensitive situation in which we found ourselves, and which was never far from our thoughts during the formative years of the new school.

Mission (business) Meetings of ex-patriate personnel were held each month, and by 1955 the local Yearly Meeting was also represented. The Chairman was Kenneth Goom. The various departments and institutions presented reports, and there was correspondence with the Mission Board, as well as with such bodies as the Christian Council of Kenya. Most items led to discussion. Usually there were decisions to be made, and often there were resolutions, comments, recommendations or requests to be sent to the Board.

These meetings were of considerable value, but like most meetings of people with such varied responsibilities, concerns, ideas and backgrounds, they were not always free of contention. Accustomed as I personally was to Friends' meetings where members expressed themselves pretty directly, I had to learn how to hold my tongue, - a hard, but very salutary lesson, which came to have a direct bearing on the new school.

Against the "global" description of the Mission which I have tried to give I must now turn to the Boys' School itself, its history and its prospects.

4. – After church, Kaimosi, 1956

2. My African Education.   4.   Kaimosi Boys' School.

As I mentioned (p.41) Kaimosi Boys' School was one of the
Intermediate Schools listed by the Beecher Report for up-grading
to secondary status.   The projected devlopment was gradual, with
one form of entry to Form 3 in 1951, and two in the following
year, with the first Form 5 added in 1955;   this to be the pattern
until 1958.   The School still remained in the list for up-grading
after the Colonial Development and Welfare Fund infusion.   In
fact, the forecast development turned out differently in two
respects.   First, there was delay in implementation, because there
was disagreement between Mission and Government, mainly about
where the new school should be sited.   Secondly, from about
1954 the school accepted a two-form entry, - but there was a
snag, namely that at Kaimosi there was no accommodation for Forms
5 and 6, so that until the new school was provided, boys finishing
Form 4 had to hope for places in Form 5 in other schools.

The classroom situation for the Boys' School was quite
satisfactory, apart from the lack of a laboratory.   There was a
large brick building containing a large hall, with wooden benches,
and six very adequate classrooms, three in each wing.   Two of
these were used by the Teacher Training College, and the rest by
the school.   The whole building, which is still very much in use,
has a corrugated iron roof and an imposing tower.   There was a
small store-room and a minute staff-room where the school clerk
functioned.

The significant shortcomings were in the boarding facilities.
There were four dormitories.   Two of them were in a new,
rectangular brick building.   The other two were brick rondavels
with thatched roofs, each containing 9 or 10 double-decker beds,
arranged radially as in an old-fashioned bell tent.   They were
laughingly called "Palace" and "Parliament".   The Training College
had two dormitories in another new brick building.   During the
early part of 1956 the cooking facilities, which served both
School and College, were still under a simple 'banda', or canopy,
in the open air, where the cook prepared the food in large iron
pots over a wood fire.   There was a single stand-pipe which
served as the sole water supply for all purposes for the two
institutions.   (Fortunately staff did not have to share the
stand-pipe facility, as Kaimosi houses did have water laid on from
the dam.   They even had idiosyncratic hot-water systems.   But
some houses had large tanks, to catch rain from the roof, - a
valuable stand-by in case the main supply failed.   They became
very important after the dam burst one stormy night.)

The stand-pipe   was also used to water the cattle which grazed
on the compound.   There were one or two African-style bathrooms,
that is, plain enclosures surrounded with reed matting, to which
bathers could take their basins of water for their baths.   The

only redeeming feature of this part of the site was that to the north one had a magnificent view towards Mount Elgon, 80 miles away. The cook served both institutions. Food was collected by representatives of each dormitory in large 'sufurias' (handle-less saucepans with a 1-inch rim) and taken back to dormitories to be shared out and eaten. However, during the year a new building was completed, with a kitchen and two dining-rooms. Cooking was then done in large Alfa-Laval boilers, and food-stores were available.

It was most unfortunate that the circumstances I have just described had to persist so long, owing to the disagreements I have mentioned. There was first the reluctance, on the part of the Mission and the Mission Board, to accept the idea of a British Head for the new school. But this was a stipulation by the Government, at the request of African Friends, who felt that since the curriculum was based on the English system, the school needed to be under English direction. The second reason for the delay was failure, for so long, to reach agreement on the siting of the school. And the way in which the problem was solved tended to continue for a long time to be a thorn in the flesh of Kaimosi. But the justification for the ultimate decision was cogent.

It is clear that Kaimosi had too many institutions, - indeed all the major institutions of the Mission. It did not make sense to add to the congestion. It was not always possible to reconcile the interests of all those institutions. But there was also a political consideration.

In 1949 there had been serious trouble in connexion with the Dini Ya Msambwa, (D.Y.M.), a break-away sect with a strong anti-European bias, and what could be called an apocalyptic element, in that the leader, Elijah Masinde, regarded himself as the resurrected or re-incarnated Prophet Elijah. (I was told, in 1985, that he still thinks so, though he is in detention.) At Chwele, a village in the foot-hills of Mount Elgon, in the northernmost part of the area in which Friends had for many years been active, there had been a violent confrontation, involving a number of deaths, and Elijah was detained. His home was, and still is, at Kamusinde, near the township of Kimilili, some 10 miles from Chwele. Kimilili was the centre of a Location of that name, which included Chwele. The area had had less development than areas nearer to the provincial capital of Kisumu; for instance, it had no major institution situated in it. Government therefore decided to improve the situation and so remove some of the grounds for grievance on which the rise of D.Y.M. flourished. Accordingly, it appointed a new, youngish, out-going Chief of the Location, to liven up community life by the encouragement of sporting activities, etc. It also designated the Location as one where Africans might begin to grow coffee, a profitable, but tightly controlled crop. Finally, they said to

Friends: "This is a part of your area; you already have plenty of things going on at Kaimosi; you can have the capital if you will site your new school in this area." That did not settle the issue, because the area is still quite a wide one. Friends had a mission station at Lugulu, in the same Location, some 10 miles from Kimilili, towards the railway station at what used to be called Broderick Falls and is now Webuye. There were an Intermediate School, several primary schools and a small clinic at Lugulu, and it was the site favoured by Friends. But water supply was going to be a problem. In Kimilili Chief Henry Wanyonyi, who was very much a local man, persuaded a number of landowners to agree to sell their land for the new school, and earmarked a 55-acre plot, just outside Kimilili township. I believe that it was only in 1955, not so long before we arrived, that this was confirmed as the site on which we were to build. I was told very recently that this plot is the very spot where Elijah Masinde first set up D.Y.M. There was a large Friends' Meeting in a large thatched church, and the members of the Meeting, who were having to abandon their land, asked that their name should be given to the new school. So it was that the school took the name KAMUSINGA, which means "The Place of the Bee-hives", because there were always a good many bee-hives, made from logs, hanging in the trees.

It was two or three weeks before we actually got to see the site for ourselves, because the rains tended to start early in the afternoon, and that meant that it was rather difficult to get to Kimilili and back, 65 miles each way, before the roads became seas of mud. However, when we finally got there our first call was at the Chief's office in the "boma", or administrative centre of the Location, to introduce ourselves to Chief Henry. The welcome could not have been more enthusiastic, because our appearance was the first real sign that something was going to happen. I have said that the area had no major institution, - and in those days, no institution was more major, carrying real prestige, than a new secondary school. So Chief Henry, a tall, exuberant, laughing personality, took us to see the site which had been set aside. The track for vehicles did not take us very far, and we followed a footpath between two fields until we reached the south-eastern corner. Then the track wound up a gentle slope between ten-foot high stands of maize and sorghum, with some finger millet, to some open pasture, where stood the large thatched church, with its little salvia-edged approach paths. Beside the church stood a large eucalyptus tree, and a little further off a more modest murembe tree, (erythrina), clad in its broad round leaves. Here and there were low mounds, ancient ant-hills, which provided me with little platforms from which to take the first photographs of what was to become a "small city set on a hill", and our home for most of 8 years.

The 55 acres formed a more or less rectangular plot, with the
church at the centre. The middle area was quite large and
flattish, open pasture interspersed with scrubby bushes, - typical
savannah country. The land sloped away in each direction, so
that the whole site had the conformation of an up-turned (but
square) saucer. From all points there was a splendid view of
Mount Elgon, which dominated the whole of the horizon from north-
east to just south of due west. The crater-rim of the summit
rose 30 miles away, and about 8,500 feet above us. (Kamusinga
lies about 5,600 feet above sea level.) But the foothills began
only a mile beyond the coppice of gum and wattle trees at the
edge of the school site. And above a village perched on a ridge
at about 7,000 feet lay the forest, which covered the slopes up to
about 11,000 feet, as we were able, a few years later, to see for
ourselves. Elgon is the third of the great mountains of Kenya
and can often be seen very clearly from 100 miles away. (Just
as Kilimanjaro is on the boundary of Kenya and Tanzania, half of
Elgon is in Uganda.)

To the south the white buildings of the Kimilili boma were visible
among the trees. On the site there was only one remaining hut
to be seen, quite deserted, and a few goats grazed here and there.
A local woman passed by on her way between her home and the
township, which lay, with its shops and market, about half a mile
beyond the boma.

It was very exciting to see this place for the first time, and to
begin to imagine what it might look like when it had become a
busy community. It had an openness and a grandeur which a
present-day visitor might never suspect, now that Kamusinga has
become famous for its trees, which actually make it impossible,
except from two elusive points, to see the summit of Elgon.

But laying out the campus was still, in September 1955, some
months in the future. And during those months I was not only
chasing up the project, but also getting immersed in school.

5. Kamusinga
1955

KAMUSINGA LAY-OUT 1963

Eucalyptus trees

Footpath to
Kamusinga
Intermediate
School

H.M.'s cook's
hut

Eucalyptus
and
wattle
coppice

Coffee
plantation

3

3

2

HM
3

2

2

3

3

3 (62)

3 (62)

2

New
playing field

Old playing
field

N

"School tree"

Dorm.

Clerk

Church

Dorm

Dorm

School
farm

2 labs (62)

Muremba
tree

Hall

Kitchen

Classrooms
Library,
Offices

4 classrooms

2 labs

4 classrooms

(62)

2 Dorms

2 Dorms

Water
towers

3 (62)

2 Dorms
(62)

3 (62)

Powerhouse

Young Farmers'
Shambas

3 (62)

Power-house (62)

Nyapara's
hut

Manual workers'
huts

Road to
Kimilili

Footpaths, gardens and tree planting not shown

Figures 2 and 3 indicate number of bedrooms

(62) indicates 1962 additions

Total area: 55 acres.   Each boundary about 500 yards

3. – Plan of Kamusinga Lay-out, 1963

During that third term, while plans and negotiations were under
way for the building of Kamusinga, the classes at Kaimosi Boys'
School were hard at work with the ordinary business of study.
In 1955 the staff consisted of the Head, Onni Rauha, and 5 African
teachers.   As is not uncommon in the mission Field, Onni had
really been rather lumbered with the school.   By profession he
was a scientist, not a teacher.   But he was very much liked and
respected   by   everybody,   and   was   a   very   dedicated   and
conscientious person.   When the school began to become secondary,
in 1952, an American missionary was in charge, who was much less
well qualified than Onni.   But in 1953 he left the Mission, and
Onni was asked to hold the fort until a permanent Head could be
appointed.   I have already explained why that took so long.
Onni was looking forward to returning to Finland in the new year.

The senior African teacher was Fred Kamidi, a prominent member of
the East Africa Yearly Meeting, whose association with the school
went back a good many years.   It was he whom I had met in 1952
at the Woodbrooke conference, and who had given the stimulating
talk about Friends' Schools in Kenya.   James Maura had an Indian
degree and Godfrey Awimbo, trained at Makerere, had spent a period
in England.   Moses Simani, a former student in the Boys' School,
had been trained in Kenya.   Unfortunately I have no record
concerning the sixth member of staff.

With four classes and 6 teachers the school was not under-staffed,
and I involved myself very little with it.   I was anxious to
devote most of my time during that term to getting things moving
as far as Kamusinga was concerned, and to familiarising myself
with some of the background to the secondary schools.   So Mary
and I spent three weeks at Lugulu, staying with Edith Ratcliff,
the missionary-nurse who ran the busy clinic.   I taught in the
Intermediate School, and also visited a number of other schools
with Jotham Standa, who was Schools Supervisor for the area,
working in Kenneth Goom's team, and who lived near by.   He was
also the Presiding Clerk of East Africa Yearly Meeting.   We were
able to make the acquaintance of the local Friends, and to get
some sense of the nature of the Yearly Meeting beyond the
boundaries of the Mission at Kaimosi.

In late October we jointly wrote an article which was published in
"The Friend", of London.   Here it is :-

"Jambo ! Jambo !"   "Mirembe muno !"   and all that.

In Africa it is natural for folk to greet one another, and as one
drives along the roads the children shout "Jambo ! Jambo !"
("Hullo") and wave their hands.   "Mirembe !" ("Peace") "Mirembe
muno !" ("Peace in abundance") is the greeting used daily by folk
in North Nyanza as they raise one or both hands, and then shake
hands in one of several cordial fashions.   And if you introduce

yourself the reply is always: "O sante !" or even, in English, "Oh thank you, thank you !"

During the last three weeks we have been hearing such greetings here near Mount Elgon, where we have been staying in the Mission House at Lugulu. Allan has been teaching in the Intermediate School, to gain first-hand knowledge of the background of boys coming to the Secondary School.

Nominally Primary Education in Kenya runs from 7 to 11, Intermediate from 11 to 15 and Secondary from 15 to 19.) All the teaching is in English. The age-range of the top form, (38 boys and 1 girl), is about 12 to 18. Allan found it surprisingly like teaching an English Fifth Form. Sooner or later the lesson turned into a barrage of questions, mostly, after the first few lessons, when England was the subject, technical questions about English. Often it was still raining at what should have been the end of afternoon school, but Allan found himself detained for up to an hour by the class. Only a day after he had corrected and returned a set of compositions he was begged: "Please can we do another composition, sir ?" - They did three in a fortnight !

In the third week Allan has been paying short visits to other Intermediate Schools. He has stood before strange classes, very like the one at Lugulu, and been cross-examined on all sorts of subjects. "What are the principal exports of England ?" "How much land does an English family own ?" "Do you have dowries ?" "How do we know that the world is round ?" "What is the House of Lords ?" What is your name, please ?" "Your age ?" "Your qualifications ?" "Your wife's name ?" "What does your Father do now ?" And nobody wants to stop when the bell goes. And when it is really time to finish, and Allan has said "Good-bye", one boy insists on asking still: "When will you come again ?" This is perhaps the nicest greeting of all.

Mary has visited two schools and spoken to girls between 12 and 16 who have a course on child-care. In each case she has gone for one lesson and only emerged after nearly two hours. Here the approach of African girls is probably more direct and un-self-conscious than that of English girls. The bearing and raising of children faces some of these girls within two or three years, (quite a lot marry at about 16), and they want to know all about the problems involved, including pre-natal exercises, baby feeding, chastisement of infant offenders, and so on.

Every day we meet new people, and invariably there is one question:- "When will the new school begin ?" We hope to begin building in the New Year, and to take possession in January, 1957. At present the maize stands ten feet high on some of the land. "We have waited for many years. Please try to make it quickly !"

Despite our linguistic shortcomings we are beginning to feel remarkably 'at home'. The sun blesses us daily at Lugulu, and at night we are caressed by the wind which breathes all the time through the tall gum-trees, and by the sweet scents of the garden. "Jambo ! Jambo !" says Kenya, and   "Mirembe muno !" Nyanza.

‡   ‡   ‡   ‡   ‡   ‡   ‡   ‡   ‡

So even in the Intermediate Schools the teaching language was English.   It was not actually essential, from the class-room point of view, for me to learn Kiswahili or one of the local languages such as Lubukusu or Luragoli.   In fact I made no attempt to learn either of these, but confined myself to trying to learn a certain amount of Kiswahili.   This had two uses.   First, as "Kitchen Swahili", it provided a means of rather crude communication with neighbours, employees of the school, and our own household and garden helpers.

The second useful aspect of this modest study was that I learned a little about the mode of thought which permeates African languages, and which explains some of the very unusual idioms, syntax and vocabulary often used by students when writing English, and to which I shall come later.   I have sometimes sensed a feeling of mild reproach because, although I am a graduate linguist, I never became proficient in Kiswahili, and learned only a few words of the local languages.   I always plead that after those first few months I was so pre-occupied with the manifold responsibilities and problems which daily demanded my attention that I lacked the additional time and energy required.

At the end of the school year we were back in Kaimosi, and I had the job of invigilating the Kenya African Secondary Schools Examination (KASSE).   This was the instrument used in selecting the students in Form 4 who might proceed to Form 5.   It was thus the final bottle-neck on the way to the COSC.   I disliked being involved.   But fortunately this was the last year when the examination was held, because by the next year enough places in Form 5, (to be re-named Form 3), would be available for everybody to continue the course.

Before the school opened for the new year I had my first experience of the recruitment of new students.   This took place at a sort of scholastic market-place in Kisumu, under the supervision of the Provincial Education Officer, (PEO).   Copies were available of the KAPE (Kenya African Preliminary Examination) mark lists for Nyanza Province, and the Heads of all the Nyanza Secondary schools, each with a colleague or two, were in attendance.   The PEO began at the top of the list and we learned which school each candidate hoped to enter.   Many of those at the top of the list had already been offered places at the

Alliance High School, Kikuyu, whose Headmaster recruited colony-wide. (The exam itself was a national one.) After this creaming process, each student in turn was offered to the school he preferred, and the Head accepted or rejected him as he thought fit. The process continued until all schools had accepted as many students as they could accommodate. People from south of Kisumu mostly went to the Government Schools at Kericho or Kisii. Catholics went mostly to St. Mary's, Yala. Girls who had not been offered places at Alliance Girls' School could hope for a place at Butere. The two best-known schools north of Kisumu were the C.M.S. School at Maseno and the Government School at Kakamega. Both were well established and by this time had completed their development to full secondary status. Kaimosi was very much a poor relation, since it was only half-grown, had had no chance to establish an academic reputation, and had those rather primitive boarding facilities. So as selection proceeded, other schools completed their lists long before us, and we were left to complete ours after they had gone.

It was not quite so simple as just going down the list and accepting the students in order. Some were obviously too old, even on their own assessment. I came across the names of several boys I had actually met in their Intermediate Schools. One of these presented a particular problem. He had been awarded a certificate despite a fail mark in English, because good marks in his other subjects had earned him a 'compensated pass' in English. (KAPE, like the School Certificate was a group exam. not a subject exam like our GCE.) Knowing him, I put him on my list. "But you can't take a chap who's only got a compensated pass in English !" said the PEO. So - a day or two later I was in Nairobi and asked the Deputy Director of Education: "Please tell me; is the qualification for secondary education a KAPE certificate, or is it a pass in English ?" "A KAPE certificate", he said. So I returned to Kisumu, and admitted my student. He is now an Under-Secretary in the Civil Service. Amongst the others whom I selected that day, one is Professor of Histo-pathology at Nairobi and in 1980 was President of the Kenya Medical Association. Another, in 1980, was Chief Economic Adviser to the Ministry of Agriculture, and was then seconded to the U.N. Food and Agriculture Organisation and stationed in Lagos. Others were the Principal, in 1980, of Kaimosi Teachers' College, and the very successful Head of Kakamega High School, who is now Deputy Director of Higher Education in the Ministry in Nairobi. Several others are Heads or in high-power managerial posts. But most pleasing of all is that for the last 5 years Alfred Ndukuyu Kimunguyi has been the very excellent Head of Kamusinga itself; he is even one of those whom I taught at Lugulu. In the late autumn of 1985 he and another Head, also a former Kamusinga student, were on a course in Bristol, and we were able to have them spend a week-end in our home. The "poor relation" of January, 1956 has thus had some eminent descendants.

In the middle of January the students arrived. Last year's Form 3 were now Form 4, and the students chosen at Kisumu were the new Form 3's. There were about 50 in each group. On the first evening I gathered together the new boys. Many of them, perhaps even the majority, regarded the school as a poor alternative to the preferences they had stated on their KAPE entry forms. It was important to try to encourage them to make the best of it and to feel that they were welcome. I remember that I began by telling them that I was as much a new boy as they were, but that as far as I could I would try to answer their questions. I know that we talked for quite a long time, and that I told them what I could about the plans for Kamusinga, but I only remember one of the questions. This came from a youth who lived near Maseno School, which actually lies exactly on the Equator, as a board on the compound states, whereas Kaimosi lies perhaps 10 miles inside the northern hemisphere. He was very disgruntled, obviously because he had not got a place at Maseno, so his question was :- "Sir, my home is on the Equator; so please could I be transferred to a school on the Equator, because I feel cold up here in the north ?"

‡   ‡   ‡   ‡   ‡   ‡   ‡   ‡   ‡

1956 was a year in which opportunity and frustration, teaching and learning, as well as construction, both physical and in terms of staff and other relationships, were ever-present pre-occupations.

The classroom was the least daunting of these. In principle, classroom discipline was ideal; everybody wanted to learn and nobody wanted to be a nuisance. The attitude of students was mature, - I doubt if any of those in Form 4 was under 17, - and it was in no way difficult to establish good relationships. The basic problem was cultural. I learned this, for instance, when, after the departure of Onni Rauha, a few weeks into the term, I found myself as the nearest approach to a scientist on the staff. That is to say, I knew Ohm's Law; and to keep the gateway to science open by at least a chink, I thought I had better try and pass on all I knew to the students.

As an illustration of the cultural problem, consider how one approaches the teaching of magnetism and electricity, as part of the School Certificate course, when none of the students has seen a telephone or an electric bell, and probably few have even used an electric torch. Students had so little of the background experience which can be taken for granted in even the youngest of 'European' children. The answer to this particular problem is, of course, that you have to provide the experience as best you can, - which is a stimulating requirement, especially when, as I have explained, you have no laboratory and no equipment. The stimulation is all the keener if you are not a scientist anyway.

Magnetic fields were easy enough, - but I can remember feeling less confident about a make-shift device designed to explain the motor principle. However, there would be two later years, hopefully with a laboratory and equipment available, when a real scientist might be able to make up for lost time. Meanwhile one must keep one's foot in the aforementioned chink.

Geography and History also presented problems, since the School Certificate syllabuses, although they made allowances, opened up horizons far beyond those in view of our students. Fortunately these subjects were taught at this time mainly by African members of staff, who fully understood the problems faced by students. Mathematics and biology were also less of a problem. Arithmetic, Algebra and Geometry were all within the grasp of any reasonably intelligent person, regardless of background. Furthermore, biology could more readily be based on personal experience than any other scientific subject. Crops and cows, for instance, had been a part of every student's life from infancy.

The most subtle problem, however, was English, - and the most important, since it underlay the whole of the curriculum. And it was the field in which most was required of me and, at the same time, in which I had so much to learn.

By 1956 the second-year students with whom I was concerned had been taught in English for 5 years, - but never, on a regular basis, by a teacher whose mother-tongue was English, and only in the year since they came to Kaimosi by an African teacher trained at Makerere who had first-hand experience of England. So it came about that linguistic limitations of teachers in previous schools, (who were in any case less highly trained themselves,) tended to be perpetuated and intensified in the students. This not only meant that they had difficulty in expressing themselves, but also that I was often baffled by what they were trying to say or write. That they had something to say was certain, something which I could not have said. I saw it as my job to insist that they should hold fast to this, and not simply try to reproduce the sort of material a 'European' might favour; and I had to help them to use the language in such a way as to make their contribution more effective. I began to appreciate this quite early on.

I have in my possession a composition written by one of these students as early as 1955, when I did spend a few days in the school, before I became the regular English teacher of the class. I have omitted the proper names, in order to preserve anonymity and to avoid any possible present day embarrassment. But I hope that the author, if he ever reads it and remembers it, will not mind my quoting it. The set subject was "My Home", and I have not altered it in any way. Here it is :-

My Home.   by * * * * * *   IIIa   Kaimosi S.S.

My home is in a sub-location called * * * * ; in a
village called   * * * * *   The place is far from
the big market of * * * * It is situated at a place where
people are still below the standard of civilisation.   The reason
for this is that no big or main road passes nearby.   A few years
ago many people around were not willing to sent their children to
school.   They were people who could not cooperate.   All these
things made them to remain behind.   It has been very recently
when many of them started knowing what education is.   All these
things of dis-organized people included my parents.

My parents are not people who are so old, they are people of
middle age.   The parents of my father were poor; so far when
they died did not leave my father anything to keep him up.   My
father married.   Mother was from a well to do family.   The
parents of my mother were capable of the things which were going
on in the country.   Mother encouraged father do work hard so
that they may keep up a better standard of living.   My father
has a family of eight including himself and mother.   He has four
sons and two daughters.   Two boys learn in * * * * in
different intermediate schools.   One daughter is still in Primary
school.   The other two one boy and a girl are still in the home
because they are below the school age.

My father has three houses.   They are all built of poles, grass
and mud.   One of these houses belongs to father and mother, the
other is for our cattle and chickens.   The remaining one is for
his sons because it is a custom that children over ten cannot
sleep in the same house with their parents.

My father is not well educated so he has not got good employment.
He works as a farmer though he has no big land.   My mother do
not have any employment but she looks after our cattle.   After
this work in the evenings and other times when she is not looking
after cattle she cooks for us.   These simple occupations make my
parents to run their family properly.

My home is a very lovely home.   I do not like to stay away from
my home.   The life and everything is so smooth that I do not
think of leaving it to go and live at a different place.   When I
am at home I help my father on the farm and sometimes look after
the cattle.

        *   *   *   *   *   *   *   *   *   *

This essay impressed me so much that before correcting it and
handing it back I typed out the copy which I still have.

Writing English compositions was at the heart of the training that was required. The essay subjects set by the Cambridge examiners in English Language could easily prove the undoing of any of our students. For instance, sport, current affairs and many other subjects were traps, because they usually involved the use of technical expressions which, from an examiner's point of view, had not been mastered. And in any case, such subjects were so commonplace that they risked boring the examiner. For most of 3 years, therefore, I was exhorting students to choose their essay subjects well. They should be subjects, I insisted, on which they could write with authority and, as far as possible, with competence, subjects which would give the examiner something fresh to read, of real interest to him.

The writer of the composition I have quoted, (let us call him Mark, though that was not his real name,) was amongst those who sometimes liked to venture into difficult subjects, and I feared he would fail. But he made no mistake 'on the day'. After the English Language paper in 1958, when he was a candidate, I went round the examination room, picking up the rough paper left behind, as required by regulations. On the floor beside Mark's desk I picked up the rough copy of his essay. He had chosen to write on : "Three treasures of my country". The first sentence read :- "Three treasures of my country are children, the land and cows." I needed to read no further. I rushed home to Mary in huge delight: "Mark must have passed !" I declared - and he had, as we discovered in due course.

We met "Mark" in 1980. He is now a very well-known and highly respected figure in a very responsible job. We talked much about the school days over 20 years ago. After we got back to England we had an unexpected letter from him; (he had told us he only wrote in reply to letters received.) It contained perhaps the most gracious compliment we could ever have received, for it began: "Dear Mum and Dad".

Reading and literature also presented problems. Even before we moved to Kamusinga and began to think about the set books for the English Literature exam we were reading and studying books which had been set in the former KASSE. I remember that we had a book of "English Narrative Poems". These ranged from various short ballads to "The Pied Piper of Hamelin". There were maidens with raven hair or flaxen locks, cherry lips and cheeks like apples, - not to mention snowy bosoms. - "Question sir ! What is a raven ? What is flaxen ? What are cherries and apples ? What is snow ?"

"Ah !" said I. "Well - - - - now just read on for five minutes and make a note of any other questions. I'll be back." And off I dashed across the compound to our house. "Mary !" I cried, "Doesn't the frig need de-frosting ?" "I suppose so" said she.

So I went to work collecting some lumps of ice. With an old knife I shaved the ice, producing a little pile of something like snow-flakes. Then I dashed back to the ever-studious class to exhibit the result and enable them to see the whiteness of the snow and feel its coolness. Grand finale - a few small snow-balls flung across the room at unsuspecting youths ! Another day, at my request, Mary had bought some of the rather pathetic apples then available in Kenya. I took them to class and exhibited them, giving a demonstration of peeling one, casting the peel over my shoulder to find my sweetheart's name, - and so on. A hand shoots up at the back of the class: "Question, sir ! Is it palatable ?" "You shall judge for yourself," say I, and everyone in the class has a small slice of apple to taste.

And there were the delights, after ploughing through pages of verse with a view, in the first instance, to comprehension, of reading aloud to the class. I remember giving a rather uninhibited rendering of "The Pied Piper" to an attentive audience. I believe it was on this occasion that I had the reward of hearing one student, with eyes agog, exclaiming: "Oh, what a sensation ! What a sensation !"

But the most insistent problem in the English class was syntax. African languages have a totally different word and sentence structure from those usual in English. I mentioned this earlier, when I confessed that I never became proficient in Kiswahili. But it was only as I made some modest progress in studying it that I began to appreciate some of the difficulties encountered by students, conditioned not only by their own languages, but also by the English used by many of the less well qualified teachers in the schools they had previously attended.

Idioms and vocabulary naturally presented problems, as they do between any two languages. Some African modes of thought are actually opposite to our own. For example, if I say to Wafula: "Have you not taken your medicine ?" and he replies "Yes", this means, "Right, I have not taken it." Whereas if he says: "No" he means: "Wrong, I have taken it." The trick is, of course, to avoid using the negative in the first place.

In the African mode of thought the normal way to describe some incidents concerning inanimate objects is also interesting. For instance, a bicycle accident may well have happened because "a stone got in the way."

As to vocabulary, Kiswahili has, for historical reasons, a much narrower range than English. The same word may be used for anything from a serious crime to a spelling mistake. I well remember one student telling me that he was unable to bring fees because his brother had "made a mistake" and the money had been used to pay his fine. On the other hand, the meaning of some

words is enriched in English by the way in which they come to be
used. But one may be rather puzzled, for instance, when somebody
refers to his "follower". He means the brother or sister born
next after himself.

The ex-patriate teacher had, and no doubt still has, much to learn
about African relationships. Students appear to have several
fathers and several mothers, - as, indeed, in African terms, they
have. Again, not all "European" uncles and aunts would be so
defined by African custom. Then there is the fascinating subject
of names. I remember one of the early classes I visited at
Lugulu, in which there were 5 boys called Simiyu. - no girls. It
was not long before I discovered that the one certain fact was
that these 5 were not brothers. On the other hand, they might
all be roughly of the same age, since Simiyu means, amongst the
Bukusu, "born in the dry season"; a girl born at that season
would be called Nasimiyu. Simiyu was much more likely to have a
brother called Wafula or a sister Nafula, both of which names
mean "Born in the rainy season." But this is not the place to
expand on the meanings of names, fascinating though I have always
found the subject. I refer to it as one of the features of our
new environment which it was necessary to recognize.

It was usually difficult to connect students' names with those of
their parents, since a boy was more likely to be given his
grandfather's rather than his father's name. Thirty years later,
however, I hear of a number of former students who have reverted
to the use of the patronymic.

As the last sentence implies, name changing is quite common, and
could be a problem. Perhaps this is a good point at which to
explain the difficulties in which it landed us for several years,
and the way we tried to overcome it.

It was very common for students to say to me that they wished in
future to be known by a different name from that by which I knew
them. This arose particularly when the Cambridge entry forms
had to be completed, and it can readily be understood that it
would be administratively most irritating to be asked to sanction
the use, for official purposes, of a name quite different from that
used in previous records. The reason was most often that the
student wished to begin to use his father's name as a "surname",
or to cease to do so. So in the 1980's the names by which many
of my former students are very well known are not those which
appeared in the school records. Indeed, the present Head of
Kamusinga, A. N. Kimunguyi, entered Form 3 in 1956 as Alfred
Ndukuyu, which names he now uses as christian names.

In order to tidy the matter up from an administrative point of
view I eventually adopted a system which seemed appropriate.
When new pupils first arrived at the school they were required to

bring with them their KAPE certificates. These were retained by the school, to be returned, together with leaving certificates, at the end of the students' school careers. However, the new entrants did not always want to use the same name as that on the KAPE certificate. So each one was interviewed and given a few days to make up his mind what his name was to be for all school purposes, including registration and fee accounts, examination entry and certificate and leaving certificate. The choice was free, but as far as the school was concerned it was irrevocable. This was convenient, and I believe it worked. But of course, what people did after they left school was their own affair.

There is one story about what happened to a student before he entered, which caused amusement for years. In 1956 one of our new entrants was called Henry Egalo; (I have changed it, of course !) That was the name on his KAPE certificate and on the school register, and we always called him Henry. The time came for Cambridge entry, so I drafted out the forms, including Henry's. Henry then approached me with some concern. "Sir," he explained, "that is not my name; please will you write Kongoni, (changed, for this story,) which is my real name ?" There followed an argument, and then the explanation emerged. Two years before he came to us he had sat KAPE as Kongoni and failed. So he went to another Intermediate School, span a yarn, and got a place in the top class as Henry Egalo. This time he passed KAPE and we admitted him. But he was stuck with "Henry" for daily life, and long after he left he would always rise to the bait whenever we so addressed him.

Boys' ages were sometimes indefinite or as changeable as their names. Let me give an example of each, which I still laugh about. In earlier classes there were a good many who did not know their actual ages, or who used different ages for different purposes, as might be convenient. The first example concerns a student, (probably the oldest, I fancy), in our first School Certificate class, in 1958. When it came to completing the forms, Cambridge required to be given a date of birth for each candidate. This student genuinely did not know his d.o.b. so I told him he had better choose one. "September, 1938," he said. "But you will have to have a day as well," I pointed out. He then paced thoughtfully up and down the room, and suddenly exclaimed, with much self-satisfaction :- "Friday !"

The other case was a little more subtle :-

It became my custom, towards the end of each school year, to pay visits to as many as possible of the Intermediate Schools from which we drew students, and to ask Headmasters to introduce me to the most likely candidates. I then had an interview with each of these. Amongst other things I asked each one to tell me his age, which I noted down. I also noted my own estimate, which was

often somewhat higher.   (I used this information when I was at
the annual selection meeting, because it was my aim to find the
youngest possible recruits).   One year, not long after the new
boys had entered the school, a register of electors was being
compiled, and anyone over 21, which of course included a number of
older students, had to be given leave to go and register. One of
the first formers also asked for leave, so I consulted my notes.
"But you told me three months ago that you were 16," I said.   He
was quite crest-fallen when leave was refused.

*   *   *   *   *   *   *   *   *

The fore-going digression took my account into later times, but I
must return to the experiences of 1956.   Outside the classroom I
found myself in a field where I had practically everything to
learn.   I was responsible for the financial administration of the
school.   This began with the collection of fees from students,
which was the most unpleasant of all my duties.   The budget of
the school was drawn up before the year began, based on the
number of students, with per capita allowances under various
heads, the principal ones being boarding and educational
materials, and also pay for African teachers and for non-teaching
staff.   The fees to be charged were laid down, and the total to
be collected was deducted from the total estimated expenditure.
This gave the amount which would come to the school from the PEO.
So unless fees were collected in full the school would have
insufficient funds to meet essential expenditure, which meant that
pressure on students had to be unremitting.   Most students were
awarded bursaries by their District Councils, and these gave some
alleviation.

I myself handled some petty cash, but at that time all monies
passed through the Mission offices, both outgoings and receipts.
I can remember becoming less and less efficient and more and more
confused.   Fortunately   a   guardian   angel   appeared,   a
septuagenarian retired accountant from the S.C.M. bookshop in
England, by name Fred Reader.   Apart from shedding sweetness and
light all about him in the Mission, he gave me my first lessons
in coping with accounts.

By the end of the year at Kaimosi Fred had taught me enough for
the accounts to be detached from Mission accounts and made my
personal responsibility, but for a long time I continued to lean
on his counsel.   It was not until September, 1958 that I was able
to hand over the book-keeping to somebody else.

I was of course in no way qualified to cater for the students, and
this was the job of my colleague, Moses Simani, who supervised the
cook and the menus.   Maize was a constant problem, – obtaining
it, storing it and milling it.   In the background were government
controls, requiring authorisations to purchase.   In addition,

storage and milling had to be agreed with the Industrial
Department, sometimes a delicate problem, as other Mission
institutions were involved.

6. – Family picnic on
Mt. Elgon, 1956

7. – Leaving Kaimosi, January 1957

2. My African Education.   5. Management.

In every new and expanding school the appointment of teachers is
bound to be a particularly major pre-occupation of whoever is
responsible for finding them.   And it was in attempting to build
up the staff that I very soon found myself in serious difficulty.

In the year 1956 we were well placed.   We had only one change
during the year.   This change arose because a young English
teacher, whom we had recruited before we left England, came to the
conclusion, at the end of the second term, that he and his wife
should return to England, where he wished to follow his vocation
to be trained as a Baptist minister.   So he was released, and we
were very fortunate to be introduced, through the Christian
Council of Kenya, to Estelle Hollinshead, whom the C.C.K. seconded
to our staff in September.   She remained with us as a tower of
strength for several years.   She had already served for 20 years
in East Africa in the Missions of the Bible Churchmen's
Missionary Society at Kapenguria in Kenya and Karamoja in Uganda,
and spoke fluent Kiswahili.   Her experience and her most cheerful
and amiable personality were of immense value.

The first problem was to recruit as many suitably qualified
African teachers as possible.   Fred Kamidi and Moses Simani were
to become colleagues of Kenneth Goom in the management of
Intermediate and Secondary Schools.   For family reasons James
Maura felt that Kamusinga was too far from his home in South
Nyanza.   Godfrey Awimbo was appointed to the Administrative
Service of the Government.   This meant that we had to recruit an
entirely new group of African colleagues, if possible graduates, or
teachers trained at Makerere.   As it happened we were very lucky.
Ezekiel Minjo, at that time the only Kenya African teacher with a
Cambridge degree in Mathematics, agreed to transfer from Kakamega
School to Kamusinga.   From Makerere we recruited three newly
qualified teachers.   The first was Filemona Indire, a Kaimosi
student before he had gone to Maseno for his secondary course,
who specialized in History and Geography.   The second was Henry
Owuor, another former Maseno student, whose home was in Central
Nyanza, and who was attracted by the prospect of taking part in
the pioneering of a new school.   He specialized in English and
Geography.   The third was William Okech, a schoolfellow of the
other two, whose home was near Maseno, and who was a biologist.

(When we were in Kenya in 1980, Ezekiel Minjo was teaching at
Chavakali Secondary School;   Filemona Indire was Professor of
Education at Kenyatta College, Nairobi;   Henry Owuor, now using
the name Anyumba and having a Cambridge degree, was Chairman of
the Department of Literature in the University of Nairobi;   and
William Okech was a senior inspector in the Ministry of Higher
Education.   -   Higher Education was defined, at that time, as the
final four years of secondary Education.)

These appointments still left us with a need to recruit ex-
patriate teachers. The Mission Board in Richmond was successful
in recruiting John Caughey to take overall charge of the Science
teaching. He came to us from the staff of Barnesville Friends'
School, Ohio, and arrived in late November, with his wife, Polly,
and their three eldest children, in time to help with the move to
Kamusinga.

A fundamental requirement for the new school still remained,
namely an English teacher to take charge of all the English
teaching. Estelle Hollinshead, excellent teacher though she was,
had no professional qualifications for teaching English up to
School Certificate. I myself had only a limited capacity to
undertake the work, and in any case I was, in effect, not only
headmaster and class teacher but also bursar, secretary and clerk-
of-works for the new building. According to government
regulations the staffing establishment of the school both
justified and required an appointment.

I therefore wrote to the Secretary of the Mission Board in
Richmond, asking for the post to be advertised by Richmond and by
Friends House in London. I received the reply that the Mission
Board, for financial reasons, could not give approval.

This was the beginning of a long and difficult problem. In 1981
I received from Richmond a copy of the document known as the
Elliott-Lampman Report, which had been drawn up in 1953 by
Charles Lampman, Secretary of the Board, and Errol Elliott, a
leading member of the Five Years Meeting and of the Board, with
the help of Walter Chinn, Director of Education of Coventry, after
a visit to Kenya. There are sections of that report which make
it plain that my difficulty ought never to have arisen.

The two Friends whose names the report bears had interviews with
government officials, members of the Mission and members of East
Africa Yearly Meeting. The most important concern which had led
to the sending of this deputation was that American Friends
feared lest government should intend taking over the educational
work of the Mission. I will only quote from what the two
American Friends themselves wrote, although Walter Chinn's
additional comments addressed and underlined the same issues.

A part of a review of "Basic Issues Considered" deals with what it
describes as "Problems of Devolution", including the following :-

"At Nairobi and in the Provincial offices we were reminded that
the central government has no desire or policy to take over
schools from missionary control, but much prefers to continue the
present practice of setting educational standards, financing
buildings and certain salaries and furloughs of missionary
teachers in specified categories. They cannot, however, allow

sub-standard work by Missions, and in the event of the failure of
any Mission body to carry out its work adequately, government or
another Christian body will take over.   No mission body should
resist this requirement of good educational work.   It is at this
point that our particular mission must accept a program of
reconstruction and advance as outlined elsewhere in this report."

Later the report continues :-". . . government grants are quite
liberal for the payment of personnel and the erection and
maintenance of required buildings.   From the viewpoint of the
increasing number of buildings and their maintenance it can be
said that buildings approved and paid for by government do not
constitute a potential burden on American Friends, nor does the
added number of personnel, so long as they fall within the grants
from government, except in so far as the cost of such personnel
may include extra expenses for long distance furlough travel and
the longer furlough salaries required for a one-year stay at home
by Americans."   So when I replied to Charles Lampman's refusal to
authorize additional staff, and pointed out that the Board of
Missions was actually under an obligation to staff the school
properly, I was only saying what he himself had written in his
report, but had evidently not taken into account.

The managerial arrangements for the school at that time were not
simple.   The local body to which regular reports were submitted
was the School Committee.   This consisted of nominees of the
Provincial Education Officer, (usually himself,) the Mission and
the Yearly Meeting, and the Christian Council of Kenya, the
majority being, Friends.   But the Committee had no real powers.
The purse-strings were held by the P.E.O., who also, in the last
resort, controlled the allocation of African staff.   Everything
else, except the purely professional aspect of the school, was
subordinate to the Mission Board.   Friends Africa Mission was
kept informed, and the school's affairs, like those of other
mission institutions, were discussed at Mission Meetings.

I did not believe that it was possible to staff the school
adequately unless the appointment of teachers was under local
control.   At the same time, it was important to relieve the
Mission as much as possible of financial responsibility for ex-
patriate staff.

At about this time developments were beginning to take place in
the management of secondary schools and colleges established by
other Missions.   There were consultations between the Ministry of
Education and the Christian Council for Education in Africa, which
had recently been formed as the educational wing of the Christian
Council of Kenya.   This was to lead to the gazetting by
government of constitutions for autonomous Boards of Governors
for these schools.   The boards were to be made up, like our
school committee, of representatives of government and missions

and churches, as well as the community, and they would fully control the schools, subject to financial regulations and the educational functions the schools were required to fulfil. The balance of representation strongly favoured mission and church interests.

It was therefore not long before I reached the conclusion that it would be the right thing for our school to have its own Board of Governors. This could be so constituted as to give Friends, African and from the Mission, the dominant voice. The Ministry of Education would encourage such a development. But when the idea was put forward in the Mission, opposition to it was very strong, and feeling ran high. A working party was set up to examine the suggestion, but in general the proposal was regarded as a move to "steal" the school from the Mission and turn it into a government school. I myself was even asked why I had come to do this to the Mission. I could not very well reply that the pressure to come had not been by me but upon me. I soon realized, (my education again !) that there was no possibility for me personally to persuade the Mission to accept the idea, and I was discouraged. So I spoke with Benjamin Ngaira, who was Chairman of the School Committee.

I told him of my failure, and said that I was withdrawing the proposal I had put to the Mission, because of the ill-feeling that it was causing. I said that if any change was to be achieved it would have to be as the result of action by African Friends.

There the matter rested for a good many months. The Yearly Meeting did take up the issue, supporting the idea of a Board of Governors for the school, and the Education Secretary of the Mission eventually agreed to make the necessary application to government. But it was not until 1960 that the Board finally came into being. Benjamin Ngaira became the first African Chairman of Governors of a Secondary School. (He later became the first African Chairman of the Kenya Public Services Commission, but he died after a sadly short period in office.) The Board had 14 members, representing Friends Africa Mission, East Africa Yearly Meeting, the local community, the Christian Council of Kenya, Makerere College and the Government, with 3 additional co-opted members.

Alongside the administrative evolution there took place changes in the way government was prepared to finance the appointment of expatriate staff. From 1958 onwards the Mission was no longer involved in paying the salaries of new appointments to Kamusinga. For several years there was a scheme which involved the school in receiving the appropriate grant and paying salaries and travelling costs between the United Kingdom and Kenya. Still later, expatriates were appointed to government service for secondment to Kamusinga, and were paid direct by government. These later arrangements did not prevent me from obtaining individual colleagues whom I wished to recruit, and who greatly strengthened the school.

I must concede that it was no doubt inevitable that tensions between Mission and School should arise on the matter of the Governors, and that I should find myself in the middle of it. Not only was the British colonial system being phased out, and very rapidly, during our time in Kenya, but the status and function of Missions were also being radically modified. As early as the beginning of 1957, in the preliminary papers for an educational conference of the Christian Council of Kenya, actually held at Kaimosi, the opinion was being mooted that District Education Boards should begin to relieve the Missions of some of their responsibility in the field of Primary and Intermediate Education. It was even being suggested that denominational rivalry in education could be reduced in this way.

The extent of the change can be interpreted as a measure of the success of Missions, at least in their function as the bringers of secular education. In the space of little more than 50 years their field had changed from educationally virgin soil to one bearing an increasingly heavy harvest. This had already made possible, as far as Friends were concerned, the establishment of East Africa Yearly Meeting, although it was not until 1956 that the Y.M. ceased to have a missionary as its Superintendent. And it must be said that F.A.M. always had a proud record in the field of education and training, and of encouraging the advancement of African Friends. It so happened that the time of our arrival coincided with a considerable acceleration of the process. Our 'offence' was that we did arrive at this stage, and were seen as the challengers of a status quo, although it was changing anyway.

We also caused some discomfort because there is an in-bred sympathy amongst Americans for the people of a colony and an unspoken reproof for any representatives of the colonial power, - and yet here were we, the colonialists, hinting at an imperialist outlook in Americans !

A fundamental reason for the misunderstandings and misgivings which arose on either side was the difference in attitudes to state education. In America there are states where religious education and worship, indeed the very mention of God, are banned in state schools. It is therefore understandable that many American Christians should be alarmed by the thought that the state might control a school. In England the position is different, because religious education and worship are legally built into the system. Furthermore, there are many schools run by churches with considerable state support. From an English point of view, the possibility of running what amounted to an independent Quaker school with almost 100% government grant-in-aid seemed ideal, and a very great privilege.

In December, 1959, during 'furlough', I visited Richmond, Indiana, and one Sunday morning I was invited to speak to quite a large forum of Friends.   I was at some pains to explain to them our responsibility and our opportunity.   They showed great interest in the completely unfamiliar scenario which I described. Evidently the Elliott-Lampman Report had passed un-noticed.

Another aspect of our problem had to do with how we saw the purpose of our being in Kenya.   The reason why American Friends were at Kaimosi and elsewhere was fundamentally evangelical; they wanted to be 'missionaries', and they saw themselves as bringing their message through their work.   The professional aspect of their work was sometimes of secondary importance, and in the past several people had found themselves undertaking responsibilities for which they did not have very appropriate inclinations or qualifications.   This was in no way to their discredit; the jobs had to be done by the people who were available.   The reason, on the other hand, why I had come to Kenya was that I was a professional person who was also a Friend, and that I was happy to exercise my profession amongst Friends in Kenya at a time when I could be useful. My purpose was never evangelical, and it was embarrassing to me to accept the description 'missionary'.

It was difficult for us to reconcile the two points of view, but 1956 was the year when they clashed most markedly as far as Kamusinga was concerned.   As time passed we all learned to make allowances for one another, not least because it was in the interest of African Friends that we should all do our work effectively.

It was just at this time that the weight of Africans was beginning to tell ever increasingly in the Quaker community, just as it was in the political life of the country.   Yet even at Kaimosi there were still distinctions between Africans and 'Europeans'.   In particular, there was 'European housing' and 'African housing'.   (The main reason was that much of the housing was intended for teachers, and government funding made a distinction between African and 'European' housing.)   Happily we could avoid this at Kamusinga.

But we were astonished to learn from the Presiding Clerk of the Yearly Meeting, when he had a meal with us in our house at Kaimosi, that he had never before sat at a table in a 'European' home.   And even in 1959, when I was having a very friendly talk in America with a former Kaimosi missionary, he felt able to say to me, referring to the time when I had withdrawn my proposal for a Board of Governors and spoken with Benjamin Ngaira: "But you did go behind the Mission's back to the Africans, didn't you ?"

I do not think I actually returned the counter-question: "Whose school was it, anyway ?" It was very difficult, even for such an admirable person as this one, to see the school and the whole educational system in any other than an evangelical setting.

I must not, however, leave the impression that life in 1956 was full of unremitting tension. It was far otherwise. Late in the year I was asked to write an article for a tiny periodical called "Here and There", published by the Friends Service Council for children in England. With that readership in mind, the article became a letter from our dog, Dandy. Here it is :

To All Dogs Everywhere

Dear Dogs,

I have heard that certain cats from Quaker Centres have been writing to one another. What I say is : "Every dog should have his day" so I am raising the first bark.

I live in East Africa at Kaimosi. To find me, you follow your nose roughly north-east for about 25 miles from Kisumu, on Lake Victoria. There are lots of us here, mainly Alsatians; but I am a Dachshund and my wife, Midge, is half Dachs and half Sealyham. (She has just presented me with four charming puppies.) At Kaimosi Mission the human Quakers are even more of a mixture than we dogs, coming from America, Germany, Denmark, Wales, England and East Africa. I sometimes sniff around to see what is going on. Now in the holidays it is quiet, but soon there will be 100 girls at the Girls' Boarding School, about 30 young women training to be teachers, about 50 young men doing the same, and 100 boys in the Secondary Boarding School. There is a small school where grown-up humans study the Bible, and near our house is a Hospital with beds for 100 sick people. (There are usually nearly 120 there; they just have to put the extra ones on the floor between the beds.) Near the Hospital some little houses are being built by a Work Camp. These are for people to stay in before they go home after being treated in the Hospital for tuberculosis. There are African, American, English and Danish young men doing the work.

The humans in our house talk a lot about the Secondary School. They say there will be a new one at Kimilili, 65 miles further north, near Mount Elgon. We sometimes go there. There are a lot of cement patches on the ground, with walls beginning to grow on them. The first walls I had a chance to sniff at are the walls of the house where my humans and I are going to live. Before Christmas there will be several houses for teachers, a place to make electricity, four big bedrooms with bathrooms, and a big kitchen and dining-room (my nose quivers to think of it !) Later there will be some classrooms and laboratories, but they'll have lessons in the bedrooms and the dining-room to begin with !

I believe my humans like talking about all this.   They have a
funny habit of smiling and looking up towards the top of Mount
Elgon, or else away into the distance, and saying what they can
see 50 miles away.   Personally I prefer the sights and smells
which are on the ground near at paw.

There are lots of these latter in the great Meeting House which
stands beside a gum-tree near the middle of the new school.This
is made of wooden poles and mud, and has a thatched roof, with
wooden shutters for windows, and the floor is beautifully smeared
with clean, dry cow-dung to keep the dust down – it's wonderful !
The School and the local Meeting are going to share this house
for some time, and the school will have the same name as the
meeting, which is Kamusinga.

We went up one Sunday, and do you know, I found the whole place
swarming with thousands of humans, chiefly in the very nice shady
little clump of trees right in what will be our garden !   I led
my humans into the crowd, and I found myself right in the middle
of Meeting.   My man says this was the biggest gathering of East
Africa Friends Yearly Meeting, and that it's rather different from
the meetings your humans have.   These Friends were sitting on
the ground or on school benches or desks.   There were hymns in a
language called Luragoli and Bible readings and prayers, and an
address by a very nice tall American Friend, Levinus Painter.   He
spoke each sentence in English and then an African Friend said it
in Luragoli, (the language spoken by most people in this part of
Africa).   He reminded the African Friends that he remembered the
starting of their Yearly Meeting 10 years ago.   Now it has more
members than London Yearly Meeting.   Quakers came to East Africa
for the first time 50 years ago, so they have spread fast, haven't
they ?   And did you know there were about 300 Friends' Schools
in East Africa ?

Before the end of the meeting some Friends stood up – the Clerk
and his Assistants, the Treasurer and others – and sang a hymn
together for the rest of the Yearly Meeting.   Ask your humans if
they wouldn't like to hear the Clerks of their Yearly Meeting do
that !   Just after the end I heard a rumble and saw a flash, and
our usual afternoon thunderstorm began.   In no time it was
raining absolutely boys and girls, and I was glad to get inside a
motor-car.

Well, that's how Yearly Meeting came to our garden.   I don't
expect many of you have had that happen, have you ?   But I am
sure you have had some pretty scent-sational experiences, so get
your humans to write to the Editor of HERE and THERE about them
some time.

Your sincere friend,
     DANDY

8. – Dandy

9. – Open-air Friends' Meeting

10. – The Family at Kamusinga
with our cook, Jeremiah,
January 1957

11. – School site, August 1956

12. – Classrooms and laboratories, late 1957

13. – Headmaster's house, late 1957

In parallel with day-to-day activity in the school at Kaimosi I was constantly concerned with the provision of the new facilities at Kamusinga.   In the latter part of 1955 I had met with the architect on the site and we had agreed on the overall lay-out of the required buildings.   He then drew up designs.   But before we could proceed we had to get these approved by the Public Works Department in Nairobi, since public funds were involved.   It was only after discussions and adjustments had culminated in agreement that Government released the first instalment of the £50,000 allowed for Phase I of the programme.   This was in April. We first paid compensation to the dispossessed land-owners and then went out to tender.   In the second week of May a contract was signed with Electrical Limited of Kitale.   This was a firm directed by two Sikh cousins, Dalip Singh and Pyara Singh, who lived in Kitale, which is about 33 miles from Kamusinga.   It was our shopping town, which we frequently visited.   We got to know Dalip Singh and Pyara Singh very well over the next 5 or 6 years, more than once visiting them in their homes.

The school was due to move to Kamusinga in January, 1957.   There would be 150 students, because we should be able to add a third-year pair of classes to the first- and second-year pairs, and there would be 7 teachers, including myself.   Since January was only 7 months away it was essential to draw up a very careful programme for the building, with firm priorities.

We decided that the target for January should be 5 staff houses, 2 dormitory blocks, the kitchen/dining-room/hall, and a power house for the electrical plant.   By the middle of 1957 we expected the completion of Phase I, which would include 4 class-rooms, 2 laboratories and 2 more staff houses.   In fact, the £30,000 for Phase II was very considerably reduced because of the on-going economic difficulties consequent upon the Emergency in Kenya, so our ideas for the additional class-rooms, library and administrative block had to be telescoped into one very tight building, whilst instead of two dormitory blocks, each with two dormitories, we got 3 individual dormitories of a different design.

The most notable feature of our order of priorities was that it involved a deliberate decision to start the new school without any class-rooms.   This was without doubt a right decision, as the disadvantages were far out-weighed by the advantages.   It was obvious that the whole school could not be completed by January, but it was imperative that we should be able to accommodate 150 students;   otherwise the school expansion could not take place. So we accepted that we should have to improvise, within the facilities available in January, in order to carry on with studies. As it turned out, the experience of that first term without classrooms was of vital importance in developing the enterprising character of the school, which meant a great deal to all the participants.

Once the building had been started I made periodic visits to the site, to keep an eye on progress, sometimes meeting with a representative of the architect, who came up from Nairobi. It was also necessary to arrange for furniture of all kinds, since there was nothing we could take with us from Kaimosi. Principal requirements were for beds, desks, chairs, tables and benches, and cupboards for the dormitories. Equipment had also to be ordered, - Alfa-Laval boilers for cooking, sufurias for serving food, cutlery and table-ware, mattresses, blankets and sheets. And of course there were also all the scholastic requirements for the new classes, text-books and stationery. I found that some of the furniture could be obtained most economically from the prison near Kisumu, and a type of desk was designed which we hoped would be appropriate, though in fact it was extremely heavy.

There was really little chance of delegating much of this responsibility, so that I found myself quite fully occupied, and continually under necessity to learn new roles. One of these was that of lorry-driver. (It was not until we actually moved to Kamusinga that we began to recruit non-teaching staff locally.) The grant from government included a sum of money for the purchase of a lorry. The Mission Secretary was able to get us a Chevrolet 3½-ton stake truck at a reduced rate and have it shipped out to Mombasa. When it arrived Mary and I decided to use the half-term break in third term to go down by train and drive it back. (I had already passed the required test.) We were advised that an empty truck on the Mombasa road of those days would give us a very bumpy ride. So we arranged to collect 2 tons of cement from the Bamburi cement works just north of Mombasa, and to bring it back as ballast for the Industrial Department of the Mission. Despite delays we did set off from Mombasa rather late in the day, and on the first day only got about half way to Nairobi. After Voi, (about 100 miles), the road was severely pot-holed and more than ankle-deep in dust. During the night, which we spent in less than luxurious accommodation, it rained, - for the first time in almost a year. This time the road was more than ankle-deep in mud, and on the steep climb towards the Athi Plain there was a long column of lorries and trucks of all descriptions, slithering into ditches and sticking fast. One by one a Public Works Department bull-dozer pulled them past the worst patches, with drivers co-operating in man-handling one another's trucks. We felt admitted into the fellowship of the road. - But we could have done without the cement ! That evening we found accommodation just beyond Nairobi, and on the third day continued our journey. Soon after Nakuru we were again on murram roads, - and there was more rain. We passed safely through Kapsabet, but as darkness fell

we were still about 5 miles from Kaimosi, - and we subsided
helplessly off the crown of the road into the bank. My first
thought was to leave Mary safely in the cab and to make my way
on foot to Kaimosi, hoping to get hauled out by tractor. After
walking a few hundred yards in the dark I began to think of the
forest through which the road lay, and remembered that it was
only a few weeks previously that Fred Reeve had shot a marauding
leopard. So I turned round and joined Mary in the cab. By the
time it was light the rain had long since stopped and the mud had
hardened sufficiently for me to drive off without further ado, -
and we reached Kaimosi at sunrise. After all that, the lorry was
very valuable for transporting to Kamusinga those belongings of
the school which did not have to be left at Kaimosi, as well as
the goods and chattels of the staff.

Before the boys left Kaimosi at the end of term we had a Farewell
Feast. This was a great occasion, attended by representatives of
all the other Kaimosi institutions and some special guests.

Fred Kamidi produced a very interesting history of Kaimosi Boys'
School, going back to its foundation in 1918, though not as a
secondary or even an intermediate school in those days. We also
had a very entertaining speech by one of the original students,
Jeremiah Segero, who by this time was Chief of the Isukha
Location, and a prominent member of the Yearly Meeting.

14. – The School Drum

As the time for our move drew near it became apparent that completion of the water supply to the school would be delayed, so we postponed the opening of the school from 17th January to 4th February. The advance party of the staff, however, moved on 10th January, and by 22nd January I somehow found time to write a newsletter to send home to England for reproduction and distribution to relatives and many other people who were interested. This is a part of what I wrote :-

"Conditions here at Kamusinga are still pretty camp-like. The water supply should be working inside a week from now, but at present we make daily lorry-trips with a couple of 45-gallon oil-drums to fetch water from the spring about a mile away. We manage to pump most of Caugheys' and Bradleys' share into the plumbing of their houses, but other folk's houses are still not ready and they just have large storage tanks in the dormitories where they are temporarily installed. They are wonderfully patient and cheerful and uncomplaining in these difficult circumstances and all are entering with the greatest interest and zeal into the plans for the future. I believe they will be able to carry the boys with them, and the prospect for this year is exciting as well as awe-inspiring."

The spirit in which the staff entered into the situation is illustrated by the wry, but very cheerful remark of one of the highly qualified water carriers :- "In my tribe this is women's work !"

Apart from the new accommodation we planned to have ready by the start of the year we also had the large mud-and-thatch church or meeting-house. But the priorities we had decided upon involved the acceptance of over-crowding in dormitories and the sharing of houses by all staff except Caugheys, (who had 3 children and no spare room: - of our own three only Ruth was at home as the boys were in boarding school at Kitale.) As I have explained we had a complete lack of classrooms or laboratories. None of the buildings was decorated in any way, and it was not until a very few days before the boys arrived on 4th February that all four staff houses became 'habitable', though two of them still lacked windows or back doors. Our generator was in operation and we were able to have electric light in the evenings, but the water supply was only connected in the nick of time, on 3rd February. However, the ablution and toilet facilities for the dormitories were not yet operational, since the septic tanks had not yet been completed. So latrine pits had to be dug at a suitable distance from existing and projected school buildings. And of course there were no roads, only tracks left by the contractors' vehicles as they moved about the site. (Chief Henry had seen to the provision of an adequate access road between government boma and the school). And naturally there was no kind of playing field

In the main school we had as yet no tables or benches or chairs, no beds or mattresses, and only about 30 desks. We did have blankets, cutlery, crockery and food. And we had a couple of cooks, who needed supervision because they were not very experienced, - so food could be prepared.

It might have been expected that when the boys arrived, as they did throughout the day, they would take one look and go back home. (This would actually not have been all that easy, since the average distance between home and school at that time was probably about 60 miles.) But in fact their response was entirely good-humoured and co-operative. We had taken the precaution, before they left Kaimosi for the holidays, of warning them what to expect, and we had even invited the new Form 1's to come and visit Kaimosi for a night, so that we could prepare them too.

The first meal in the hall was memorable. As there were no tables or benches, everybody had to sit on the floor. Outside was a pile of cubical stones, which were being used to face a part of the building. A number of these were brought inside, and the boys squatted in groups around them. Cutlery was set out upon the stones. Hardly were all seated when from one group there was a call to Mary, who was supervising the serving. "Please, madam, a complaint !" "Oh dear, Lawi, what is it then ?" "Madam," declared Lawi, "the spoons on this stone are miscellaneous !" Amid much laughter the meal proceeded, and soon afterwards everybody settled down in the dormitories as best he could.

On the following morning the whole community went into action. As one of the third-formers wrote, (we were now using the new nomenclature,) in his first composition of the year a little later on, the campus was not so much a school as a wilderness. There was no question of lessons for the time being, so we made sure everybody had a panga (machete) and set to work. During the first week furniture began to arrive, and it was no longer necessary for all to eat and sleep on the floor. The response to the situation had been splendid. The bush yielded to the pangas, and on 11th February lessons actually began.

These took place in the dining-room, the church and the four dormitories. In the morning beds were pushed to the end of the room, and the cleared end housed the class. As we worked we watched the walls of the classrooms and the laboratories begin to rise on the mere plinths that had been apparent when the year started. Two more staff houses also began to appear. For a few days the Mission's tractor-plough was on the site and broke up about 20 acres of school farm, 5 acres of allotments for the Young Farmers and various private gardens, as well as creating

our first primitive roads.   When term ended in April the dry
season was over, and there was already weeding to be done.

The very last day of term provided something of an agricultural
climax.   An area had been chosen and ploughed and terraced for
the establishment of our coffee plantation.   The number of trees
we were licenced to plant corresponded exactly with the number of
boys, - so each boy was allocated a spot and was responsible for
digging a hole, one yard in diameter and one yard deep, and
filling it with the prescribed mixture of soil and manure.

On the great day the seedlings were distributed and each was
lovingly planted, after a demonstration by Jocktan Kundu, our
driver, already an experienced grower.   Each seedling was given a
protecting mantle of sticks, leaves and grass.   I have a colour-
slide of the scene, with the backdrop of an enormous black cloud
coming round the shoulder of Elgon and promising us the customary
afternoon downpour.

Almost at the beginning of second term, in mid-May, we were able
to begin to use the classrooms and laboratories, although none of
the usual laboratory facilities were yet available.   It was not
until the first week in October that our gas generator was
functioning and the first bunsen burner was lit, - just about 13
months before the senior classes were due to sit the Cambridge
examination !

15. – Henry Owuor teaching Form 2, 1957

16. – Going into the Dining Hall

17. – Serving in the kitchen

18. – A dormitory

19 and 20. – Laboratory, 1957

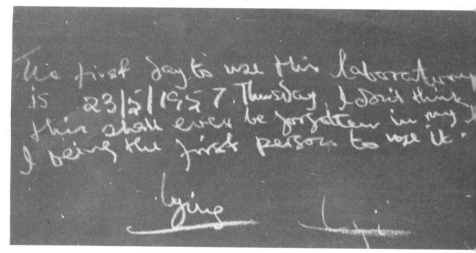

The first day to use this laboratory
is 23/2/1957. Thursday I don't think
this shall ever be forgotten in my
I being the first person to use it.

21. – John Caughey teaching in a laboratory

2. My African Education.   7. The Daily Round, the Common Task.

One grey English autumn afternoon in 1959, while we were on leave
in England, I sat down and wrote a short review and prospect of
Kamusinga, as it struck me from a distance after an absence of
about 4 months.   One passage bore the heading at the top of this
page, and others went on to describe different aspects of life in
the school.   What here follows is a series of extensive
quotations from that document, with some additional comment.

"Daily life at Kamusinga now conforms to a pretty regular pattern.
The boys rise at 6.30, just before sunrise, tidy dormitories and
classrooms, and go to their simple breakfast of maize-meal
(posho) porridge.   Before a school assembly at 8 o'clock a number
will probably have done some laundry, which is by now spread out
or hung up to dry in the morning sunshine.   Simple devotions,
consisting of a hymn, a reading and a prayer, unite us all, and
are followed by a morning of six 40-minute periods, with two
short breaks.   The fourth of these periods is for study, not
teaching.   Wednesday and Saturday are half-holidays, but on the
other days we assemble also at 2.15, after a fairly hearty lunch.
This is the time for notices of all kinds.   Then we have two
more 40-minute lessons.   After a cup of tea at about 4 there is
time for games and other activities until about 5.30, when many
boys like to have a shower-bath before supper, - which is another
square meal.   Studies, called 'Prep' or 'Preparation', go on from
7.30 till 9, when the school assembles for bed-time devotions.
Lights are out at 9.30, though the generator stays on until 10,
after which staff have to use candle-light or kerosene lamps if
they are not ready for bed.

"Half-holidays are used for games, laundry, gardening, study and
other pursuits of a voluntary nature.   The second half of
Saturday morning is devoted to communal work over the school
buildings and compound and farm, and there is usually a dormitory
inspection.   On Wednesday morning, instead of assembly and first
lesson, we have nearly an hour available for a meeting for
worship,   which we hold in the open air."

"A visitor to Kamusinga is, I believe, impressed by the self-help
which is apparent in the school.   Apart from the 4 cooks and the
5 wood-cutters/groundsmen there is nobody to do the work but the
boys themselves.   They wash, iron, scrub, tidy, dig, hoe, polish
and dust, - and they set such a good standard that I never
hesitate to show visitors round the dormitories."

(Incidentally, it will be noticed that I did normally refer to the
students as 'boys', although the word was in general use, in
colonial Kenya, to mean 'servants'.   I had consulted with the
Senior Prefect, who agreed that my use of the word in school
would not cause offence.)

"The curriculum.

"The curriculum is comparatively stereotyped, as it must be, to meet the requirements of the external examination for the Cambridge Overseas School Certificate, for which the boys are preparing, and in order to qualify them for the kinds of posts which they will be required to fill.   It is frankly academic, since the boys are of the necessary mental calibre, (they could never have gained admission if they were not of high attainments.) "Subjects studied are : (with the number of 40-minute teaching periods a week in brackets)   -   English Language and Literature (8) Arithmetic, Algebra, Geometry and Trigonometry (7 or 6) History (3) Geography (3) Agricultural Biology (4)   Physics-with-Chemistry (4)   Swahili (2 - 3 in upper forms only)   and Bible and Quaker Doctrine and History (3).   The scheme is very nearly the same for all four years of the course.   Some of the subjects have a helpful African slant, such as History, Geography and Agricultural Biology.   We are not at present able to offer options, although that is, of course desirable."

The question was often asked :   "Why do you concentrate on such an academic course, based on an examination system which is in many ways alien ?   Does it not have the effect of distancing students   from   their   own   background,   when   you   should   be encouraging them to plough back the results of their education into their own community ?"   It was this kind of thinking which lay behind the aims of Chavakali School, the second Quaker secondary school, opened in 1959, where an American I.C.A. programme provided facilities and equipment for practical training in agricultural and technical skills as well as academic subjects. Writing in 1965 in Levinus Painter's "Hill of Vision" (a history of Kaimosi), Fred Reeve stated that the motivation for this development came from the Maragoli leaders.   And in Walter Chinn's contribution to the Elliot-Lampman Report, to which I have referred, there is a passage which recommends strongly "that as soon as the present administrative problems have been resolved the Mission should press for the creation at Kaimosi of a new type of Secondary School, with a strong rural and technical bias, in order to off-set the over-academic nature of so much education in Kenya, and to serve for the area as one of the 'feeder' schools to the new Technical College being established at Nairobi and to such institutions of further education specialising in rural activities as may be established elsewhere.   In discussion with the Education Department it is understood that development of this kind is approved in principle."

(This 'new Technical College' - Walter Chinn was writing in 1952 - became, during our time, Nairobi University College, one of the three constituents, with Makerere and a new College at Dar-es-Salaam, of the short-lived University of East Africa.

It is now the University of Nairobi, which is, in the mid-1980's, the senior of 3 Kenyan universities. Its new Vice-Chancellor is Phillip Mbithi, who came from Machakos to spend 1962 and 1963 in the Sixth Form at Kamusinga. He was our Senior School Prefect in 1963.)

But the historical situation meant that priority had to be given at that time to conventional academic courses, despite their short-comings. This was, first of all, a national requirement, since rapid political advance, (and in 1959 we still did not realize how much more rapid it was still to become,) required the accelerated supply of highly qualified and capable administrators of all kinds. And as the privileged few who had been admitted to secondary schools, boys themselves demanded concentration on the attainment of qualifications which would enable them to take their places on the various ladders of advancement. They constantly referred to themselves as the future leaders, and this was also the role the community expected them to play. In the circumstances we accepted the academic responsibility as we understood it, although we were at pains to exploit as many ways as possible of broadening the base of our work, ways which I shall later describe. I took the view that Chavakali was too far ahead of its time in those days, and that it would be difficult to satisfy pupils by stressing practical courses when they knew that they would eventually be competing with people who had more conventional qualifications. By 1980 the situation had entirely changed, and I believe the school is now run with aims much more like those originally intended. Indeed, I was delighted, in 1980, to find a former Kamusinga student as Headmaster, and an enthusiastic believer in those aims.

I return to quotation from my musings of 1959.

"Money, money, money.

The economic aspect of the school may surprise people in other countries. The approximate cost of educating a boy at the school is 2000 shillings a year (£100), covering staff salaries and all other recurrent expenditure. From 1960 onwards each boy has to find 300 shs. in fees - with an extra 100 shs. in the fourth year, for examination fees. It costs each boy an average of 40-50 shs. to travel to and from school each year; there are three holidays.

"The lowest paid African teacher on the staff earns about 500 shs. a month. Those coming straight from Makerere start at about 675 Shs. a month. Our school clerk, one of our first 'graduates', started at 350 shs. a month. The head cook gets about 100 shs. and the lowest paid labourer about 50 shs. plus mid-day meals.

"The annual boarding grant per student is 400 shs., out of which the school has to provide food, 2 uniforms and (spread over 4 years,) 2 blankets, 3 sheets, 1 mattress, 2 games shorts, 1 panga, 1 jembe or hoe, as well as firewood, washing and toilet soap, toilet paper, disinfectants, laundry irons, replacements of cutlery and crockery and so on.   Rough prices, in shillings and cents. (1 sh.=100 cents) of some of the items we use are :- Meat 1.20/lb, cabbage 12 c/lb, carrots 18 c/lb, maize 35 shs/200 lb. bag. (Each boy eats about 350 lbs of maize a year.)   The actual cost of the food we give the boys, apart from all fuel and labour costs, is about 1 sh. daily, and yet mostly they feed better than at home.

"It is easy to see, from these figures, that the 300 shs. fees, plus, say, 50 shs. travelling, is a great deal of money for an African boy to raise, even if he is lucky enough to get a helpful bursary from his African District Council.   Add to this the fact that the majority of people in Nyanza still do not live on a cash basis, but count wealth in terms of cows, minor stock and land. There is an African song which has as its refrain : 'Cows are the root of all evil !'   We are often in a difficult position, having to put pressure on boys because if we don't collect the fees we cannot give the students the diet, books, etc. they need."

As a background to this particular account it may be interesting to recall that total government expenditure in those days was of the order of £33M a year, - quite a considerable increase from the £13½M quoted for 1950 in the Binns Report.

"Home and School".

"The same circumstances force many students into self-sufficiency, because the parents are unable to provide the financial support the boys need.   Similarly, it is a small minority of parents who can enter understandingly into the lives of their sons who are students in the school.   Very few speak English; a large number are still illiterate.   For this reason, and because most of the students come from a distance of 50 miles or so, we do not see much of parents."   (But we did do something about this later on.)

"The gulf between home and school is evident, again, when health is considered.   At the beginning of term sick parade is usually too well attended each morning, with ulcers, digestive trouble, etc., much in evidence.   As the term wears on the balanced diet and regular life have their effect, and sickness is much reduced. For the most part a 'staff wife' deals with sick parade, and issues remedies for the commoner complaints, such as coughs, bruises and malaria.   It is difficult to keep invalids in bed, as they dislike missing lessons !   Any more serious or persistent trouble is referred to the local Health Centre, which sometimes sends boys off to the Hospital at Bungoma, 25 miles away. One boy, by the way, is usually appointed orderly, calls himself 'dispenser', and dispenses cough mixture and epsom salts as required, with aspirin and anti-malarial drugs which the lady in charge will sometimes prescribe and supply."

For much of the time the lady in charge was Mary. There are countless stories which she can tell, – and even some which are told about her. During a visit to the Kenyatta Hospital in Nairobi in April, 1980, the President of the Kenya Medical Association, who is also Professor of Histo-pathology in the University, introduced her to a professorial colleague with his usual twinkle: "This was my doctor !"

With professional medical aid not always readily accessible, resourcefulness was at a premium. Another tale illustrates this:– Another Old Boy, now quite a senior Civil Servant, told Mary four or five years ago that he had waited 20 years to ask her why, when he had a bad cold, she had given him a couple of aspirins and told him to go to bed with lots of blankets, having first drunk 6 glasses of water. What was all the water for ? – The reason appears to have been, in the first place, to keep his mind occupied, but no doubt the physical effects were also beneficial !

On another occasion a boy was suffering from a high temperature and various aches, and did not respond to the normal palliatives for malaria, so we thought it best to take him to Bungoma Hospital. The M.O.'s eyes were better trained, and in due course he diagnosed measles, no spots having been apparent to Mary !

Occasionally we had more serious problems. One very large first-former had a severe attack of cerebral malaria, which caused what amounted to violent fits. He had to be injected locally, lashed to a spare door, and transported by Land-rover to Bungoma Hospital, with several boys ready to restrain him if he revived before we got there. Happily he largely overcame the affliction later on and for several years was an air-line pilot. He is now a very successful business man, and still holds his pilot's licence.

22. – The flag-pole arriving

91

23. – Sick Parade

24 and 25. – Saturday morning work, harvest time

2. My African Education. 8. Getting the teachers.

The manner in which staff were recruited changed considerably over the years, as I have already briefly indicated.

African staff, it is true, continued to be appointed to the Kenya Teachers' Service, and to be deployed by Provincial Education Officers.   However, there was never any serious difficulty if a school and a teacher were agreed about the desirability of an appointment.   The six or seven P.E.O.'s with whom I had to deal between 1955 and 1964 were always very co-operative in this respect.

There was only one really difficult period when our internal staff relationships came under strain.   This was in 1958, and was not fundamentally of our making, since it resulted from new official conditions of service for African teachers.   These contained provisions for the dismissal of African teachers for certain offences in their private lives.   There was no provision about such offences, (which concerned relations with women,) in the conditions of European Government service.   This caused considerable resentment, and three African teachers at Kamusinga refused to sign the new conditions.   A very tense situation arose, partly because, as I now believe, I allowed myself to get into a position of apparently supporting an unfair regulation, instead of side-stepping the problem by not following to the letter the then P.E.O.'s advice.   Our local member of the Legislative Council, Masinde Muliro, was called to the school to arbitrate, and he took the view that the problem was a national one, which could not be solved by one school, and he proposed to deal with it in Nairobi.   After he had spoken to the school the crisis subsided, but we did lose one valuable member of staff, who, for reasons arising from personal experience, remained unhappy and unsatisfied.   At that time there was only an embryo Teachers' Union*.   Otherwise Kamusinga might not have been afflicted in this painful way.   When the much strengthened K.N.U.T. organized a national strike some years later we had the same problems as everybody else, but they did not again threaten the school.

The largest number of African teaching staff we ever had up to the time when I left Kamusinga, and indeed for sometime afterwards, was 6; yet at the end of 1963 we had the equivalent of 17 full-time teachers.   And in order to achieve as many as

* In a paper presented to the conference on Christian Education in 1957, to which I have referred, the writer actually posed the question :-
    Does Kenya need a Teachers' Association ?
    If so, what should we do to foster it ?

6 Africans we accepted qualifications lower than those of our first African colleagues. We not only had teachers with no more than two years of training after School Certificate, but in 1964 we retained one of our first Sixth Formers to help us in the interval between school and university. I do not imply that these people were not excellent colleagues. And in mitigation of this reduction in the level of qualifications available there was a bonus, because we were beginning to recruit to the staff former students of the school, who brought with them valuable understanding and loyalty and, indeed, good counsel.

The reason why more highly qualified teachers were not available for Kamusinga and other schools was the rapid political advance being made in the country. Many of the Africans who moved into administrative and various other types of managerial posts were drawn from the teaching profession. Until then this had been almost the only field open to those who had had the most extended education. It is true that more and more schools were being opened, or promoted from intermediate status, - but it was a good many years after Independence before supply began to catch up with demand, so that there were enough African teachers to enable the schools to do without ex-patriates.

(But even in 1986 I know that Harambee schools have been only too pleased to have help from English students putting in a year between school and university.)

Meanwhile the need for ex-patriate teachers in all secondary schools persisted, and their recruitment for Kamusinga was amongst my most important responsibilities and pre-occupations. And the emphasis in recruiting was shifting. It was no longer the government schools alone who needed teachers with good academic qualifications. Schools under the wing of missions could not give exclusive emphasis to religious zeal in their new staffs. It is true, of course, that there were in Kenya very many Christian teachers who also had high qualifications and gifts, but there were not enough.

By 1958 the Mission Board in Richmond was no longer putting difficulties in our way, and our ex-patriate recruitment was concentrated through the Personnel Department of the Friends Service Council in Friends House. Other 'mission schools' were recruiting ex-patriates through the Overseas Appointments Bureau, (O. A. B.) in London, whose precise function it was to recruit staff for overseas schools associated with missions. We were able to get approval for F.S.C. to act in a similar way on our behalf. I have already referred to the way in which the employment of such recruits was funded; it was described as "O.A.B. terms", and it served us very well up until 1961.

But until August 1958 we were always struggling to fill the last couple of vacancies on the staff.   We had our disappointments, but also much loyal help from both African and European staff who came to us on a temporary basis.   We were particularly fortunate to have P.T.C.(Paddy) Lewin with us in the earlier part of 1958. He gave us two invaluable terms while he was waiting to take up an appointment at Alliance High School.   His energy and his enthusiasm and his gifts as a teacher helped us to survive a very difficult period.

The September term of 1958 started with our first "O.A.B." colleagues, namely two full-time teachers, one full-time teacher-bursar and two part-time teachers, who all arrived together for a 4-year tour of service.   These were Michael Wardell and his wife, Mina, Alan Davies and his wife, Anne, and my cousin, Helen Bradley.

All five were fully qualified graduate teachers with good experience.   (See page 98)   This injection of new talent and energy made an immediate impact upon the school, which began to hum, as a Place of the Beehives should, not only in the class-room, but also in many other ways.

I have said that the emphasis in recruitment had shifted.   In illustration I quote some notes I sent, in June, 1957, to George Whiteman, Personnel Secretary of the Friends Service Council, for his use in dealing with enquirers :-

"To any man of suitable qualifications who seeks a satisfying job, Kamusinga offers a wonderful opening, as the school is still in its early childhood.   And to a Friend who wishes to work for and amongst Friends of several different kinds, the stimulus is perhaps even greater.   Wives, too, will find that they can help in many ways; indeed, unless his wife is as keen as he, and is prepared to face problems cheerfully, as they come, a man had better stay at home."   I should add that on another occasion I wrote :-"Those who come will find themselves, excited, shaken, moved, shattered, challenged, depressed and uplifted, in bewildering succession, - but never, never bored !"

The process of appointment was a long one and we did not normally expect to see a new ex-patriate colleague until at least 6 months after we asked for one.

During 1961, as progress towards national independence gained momentum, so did the need for more ex-patriate teachers.   A new scheme was devised for recruiting young English and American graduates.   "Teachers for East Africa" (TEA) was a crash programme designed to supply potential teachers for Kenya, Uganda and Tanganyika, (as it still was,) on what might be called a 'wholesale' basis.   In America the project was handled by Columbia University, in England by Bristol University, and in East

Africa by Makerere College, in conjunction, of course, with the appropriate government authorities in each country. The recruits came in three categories. First, there were trained graduate teachers with teaching experience. Secondly there were trained graduate teachers with, as yet, no teaching experience. And thirdly there were newly fledged graduates who were willing to do their year of training as teachers at Makerere College, followed by two years of teaching in East Africa.

For the first, and smallest, category there was a very brief orientation course at Makerere. For the second there was an orientation course which lasted several weeks. And for the third there was a full teacher training course, including periods of teaching practice in secondary schools.

The allocation of TEA teachers to territories and provinces was done through appropriate channels, but preliminary contacts between schools and recruits were not impeded, so that we at Kamusinga were able to identify the candidates who would be happy and useful with us, and to request their appointment.

Our first recruit was in the second category, and he joined us at the beginning of 1962. This was Joe Timmons, from Indiana, who was to share the English teaching. Meanwhile we were in touch with Paul Hargrave, a Science graduate from Colegate University, who was in the third category, and he joined us later in the year.

During the first term of 1962 we were also host to third category students, including two young ladies, for purposes of teaching practice. Certain embarrassments which arose from the arrival of Joe Timmons and the student teachers were traumatic, but can be more appropriately recorded later, in another context.

These TEA colleagues had the status of Government Education Officers, seconded to the school, and their appointment in no way involved any other body; the school handled neither their contracts nor their salaries. It was therefore a great satisfaction to find how well these colleagues entered into the spirit of the school and earned the warm appreciation of the boys, as well as of their colleagues. In 1964 we welcomed a third TEA colleague, this time from the first category. This was Bill Cooper, an English teacher to replace Joe Timmons. He was a member of a Californian Yearly Meeting, as I discovered when I first scanned the lists of new arrivals. Both Joe and Paul were single, but Bill Cooper brought his wife Katherine and their baby.

There were two other ways in which we obtained temporary expatriate help which proved most valuable. Some time in 1962 two of our Sixth Form boys had joined a party of English Sixth Formers on a Brathay Park expedition in Uganda. One of the leaders was a master from Rugby School. Towards the end of the

year he wrote to me, asking me if we could make use of a Sixth
Former from Rugby who had completed his Cambridge entrance
requirements by December, was a very good mathematician, and had
two terms to spare. We were able to make the necessary
arrangements and in January, 1963 Jimmy Hase, fresh from school,
and totally untrained, began to teach, especially in Form 3.
When he left there was the customary feast in honour of departing
staff. (Henry Owuor was also off at the same time, to Cambridge,
to read English.) Speeches were made, and I well remember how
the Third Form orator lamented the departure of Jimmy, describing
him as the very personification of mathematics ! What Form 3
never knew was that there was probably not one of them who was
younger than this famous teacher, who was 17 at the time ! (But
it has to be admitted that such use of school leavers is
hazardous, and can lead to disappointment and distress, as we also
experienced on one occasion.)

The most unusual recruitment we had was a very great success.
John Peirson, a master at Rugby School, was due for a sabbatical
year, and he had heard about us from the colleague already
mentioned. He asked about the possibility of our having him
with us for a year. There was no way in which he could be
fitted into the usual procedures and terms of appointment, so I
believe we arranged with the PEO to claim the old-fashioned flat-
rate grant, ("mission terms") and appointed him as though he were
a missionary. This was enough to make the proposal feasible,
and John and his wife Rosamond and their children came to spend
the academic year 1963-1964 at Kamusinga. (See page 98) Quite
apart from the great expertise which John brought to the science
department, the musical talents and enthusiasm of Rosamond and
himself made a tremendous contribution to the life of the school.

By 1962 the normal basis for the appointment of ex-patriate
teachers was in line with that for the TEA teachers. They were
appointed as Government Education Officers seconded to Kamusinga,
and had two-year contracts, though we always hoped people would
stay for two tours.It was generally agreed that most ex-patriates
needed two years to reach their full effectiveness in the Kenya
environment. We were still able to do our own advertising and
interviewing in England, but once candidates and ourselves were
agreed, all formalities became the responsibility of the British
and Kenya Governments, with whom we maintained as close a liaison
as possible. Amongst other things the school was relieved of a
very considerable accounting burden. This method preserved the
possibility for us to recruit people who were not only
professionally well qualified, but also in sympathy with the
general philosophy and practice of the school. It also had the
spin-off effect that there was no reason, if all the parties
agreed, why an Education Officer in a government or other school
should not transfer to Kamusinga. In 1964 John Williams did, in
fact, join us from Kakamega by such an arrangement.

By the beginning of 1964 13 of the full-time staff were graduates and two wives who were graduates were teaching on a part-time basis. The total staff at that time was equivalent to 17 full-time teachers.

(Some biographical details about ex-patriate teachers just mentioned.

Michael Vardell had been a pupil at Great Ayton and Bootham Friends' Schools, had a Manchester Geography degree gained at Dalton Hall, the Quaker college, and had been teaching in the Friends' School at Ackworth, near Pontefract.

Mina Vardell had a Manchester degree in French and had been teaching in a Grammar School at Normanton.

Alan Davies had an Oxford degree in English and had been teaching in a Grammar School in the Liverpool area.

Anne Davies had a Leeds degree in English and had been teaching in the Friends' School at Sibford, near Banbury, Oxfordshire.

Both Alan and Anne were Friends.

Helen Bradley was a B.Sc.(Econ) of the London School of Economics and also had a year's secretarial training. She had spent four years training and practising as a teacher in Queensland, Australia, and had recently been teaching in Devizes, Wiltshire.

John Peirson had a Cambridge degree in Biology, having been a pupil at Marlborough School. He had taught for many years at Rugby School, where, on his return, he became a housemaster. He was also a gifted musician (instrumentalist).

Rosamond Peirson, daughter of a Rugby School master, was herself a graduate musician, also an instrumentalist.)

2. My African Education. 9. Shambas, Shenandoah, Shakespeare and
other Shows.

The academic work was at all times the top priority in the minds
of the boys.   But there were other strands woven into the texture
of life in the school.   Foremost was the fact that the school was
a Quaker foundation.   This had much to do with the importance we
attached, not only to religious matters, but also to the
encouragement we gave to every possible type of activity which
would broaden the educational experience of boys beyond the rather
circumscribed field of preparation for examinations.   But a
backdrop to the life of the school throughout the whole of the
period of which I am writing was the rapidly changing political
scene, of which everybody was at all times acutely conscious, and
in which we were all, in fact, directly involved.   But before
writing about that aspect of our life I must first give an account
of some of the broadening activities to which I have referred.   I
do not mean to infer that such activities were foisted upon boys.
The response to opportunities offered and the initiative shown by
the boys themselves would belie such a suspicion.   Even lectures
or talks by visitors, which were attended by everybody in the
school or in a particular class, invariably excited interest and
response.   No doubt this had something to do with our
geographical situation, which amounted to cultural isolation, so
that we had to be self-reliant if we did not wish to stagnate.

              *   *   *   *   *   *   *   *   *   *

The activity in which more than half the school were usually
involved was the Young Farmers' Club.   It had already been
established in Kaimosi days, not, as the name might suggest, for
social or educational purposes, but as a means of self-help.
Plots of land were made available on which individuals, (or
sometimes a couple of partners,) could cultivate the sort of
vegetables which were used in preparing school food.   When
harvested the produce could be sold to the school at the going
rate, (of which I have given some examples on p.90), and the
grower would have some money to help in paying his fees.

When we moved to Kamusinga we immediately allocated a suitable
area to the Young Farmers, and even had it ploughed over.   The
individual plots, or 'shambas', were allocated by the committee of
the club, and production was soon considerable.   But it was all
on a rather free-lance basis, which resulted in occasional gluts
and shortages, which benefited neither members nor the kitchen.
So the school, in its dual role as landlord and customer, required
the club to organise itself as a sort of Co-operative Society.
Naturally there were careful consultations with the club's officers
before the terms of business were fixed.   These were
approximately as follows :-

1. The school would do business with the club, not individual members. This meant that the club was responsible for all the detailed accounts of supplies to the kitchen store. The storekeeper accepted supplies in bulk and the secretary of the club kept detailed records of how much individual growers had contributed to the total quantity supplied.

2. At appropriate intervals the club secretary would hand to the school bursar a list of contributors and the quantities. The bursar would then credit the appropriate amounts to the fees accounts of the members concerned, debiting the total to the catering account.

3. The school financed the purchase of seeds at the beginning of the year. The club had to record the value of the seeds issued to each member, and report this to the bursar, who charged the members' accounts.

4. There was sometimes a tendency for members to neglect their plots, and thus to waste a possible amenity. A very modest rental was therefore charged to each member, on the principle that you take more care of what has cost you something.

5. The amounts credited periodically to each member's fees account remained purely credits until he had completed the year's liability for fees. Only after fees had been fully paid could he actually receive a cash payment. However, it was always open to him to leave his account in credit at the end of the year, as a savings account for the next year's fees.

The system worked very well, and it was possible, on the basis of a member's record, to give him special consideration. For instance, if we knew that a member consistently earned a good income from his plot we were able to be less rigid about the date-lines for payment of a proportion of school fees. Sometimes, too, we might help out with transport money at the end of term.

The volume of trade was always considerable, and in 1958, for instance, when there were only 200 boys in the school, it was about 3,500 shillings. This does not include the amount that members could quite legitimately earn in cash by selling produce to members of staff and other local people who might like to buy it.

The educational value of the experience was also not negligible. The following extracts are from a report written for the school magazine at the end of 1960 by the club's secretary :-

"The Club . . . aims at enabling the members to earn some money for fees and for other necessities, teaching them better methods of farming and how to work co-operatively."
". . . , we see that energy and wisdom, applied through proper socialism, removes fear, worry, poverty, and ensures prosperity."

It is interesting to note that the writer of this report is currently not only an M.P., but for several years was Assistant Minister for (of all things) Economic Development !

   # # # # # # # # # #

It was a corporate activity of a totally different kind which first brought the name of Kamusinga, hitherto unknown, into prominence, first (in 1957) at provincial and then (in 1958) at national level. This was the choir. It was the choir which put Kamusinga on the map.

In 1957 we were situated in what was known as Nyanza Province, which embraced the whole of Western Kenya, from Kericho and Kisii in the south to Bungoma in the north. Each year there was held at Kisumu a Music Festival, at which choirs from schools in all parts of the province took part. There were many classes, including, of course, one for boys' secondary schools. Each had to perform a prescribed song in English and an African song. The adjudicator was a distinguished musician from England, who was assisted by an African musician for the African song. In our class the choirs with the highest reputation came from Maseno and Kakamega Schools. It was therefore an enormous boost to our prestige when the Kamusinga choir carried off the trophy in 1957, (when we still had only 150 boys).

Usually the winning choir from each class would go on to compete, about a fortnight later, in the National Music Festival at Nairobi, and there would be a grant for expenses. It was too late, however, for us to arrange this, so we had to look forward to the next year.

At this time there were no ex-patriate musicians on the staff, and the training and conducting of the choir were carried out entirely by George Maleya, at that time in Form 3, the top class. But Henry Owuor was already an expert on African music and was able to help George in preparing the African song. George was simply a gifted musician with no formal training behind him. But singing was always an integral part of African community life, especially in the Maragoli area, where George grew up, and he must have participated in much musical activity there. At the end of his school career he became our school clerk, and subsequently school bursar.

The following year we were determined to go to Nairobi, and the choir prepared for both the Provincial and National Festivals. The African song could be used in both, but each had a different prescribed English song. The conductor this time was David Okuku, at that time in Form 3, and again, Henry Owuor helped with the African song. At the provincial festival we were disappointed to be narrowly defeated by Kakamega, but nothing deterred, we went ahead with our plan to make our first appearance at Nairobi, to compete with the redoubtable, and normally victorious, choir from Alliance High School.

Competing at Nairobi involved a journey of some 260 miles in each direction, and our mode of transport was the open school lorry. At that time the tarmac did not begin very much before Nakuru, so that well over the first half of our route lay along extremely dusty and corrugated roads. It was not possible to reach Nairobi in one day, so we arranged an overnight stop at Nakuru on both outward and homeward journeys. (Nakuru lies in the middle of the Rift Valley, about 100 miles from Nairobi.) We slept on the floors in the classrooms of a large Primary School in Bondeni, by courtesy of the Headmaster and of the PEO Rift Valley. We had our evening meal in a 'hoteli' (restaurant, African style) in Bondeni.

For many people in the choir this was their first long journey, and in itself an exciting adventure. The discomforts were considerable, but good humour prevailed throughout. We had road-side picnics, and even sampled novel kinds of food. Apples proved acceptable, but in those days not many boys found processed cheese very palatable. There was a lot of bread and jam.

The choir numbered close on 30, but pressure on the lorry was slightly eased, as Paddy Lewin drove his little Peugeot and was able to take Mary, (medical attendant !) and a couple from the choir. I sometimes relieved Jocktan Kundu at the wheel, and two others could sometimes squeeze into the cab. In Nairobi we were most hospitably received and lodged, for 2 nights, at the Pumwani Boys' Industrial Centre, and we were fortunate to have meals, as well as sleeping space, provided for us there.

Both in Bondeni and Pumwani every possible opportunity was taken to rehearse the two songs, until finally the afternoon of the competition arrived. Best uniforms, which had been protected from the dust, had been donned, and we made our way to the National Theatre.

The song in English was an arrangement for 4 male voices of "Shenandoah". The choir's performance in the competition was the best I had ever heard them give.

It was controlled and sensitive and very moving, and it was very well received. The African drinking song was introduced by David Okuku, who had the audience in tucks as he explained how it was possible in the song to recognize the sound of the beer going down "into the stommach" (as he pronounced it.) The performance was again finely controlled and very entertaining, with a superb bass solo by Arthur Arunga.

After all the choirs had performed the adjudicator presented his report and announced the result. Kamusinga were the winners, with A.H.S. behind them. A little later Kamusinga also received the award for the best African choir in the Festival. To have won both trophies at the first attempt filled us with euphoria.

Before we left Nairobi we went to the Kenya Broadcasting Corporation, where a recording was made of the two songs. These were subsequently broadcast, and we were also given a tape-recording. In 1959 I took the tape to England with me, and submitted it to the B.B.C. In due course I was invited to go and record some introductory remarks, and on 5th November the Kamusinga choir was heard in England. On Saturday of the same week it was heard again in the programme "Pick of the Week". The fees for these performances enabled us to purchase a suitable cup for our own annual choir competition.

On the way home, in the morning after we had overnighted at Bondeni, the pupils of the Primary School assembled in the sunshine, and the choir expressed their appreciation of the hospitality by giving a special performance of the songs. On the road the singing was almost continuous, though the repertoire was wider and the musical quality doubtless a little inferior. When the lorry reached Kamusinga in the late afternoon the school flag, which had gone with us to Nairobi, was unfurled, and the lorry drove several times round the compound, while the choir sang spontaneous paeans of victory and the rest of the school cheered them home. Kamusinga had indeed become a name that was known.

At two-year intervals the choir again went to Nairobi, and on the next two occasions they retained their status as the winning secondary boys' choir. We never again attempted the long road journey, but used the railway, - which was another adventure.

At Kamusinga a place in the school choir was as much sought after as a place in the school team in most schools. It carried with it the chance to go to other parts of the region and of the country, but it was not easily achieved. Western Kenya is the most musical part of the country, so that competition was very keen. By 1962 we had 9 dormitories, or houses, in the school, and each of these entered a choir for our annual choir competition. So we had the luxury of listening to 9 separate male voice choirs, each with between a dozen and a score of

singers, taking 4 parts. The most interesting part of this
competition was the selection of African songs which were
performed. Each choir was expected to perform a song which had
not previously been heard in the competition, and many original
and ingenious compositions resulted. It is perhaps worth
mentioning that many of the singers found themselves having to
learn to sing in an African language quite different from their
own.

$$* \quad * \quad * \quad * \quad * \quad * \quad * \quad * \quad * \quad *$$

The Debating Society may be introduced by quoting a paragraph
from its secretary's report, published in the magazine in
September, 1963 : -

"The aim of the Society is to help its members to be fluent and
reasonable speakers and the Society is beginning to a certain
extent to achieve this. This does not mean that all members of
the Society are reasonable orators, but a good number of them are.
The Society has the privilege of entertaining the whole school at
least twice a term by arranging debates which are run on
parliamentary basis. Occasionally we hold debates with other
Schools and Colleges when our football and volleyball teams visit
them or when the schools or colleges visit our school."

Debates were a lively part of Kamusinga life from the outset.
The fortnightly meetings of the 50 or so members were private
gatherings at which, amongst other things, the presiding member
of staff gave help and advice on the preparation and delivery of
speeches, as well as debating procedures. The Saturday night
debates, which could be attended by anybody in the school, were
conducted in parliamentary fashion, and were often very lively
occasions. The Chairman sat in an exalted position as Mr.
Speaker, with the Secretary at his feet. The hall furniture was
re-arranged so that rows of benches faced one another across the
gangway, and at the end facing the Speaker was the Sergeant at
Arms, ever ready to serve the Speaker by disciplining members.
Oratory was almost always flamboyant, and evoked equally lively
response from opponents. It was a favourite practice for a
member to rise ostentatiously during a speech by somebody else
and stride dramatically across the floor of the house to seat
himself on the other side. Just occasionally it might even
happen that at a later stage he would cross back again.

The motions for debate might be of almost any character, social,
educational, philosophical or political. I can recall only one
occasion when behaviour was other than correct, though it was
often eccentric. This was during a political debate held in
1961, while the minority party in the Legislative Council, the
Kenya African Democratic Union (KADU) was in office, the Kenya
African National Union (KANU) having refused to accept it because

Kenyatta was still in detention at Maralal.   But an article in
the school magazine dated August 1961 illustrates very well how
the school could re-act under stress.   I quote from it :-

"Early this term a motion was put before the whole School to
discuss.   It stated that, 'we move a vote of no confidence in the
present Kenya Government'.

It affects both the white and the black men who live in Kenya.
Boys decided to base their arguments on tribalism which of course
brought everything to failure.   But let us be realistic.   It is
expecting too much from human nature to think that all the
Africans in Kenya can obediently and unanimously come into one
party.   What drives this ?   Ambition is the motive.

"We have under tribalism abused the privilege of free speeches and
expression in the School.   Here we are to prove that we should
not follow other people blindly.   We do not want to invite the
seed of oligarchy and dictatorship to Kenya.   They allege that we
are few among many that have seen what life is about yet we still
can behave wildly and be childish too.   Thieves and scoundrels
also use the same motto.   From this we learn that even if we go
further with education we shall not uproot the tribalism in Kenya.
Men have got to be found to handle it.   We need to eradicate
ignorance, illiteracy and poverty.   But the greatest evil is
tribalism which has brought confusion in the running of the
Debating Society at Kamusinga."

Sometimes members of staff or visitors were invited to be the
main speakers, and the magazine records that in 1960 one debate
was honoured by the participation of our local member of the
Legislative Council, the Hon. Masinde Muliro.   The visits by
representatives of the Debating Society were possible because a
few extra bodies could usually be loaded on to the lorry when the
football and volleyball teams had away fixtures.   Such
opportunities were much appreciated, and of course, the
reciprocation of these visits benefited all at Kamusinga.

＊　＊　＊　＊　＊　＊　＊　＊　＊　＊

The most on-going of all the non-classroom activities was, of
course, sport.   Football, volleyball and athletics were the most
important activities.   During the first year the playing field
was under construction and of little practical use.   Volleyball,
however, requiring only a small pitch, was perfectly possible and
was always popular.   There were even occasions when it attained
considerable importance, because it was a game which could be
played with groups of visitors of the opposite sex.

The quality of the football began to rise dramatically in the latter part of 1958. Until that time the staff boasted no very skilful performer in any of the sports, so that the arrival of Michael Vardell gave an enormous impetus to the footballers. Players began to understand the meaning of the injunction to 'play football', and the effects were soon reflected in the results of matches with other schools. For long periods the team suffered very few defeats, so that Kamusinga became a respected name in sporting circles. I wish I had a list of the football team of 1960; I feel sure it must have included the name of the gentleman who, in 1980, became the very proud chairman of the celebrated Abaluhya Football Club, which enjoys a prestige in Africa comparable with that enjoyed, for instance, by Liverpool F.C. in Europe.

The quality of athletics also began to rise. The school always had outstanding performers in long and high jumps, and we also had at least two very accomplished pole vaulters. In other field and track events performances were gradually improved. The great event of the year was the Provincial Inter-Schools Athletics Meeting at Siriba College, (adjacent to Maseno School,) in June. This was always dominated by the Kalenjin athletes from Kisii. (The Kalenjin tribes produce most of the Kenyan athletes who have become internationally so well known in recent years.) Maseno, Kakamega, Yala and Kamusinga battled it out for second place. But in 1960 Kisii School was not in session at the time of the sports, and no Kisii team took part. The battle for the trophy was joined by the other schools, and it became the closest of contests between Maseno and Kamusinga. Excitement was maintained up to the very last event, the relay, in which the last Kamusinga runner reached the tape only inches in front of the Maseno boy, so completing a famous victory.

Other games were introduced from time to time by members of staff who were enthusiasts for them. American colleagues introduced softball, and for a time some people learned a little about basketball and tenniquoit.

A second football pitch and running track were prepared in about 1961, in conjunction with other developments which were taking place. These were in the centre of the compound. And at the beginning of 1964 a hockey-field was excavated, to have an all-weather surface of murram. Several years earlier some members of staff had also levelled and prepared a murram tennis court just inside the northern boundary of the compound.

That games were pursued not merely with skill, but also with eloquence, is well illustrated by the following report on volleyball results which appeared in the magazine of June, 1962 :-

"Our claim to be stronger than other volley-ball teams in Nyanza
Province and part of Rift Valley can be proved by considering
the teams we have beaten. Though a few managed to beat us, they
beat us through sweat and danger. . . . . . We are sure of
maintaining our UHURU STYLE and remaining firm."

＊　＊　＊　＊　＊　＊　＊　＊　＊　＊

Saturday evenings always offered an opportunity for relaxation
and entertainment, which took many forms. The occasions to which
staff specially looked forward were those on which the boys
displayed their own talents. We could always depend upon an
uninhibited show, with original music and original humorous and
satirical sketches. Any member of staff regarded it as a
compliment if he was the subject of an outrageous take-off.
School institutions of all kinds were burlesqued. I particularly
remember a mock choir competition, when the adjudicator sat
enthroned upon a chair on a table, to listen to performances by
rag-taggle choirs, under mad-cap conductors, rendering
excruciating versions of familiar hymn tunes. The straight-faced
and choleric adjudicator had no difficulty in awarding the trophy,
since he solemnly and severely disqualified one choir because the
conductor had a button missing from his shirt. In 1982 I
watched him sitting as presiding magistrate in a law-court not
far from where he handed down his first judgment, and afterwards
we enjoyed the memory of it together.

Characters in the sketches were often wondrously attired. On
one of the visits we paid to Nairobi Mary bought up a whole
bagful of old hats, the remnants of a jumble sale at Ofafa Friends
Centre, and added them to the props cupboard for dramatic
occasions. They proved enormously popular, since to wear one, so
it seemed, was to add dignity to the appearance of any conceivable
character, - and if two could be worn, so much the better.

The boys included many gifted impromptu actors, who loved
mimicry, and who usually took special delight in playing high-
pitched female roles.

It was in 1959 that these gifts were first harnessed to the
presentation of a serious drama, namely "Everyman", which was
produced by Alan Davies.

The stage consisted of a number of tables, assembled in the
washing-up area between the kitchen and the dining-hall. The
very effective costumes were concocted from the simplest of
materials, ingeniously adapted with the help of some of the
ladies, led by Anne Davies. Everyman himself was dressed in
khaki shirt and shorts, bedecked with a few coloured ribbons, and
he carried a rucksack and a staff. Death wore only a pair of
shorts, but broad white ribs were painted on his brown chest.

Another character wore a white surplice, made from sheets, with green trimmings. God himself wore a long white robe with coloured stripes and a resplendent halo. The robe was, in fact, a bedspread, and the halo a pleated lamp-shade which had been opened up and secured to his head by means of a ribbon bound round his brow.

The play held the audience spell-bound, and I can recollect no more dramatic and moving moment than that when Everyman stepped down into his grave from the front of the stage.

The play made such a strong impression upon me that I began to wonder how it could be presented to a larger audience. Miracle plays were performed originally for the ordinary people in public places and in the open air, perhaps on an open cart. What about Kimilili Market on a Thursday morning, and on the school lorry ? - But nobody on the market was likely to make much of a performance in English.

It happened, however, that the two Makerere students who were just beginning their teaching practice at Kamusinga both came from Tanganyika (as it then was) and were therefore Kiswahili speakers. They agreed to translate into Kiswahili an abridged version of the play which Alan Davies arranged. And this we decided to present. It was as near as we could get to the Bukusu language, because even if a Lubukusu version could have been written, not all the actors would have understood it.

In due course, one Thursday morning, the actors, (with a slightly changed cast), donned their costumes and climbed on to the back of the lorry, and we all went to market. The lorry drew up at the edge of the market area, the sides of the lorry were removed, and a form placed in position to serve as a step up on to the stage. But before the performance began it was necessary to attract attention, and then to make some announcement. So the most voluble of our Bukusu boys stepped up on to the lorry with the big school drum. Bang ! Bang ! Bang ! A greeting, and a call to gather round. As the crowd assembled he gave the people an explanation of what they were about to see and hear. And then, after a short overture from two guitarists, the performance began. What the people made of it I do not know, but the photographs I took at the time, as I moved about behind the crowd, are good evidence of the interest which was aroused.

Reading the school magazine of June, 1967, 8 years later, and after our time, I came across the following :-

". . . . . It was realised that drama could be used as a means of co-ordination between students and the local people, so that the masses could witness some of the diverse activities the school undertakes.

"So this year's production of 'Julius Caesar' by Mr. R. D. Pettit was an experiment in a new field. It was performed at Kimilili African Market on 29th March. Members of the cast in costume went round and explained what was going to happen. An audience of about 200 was gathered by the sounding of drums and the horn, and it kept increasing. The performance commenced with Rombosia's translation of the plot into Kibukusu.

"There is no doubt that the market people enjoyed the play. Women traders left their stalls and the cattle market virtually stopped selling . . . . .

"A good number of the audience believed that the murder and the suicides were real. In fact one woman came to check on Titinius crying 'They have killed my aunt's son. That last one they carried out is my aunt's son . . . Vooowi ! Where shall we go ?' "

To return to our own time at Kamusinga, - at the end of 1959 came a more ambitious production, presented in the church, (which had almost perfect acoustics.) This was "Macbeth", performed in an African, not a Scottish, setting. I was in England at the time, and was sorry to miss it, but reports were excellent. And the experience of participating in a play or seeing it performed was of the greatest value to students taking English Literature, with "Macbeth" as a set book, in the Cambridge exam.

From then on there was a major production each year, usually a Shakespeare play. So in succession we had "Henry V", "The Rivals" and "Twelfth Night".

With "The Rivals", in 1961, an innovation was introduced, for after the performances at Kamusinga the production was taken on tour and presented at four other schools and colleges. "Twelfth Night" also went on tour, being performed at Butere Girls' School, Kakamega and Kaimosi, but the two performances at Kamusinga, one before the tour and one afterwards, were of special interest because they were given in the open-air theatre behind the oldest classroom block. (The 1966 number of the magazine reported that the production of "As You Like It" was performed in as many as 13 schools.)

In all these productions we were fortunate to have such good relations with Makerere, since we were able to have the loan, on each occasion, of costumes from the college theatre wardrobe. Adaptations and ingenious improvisations were still necessary, but the visual effects were always colourful and enlivening.

26. – 'Twelfth Night'
Sir Andrew, Feste
and Sir Toby

27. – 'The Shadow of the Glen'

28. – Staff Play-reading

29. – Jotham Amisi, S.S.P., 1961 and 1962

30. – Washing Day – every day!

31. – Alfred N. Kimunguyi, Headmaster, 1982

32. – Alfred and Anne Kimunguyi and their younger children

In 1961 and 1962 the Dramatic Society entered in the One-Act Play
Festival at Nairobi, which provided members with valuable first
experience in a properly equipped theatre, and also gave them the
opportunity to see performances by other companies.   Our 1961
entry was "The Shadow of the Glen" by J.M.Synge, but set in an
African scene instead of an Irish one, - on the lower slopes of
Mount Elgon.   The play has four characters.

Play readings by the staff, or in which both staff and boys took
part, were quite a popular form of Saturday night entertainment,
which was also of value as a broadening of the dramatic
experience of boys preparing for the School Certificate exam.
Sometimes these were animated readings, for which the characters
donned costumes and actually moved about the stage.   The school
was highly amused, for instance, to watch the antics of teachers
and their wives in a fairly rumbustious rendering of "She Stoops
to Conquer", and the staff, for their part, enjoyed the opportunity
for a little play-acting, far removed as they were from
opportunities to visit a theatre.   On one other Saturday evening
there was a rendering of a much abridged version of "The Merchant
of Venice", with Guy Barnett, (see page 117 for biographical
details), starring as   Shylock, and Helen Bradley as Launcelot
Gobbo.

＊ ＊ ＊ ＊ ＊ ＊ ＊ ＊ ＊

Clubs in which smaller numbers participated were numerous.   For
the most part they depended upon the enthusiasm or availability
of some member of staff.   This being so, some of them tended to
fade out when a teacher's contract came to an end, but some had
acquired a momentum of their own, and the members were able to
recruit some other teacher to give them encouragement.   It must
be noted, too, that some of these clubs were very much the
province of 'staff wives', all of whom were very fully integrated
into the life of the school, whether or not they taught in the
classroom.

The earliest of these clubs was the Dancing Club.   Rather
surprisingly, as it seemed to me, there was considerable
enthusiasm for Scottish dancing, (which had been introduced
originally by an African colleague, Joseph Wanyonyi,) for square
dancing and for ball-room dancing.   For several years the club
flourished under the guidance of Nina Wardell.   It continued
after she left, her mantle falling upon Brenda Bradstock.

At a later stage the Fine Art Club, started by Anne Davies,
received a tremendous impetus when Tessa Beaver came to Kamusinga
with her husband, Harold.   She is a distinguished artist herself,
who delighted everybody with the paintings and woodcuts in which
she interpreted, I might say, celebrated, the Kamusinga scene.
There was a ready response to the opportunity to learn from her

in the club, but it was also possible to introduce some art teaching into the curriculum of certain classes. Everybody at Kamusinga in those days will remember how, under Tessa's guidance, the Art Club itself celebrated the coming of Uhuru with lively murals in the dining-hall.

But I must point out that the first Kamusinga artist emerged in 1958, when Elfas Webbo became one of our first three Makerere students, training as an art teacher. He has recently published a most valuable book to stimulate and assist teachers of art in primary schools. He is a tutor at Siriba College.

Another small club, the Bookbinding Guild, ran for several years from 1959 under the guidance of another lady, this time a close neighbour, Kathleen Charles. Her husband, Leslie Charles, had succeeded Kenneth Goom as Schools Supervisor, and they lived with their family in a house adjacent to our compound, just beyond the old football pitch. The Guild learned something of a number of useful crafts, and also had expeditions to Kitale, to visit Kitale Printers and see the printing process in operation.

As is the way with enthusiastic teachers, specialists on the staff were not slow to start appropriate clubs which supplemented the experience of the classroom. One of the earliest was the Science Club, which originated under John Caughey, and continued to flourish as other scientists stepped into John's shoes.

A little later came the Geographical and Historical Club, which eventually became two separate societies, both of which, as the magazine reported, were still flourishing in 1971. They had talks from staff, visitors and members, and occasional films, and whenever possible they went on excursions.

The Folk-Lore Club flourished for several years under the wing of Henry Owuor. The club interested itself in folk music and what is known nowadays as Oral Literature. Henry Owuor, better known these days as Anyumba, is currently amongst the most eminent Kenyan experts in this field. But this expertise was already much in evidence in early Kamusinga days, to the enrichment, not only of the club, but also of everybody in the school. To all of us he unfolded the variety and importance of song and dance and instrumental music and the stories and wisdom of African society, not only in his own native Luo country, but also among other tribal groups. The researches of the club overlapped the activities of the house choirs to which I have referred, and also produced contributions to Saturday night entertainments.

A related activity which flourished particularly during 1960 and 1961 was a highly practical programme of research into local history. Amongst our many visitors was Miss Zoë Marsh, an Inspector from the Ministry of Education, who was anxious to develop methods of encouraging history teaching in Primary and Intermediate Schools. She wanted to provide teachers in these schools with materials on which they could draw, and which would stimulate them to produce material of their own. She planned the publication of a series of booklets, each relating to a different area, which would record some of what had been discovered about the local past. Kamusinga, under the direction of Guy Barnett, was to work on the area to the north of Lake Victoria.

The method was, first, to review what was already known, either by the boys themselves or through existing writings which might be available. When a framework had been agreed and the holidays came, the boys, mainly third formers, returned to their homes and began to ask questions, especially of the old men and women of their communities. A week or two later Guy Barnett visited each of them for several days and the work was intensified, with very interesting results.

During the following term the information collected was sifted and arranged. It was then given dramatic form, and presented to the school in a series of scenes. These scenes vividly portrayed the social customs of an older generation, as well as salient incidents from the past, such as the first appearance of white men, which was well within the recollection of the old people consulted. In due course the booklet was published by the Cambridge University Press, with the title : "By the Lake".

*   *   *   *   *   *   *   *   *   *

The fact that it is possible, so many years later, to revive memories of so many activities which enriched life at Kamusinga is due, in no small measure, to the magazine, "The Kamusinga". This started as a wall magazine at an early stage, but to my knowledge none of this has survived. It must have been in 1958 or 1959 that a magazine proper was published. This was a home-made production, duplicated from stencils on ordinary duplicating paper, embellished with a distinctive blue cover, and bound together with staples. The earliest copy in my possession is No.6, published in December, 1960, price 45 cents. Numbers 7 and 8, which I also have, were both published in 1961, and the price had risen to 50 cents. In June, 1962, for the first time, a printed magazine appeared, inscribed Volume 1 Number 1. It was printed by Kitale Printers Ltd., and the inside cover contained several advertisements by firms with whom we often did business. After this the magazine appeared annually, usually in June or July. My own collection includes all the numbers from 1 to 7 (1968) as well as number 10 (1971). They formed a most useful aide-mémoire to me during our 1980 visit, and I have referred to them continually in writing this story. The contents of the magazine were always informative, full of variety and entertaining.

Take, for example, Vol.1,No.2, published in September, 1963.

A list of staff, teaching and non-teaching.
A list of Governors.
A list of Prefects.
A list of the Editorial Board.
A very brief Editorial.
A list of about 20 visitors to the school.
A list of all new boys in Forms 1 and 5, and their home
        Districts.
A list of Cambridge O.S.C. results for 1962.
An analysis of the tribal make-up of the school population.
An appreciative article about minor staff in the school.   (These
        included the driver, Jocktan Kundu, the painter,
        Vanyonyi, the postman, Simiyu, who cycled each day to
        Broderick Falls P.O. - 15 miles - to carry our outgoing
        and incoming   mail, the night watchman, the
        groundsmen and woodcutters and the cooks.)
Notes on 14 different clubs.
Very brief house reports.
Results of various competitions, sporting, social and cultural.
Reviews of "Twelfth Night" and "The Shadow of the Glen".
More than a dozen original articles, ranging from an account of
        religious achievements in Africa to a light-hearted
        discussion entitled :"To kiss or not to kiss", and
        including a farewell greeting in verse from a member of
        the first-ever Form 6 to 'graduate'.

Curiously enough this is the only number not including what was
normally an obligatory article by the headmaster, - he may have
been away when the magazine went to press.   Some of these may
sound a trifle factual and dull.   But they were always worth
reading.   Take, for instance, the Fox House report in December,
1960, which reads :- "Our motto is 'Aim low and surprise !'
Sticking to our motto we have progressed a lot.   This term we
have worked harder; the famous Agoi and Ford in football are now
resting under our feet.   We hope to win both football and volley-
ball cups.   We are sending out six members and we wish them a
good time there."

Later numbers indicate a strengthening of the creative
contributions, with comments on school affairs, on the home scene
of writers, on religion and on politics, with the welcome addition
of stories and poems, all of which still make absorbing reading.

I have already referred to one report which expressed thoughts
not inappropriate to the recent responsibilities of the writer.
It was not an isolated case.   For instance, in the course of an
article entitled, "If I had all the energy I needed" the writer,
who was at the time in Form 3, wrote :-

"Biologically we need to eat and get energy. All the foodstuffs are used in the production of energy. One might say proteins are not put to this use. This may be true, but they are used in the building up of more power and efficient muscles for dealing with other foodstuffs to produce the largest amount of energy. If there were another means by which to get energy I would not need any food; there would be no need for a person to have the digestive system, there would be no need for people to have muscles."

Is it remarkable that this writer became Head of the Dairy and Food Technology Department of Egerton Agricultural College, and that after research at the University of Reading he has been awarded a doctorate, and must be the foremost food technologist in Kenya ?

Conversely, it is amusing to read again the valedictory comments of a 1960 leaver from form 4, recollecting his arrival on the day the school opened :-

"We came on the scene, only to be bossed about by some old boys from Kaimosi. Newboyhood is really boring, though, certainly, educative." The educative process seems to have laid a reasonable foundation, since that writer is now a very senior civil servant, and Permanent Secretary to one of the most important Ministries.

One regular contributor, who was on the editorial board for several years, is now Managing Director of one of the largest publishing houses in Eastern Africa. The Kamusinga was also the periodical to carry the first writing of a present-day novelist and a present-day poet.

The activities described so far, as well as much to which I shall later refer, all gave great scope for the initiative and spontaneity of boys in the school. But they owed a great deal to members of staff. These threw themselves with great energy and good humour into the clubs, far beyond any mere obligation. There was no co-ercion on either side, so very genuine and warm partnerships developed, the effect of which spilled over into the rest of the life of the school. Maybe this was why the school for so long avoided troubles such as those in other schools, and when they did come, was able to recover from them.

(Biographical note: Guy Barnett. Pupil at Highgate School; degree in Politics, Philosophy and Economics at Oxford; taught history at Wakefield Grammar School. Came to Kamusinga after unsuccessfully contesting Scarborough in the 1959 General Election. Later, M.P. for Greenwich, 1971 until his death in December, 1986. Junior Minister in the last Labour Government.)

I have already referred several times to our 'Sixth Form', and 'graduates' from Form 6, though I have not explained how these additions came about.   Before I continue my account of life in the school I must do this.

Even before 1960 a major change was taking place in the relationship between East African secondary schools and Makerere College.   I have already mentioned, (p.34) that Makerere took students straight from Form 4, and that they all did a 2-year course, after which the lucky ones would go on to degree courses while most of the remainder did a 2-year teacher-training course, to emerge as what in those days were called "T1" teachers, such as the three we recruited when we moved to Kamusinga.   It is obvious that this was an uneconomical way to use a University College.   In the first place, students in the first two years were occupying places which were needed for students on degree courses. Now that so many more schools were turning out potential university students there needed to be an expansion of the facilities for training graduates.   By 1959 Uganda and Tanganyika had already started English-type Sixth Forms in several schools. It was therefore decided that such classes should be started in Kenya, and in the first instance £120,000 were made available over 3 years, for the establishment of classes in three places.   The amount of money and the number of proposed classes were subsequently increased.   In 1961 8 classes were started in 4 different schools and in Strathmore Sixth Form College, which was to serve Catholic Schools.   To Alliance High School, as senior secondary school, were allocated both Arts and Science Sixths and the other classes were shared between Kangaru, Kakamega and Shimo la Tewa (Mombasa) Schools, only one of which would at this stage be able to offer both Arts and Science courses.

Kamusinga had so far taken only two year-groups up to Cambridge School Certificate, so had no claim to be amongst the first to be expanded further.   On the other hand, having worked hard, after our late start, to bring ourselves abreast of other schools, we were anxious not to be out-distanced once again.   We knew we had a staff fully qualified to do the work.

I therefore approached the Provincial Education Officer with a question : - "Suppose," I asked, "that by some means or other we could raise the funds to provide the extra buildings required, do you think that government would fund the recurrent expenses of running a Sixth Form ?"

I should make it plain that I had no idea how to go about raising the capital funds which would be needed.   (The figure used by government was £20,000 per class, - eventually £160,000 for the whole national project.)

The P.E.O., R.A.Lake, was very sympathetic, and invited me to attend a meeting of the Provincial Education Board in Kisumu, so that I might ask the Board the same question. I did so, emphasising that I had no idea if capital could be found. The Board agreed to accept the recurrent expenditure involved in one class, if places could be provided. This was in late May or early June. Even if I got the money there could be no question of being ready by January, 1961, so the earliest possible target would be 1962.

The next problem was to discover how to raise the capital, so I needed advice. I wrote immediately to Professor Roger Wilson, Professor of Education at Bristol University. Roger Wilson was a prominent Friend, who had actually spent several days at Kamusinga. I had also visited him at Bristol during my 1959 leave. I knew that his interest in East Africa was considerable. (In fact he was one of the moving spirits behind the Teachers for East Africa project which I have mentioned.) I asked him if he could suggest any possible way in which I might go about trying to raise at least £20,000, and if possible £40,000.

The idea had been vaguely in my mind during my mind as early as September, 1959, while I was in England, and I had asked the Secretary of the Joseph Rowntree Charitable Trust what chance we might have of some help from that quarter. His reply virtually ruled out the possibility.

When I wrote to Roger Wilson I had no idea that he was Chairman of the same Trust. Acknowledging my letter, he promised to see whether the Trust might help, and shortly afterwards I received the exciting news that £18,000 were promised, some from the Charitable Trust, and some from the Memorial Trust. Less than 6 weeks after I had seen the Provincial Education Board I was able to report to the P.E.O. that we could provide the necessary buildings for an Arts Sixth to start in 1962.

This had personal consequences for my family. By 1960, when we started our second tour at Kamusinga, it had already been conceded that teachers on O.A.B. terms, (as I now was,) might have contracts for only 2 years. So we had in mind to return permanently to England in 1962, so that I might still have a reasonable chance of finding a suitable post. However, I was given to understand that it would be good if I could stay long enough to see the project through to completion. So we agreed to return to Kamusinga after leave in 1962.

* * * * * * * * *

There was a great deal of satisfaction to be gained from planning the physical extensions required. This time we had no need to go and get P.W.D. approval for our plans, since no government money was involved, and we could act at our own speed.

We decided to ask Eric Hoare, F.R.I.B.A., who lived near Kitale, to be our architect. And although we intended to put the eventual contract out to tender, we were able to have three-cornered discussions between ourselves, Eric Hoare and Electrical Limited, who had built the school so far. So it was possible for us to make realistic estimates of likely building costs.

The unit costs ranged from 17 shillings per square foot for plain classroom facilities, with no services other than electric light, and no frills, to 30 shillings per square foot for laboratories, complete with water, gas and electric circuits, or for private houses, with the necessary services. With these and interpolated figures as guidelines we were able to work out how much it would cost to build what we thought we needed; and conversely, how much we could provide with the amount of money likely to be available. The result was very satisfactory, and when tenders were eventually invited, we had no hesitation in awarding the contract to Electrical Limited

*   *   *   *   *   *   *   *   *

Meanwhile there had been two interesting suggestions. The first of these was an official invitation to start Science Sixth Form as well as Arts. We were assured of government help in equipping laboratories and certain other requirements, but we should have to raise quite a lot of extra funds for building. We agreed to offer a Science Sixth, acting on the assumption and in the faith that in some way we should be able to raise the money. We were only able to take this risk because, of course, in the first year of Sixth Form work we could manage with less accommodation, but we should have twice the number of Sixth Formers once the second year began.

The second suggestion arose from the fact that the Government had made no provision in the Sixth Form programme for girls to share in the development. We therefore proposed to make provision for girls to share in our Sixth Forms. We planned a special dormitory for them, and looked forward to becoming the first secondary school in Kenya to venture into co-education. We also attracted a most valuable addition to the staff, with a view, not only to strengthening our Science side, but also to caring for the girls we hoped to admit. This was Esther Bower, a Biology and Mathematics graduate who, for some 12 years, had been Headmistress of Bilston Girls' Grammar School in Wolverhampton. However, before we actually started the building, though after Esther Bower had joined the staff, we had to abandon the idea. This was because the Government, as a result of very proper pressures, had decided to fund the establishment of a Sixth Form at the Alliance Girls' High School at Kikuyu. At that stage there would probably have been too few girls qualifying for Sixth Form studies to fill more than one Sixth Form, and we had no wish, in

any case, to be in competition with A.G.H.S.   We had very cordial
relations with the Headmistress, Miss Mary Bruce, and were very
pleased on her account.

For us and for Esther Bower this was a great disappointment.
But we were very glad that she had the opportunity, after a period
of most valuable work at Kamusinga, to serve the needs of girls
as the Head of Lugulu Girls' Secondary School, where she is still
very well remembered with appreciation and affection.

＊　＊　＊　＊　＊　＊　＊　＊　＊　＊

Acceptance of the offer to let us add the Science Sixth implied a
further campaign for funds.   The Trusts gave us an extra £5000
when the Secretary, Eric Cleaver, visited us in January, 1961.
But we decided to launch a formal appeal in England and, if
possible, elsewhere.   We obtained the support of friends of the
school who were well-known and influential in England.   We set
up a formal organisation, with a Chairman, Philip Radley, a former
Head of Ackworth Friends School, who had visited us with his wife,
and a Treasurer, Percy Woods, whose son, John Woods, by this time
on the Kamusinga staff, became my successor as Headmaster.

The appeal brought in contributions from trusts, Friends' Meetings
and individuals.   We did not achieve our target, but received
over £12,000.   By cutting our coat according to our cloth we were
able to provide the minimum facilities that were required.   This
meant, amongst other things, accepting some congestion in
dormitories, the need for one staff house to be shared, and
contenting ourselves with the extension of the existing dining-
hall instead of the provision of a new hall which would have
relieved the pressure on the dining-hall and provided a permanent
replacement for the old church, which could not be expected to
last indefinitely.

＊　＊　＊　＊　＊　＊　＊　＊　＊　＊

Before I leave the subject of building it is perhaps worth while
placing on record, for historical purposes, some details of the
financial aspects of each of our programmes.   Learning about
them and acting upon them were indeed a significant part of my
African education.

It is interesting to note the difference in unit costs between
those approved in the original programme and those on which the
Sixth Form extensions were based.

In 1956 the prices, (in £'s) and unit costs, (in shs./sq.ft.) including 10% for P.C.'s, for a selection of the buildings were as follows :-

	Contract sum. £	Unit cost. sh.
(2 built) Dormitory block, incl. ablutions, (2 dorms. in each block)	5,450	27.06
Classroom Block (4 rooms)	5,687	49.07
Lab. Block (2 labs and prep. room)	4,622	37.84
H/M's house	4,571	45.54
3-bed-roomed house (4 built)	1,630	36.85
2-bed-roomed house (2 built)	1,241	33.00

The total amount of the contract, including also the dining/kitchen block, provisional sums and P.C. items, was £43,249.

I presume that these figures reflect the kind of allocations for different buildings which were made according to Government (Public Works Department) practice. In retrospect they greatly surprise me. The quality of the housing, for instance, was the same for all three types of house, and I can think of no reason for the different prices per square foot. It is evident that the figures were for official use only, and that the overall quality was considerably evened out in practice. This was particularly important as regards housing, since we were anxious that all houses should be suitable for either ex-patriate or African occupation, and we did achieve this.

In Phase 2 of the original building programme our plans were still subject to government approval, but we were able to profit from earlier experience in order to get as much accommodation as possible for the money available. The second batch of dormitories, in 3 separate buildings, cost considerably less. Four further classrooms, a library, a headmaster's office, a small school clerk's office, a store and a staff room all had to be telescoped into the smallest possible space. (I believe each classroom had an area of no more than 480 square feet for a notional class size of 30.) Even in the first four classrooms, the design of which resulted from an unnecessarily expensive flight of the architect's imagination, we had managed to get our blackboards for nothing. We had one wall coated, between the heights of about 3 ft. and 7 ft., with specially hard, smooth plaster, which could be painted black. We managed to include Phase 2 a small house for the school clerk. Unfortunately I no longer have in my possession any record of the details of the costs of that second phase. But as I mentioned earlier, the economic stringencies consequent upon the Emergency meant that the total capital grant for the whole of the buildings up to form 4 level was only about £73,000 instead of the £80,000 we had originally expected.

When we came to provide for Forms 5 and 6 we were able to proceed entirely at our own discretion, and the figures used in our accounts could be taken at their face value. (As the situation, e.g. with regard to adding the Science Sixth and abandoning the co-educational idea, changed, we of course sought and obtained from the original trustees approval for any proposed variations of major importance.)

The advantage of the 3-cornered consultations between architect, contractors and ourselves, to which I have referred, were very great. Not only did we keep costs down, but we got buildings and fitments of much better quality. A contributory reason for this was the political situation at the time. With the rapid advance towards independence, (Kenyatta was released while we were busy building the first of our new buildings,) business was slack, because the future contained so many uncertainties, - so prices were low. This was to our advantage also when we were ordering new furniture from firms which were glad to have orders. A good many settlers were leaving and selling up their possessions, so that by attending auction sales I was able to get many items of second-hand furniture for staff houses. (Expatriates required furnished accommodation, although African teachers furnished their own houses.)

I have in my possession a statement which I drafted when we had received in cash or promises about £35,000 from non-government sources. In round figures the list of accommodation and costs was as follows :-

	£	sh/sq.ft
2 dormitories and ablutions	5,000	c.24 †
2 laboratories	5,000	30
5 3-bedroomed houses	12,000	30
4 classrooms	3,000	17
55 kw. generator and house	2,200	(+ £800 from govt.)
Extension to dining-hall	1,000	
Furniture, etc.	5,000	
Balance, towards other needs	1,800	
	35,000	

† my approximate recollection only.

All this accommodation was more spacious than that previously provided. For example, the houses all had larger rooms and tiled kitchens and bathrooms, and the classrooms were considerably bigger.

Unfortunately this is where physical development had to stop, since it was felt advisable to wind up the Appeal Fund. The only further accommodation which we could expect to acquire was the schools supervisor's house across the football field, when it should become vacant on the transfer of supervisory duties from F.A.M. to the District Education Officer. (This house was unfortunately burned down in the late 1970's.)

In concluding this financial account I must record that the Ministry of Education, apart from undertaking all the usual recurrent costs, also provided £6,700 in all for the initial supply of science equipment (£4,000), text books (£1,500), Library books (£1,000) and Geography equipment (£200).

33. – 1957 – John Caughey plants a flame-tree

34. – 'Caughey Avenue', 1982

2. My African Education.   11. "The buildings stand out bowing, to
say 'Welcome !' "

A school in a rather isolated position, especially one which is at
the   same time very much concerned with equipping young men to
live in the larger world, and indeed to make a valuable
contribution to that larger world, needs real contacts with it, not
just teachers and books.   Any sallies from Kamusinga were
necessarily limited by travel facilities and the finance available.
Such sallies were high-lights in our experienca, whether we only
went as far as Lugulu, 11 miles away, to visit the Girls' School
there, or succeeded in reaching Nairobi for music and drama
festivals.

It was therefore one of our greatest needs and pleasures to
receive visitors.   Offering hospitality, whether for a few hours
or for periods as long as several months, was an important
feature of Kamusinga life.   Not many private or official guests
failed to be drawn into some sort of participation in that life.

Private guests included the relatives and friends of members of
staff.   The first of these, at Easter 1957, was my sister
Margaret, on her way back to England from her work for the
Friends Service Council in East Pakistan, (now Bangladesh).   And
of course she was invited to talk.   At the end of the year my
parents also came, and stayed for a couple of months.   My Father
spoke several times at Sunday services and took part in other
activities.   Later on house-guests of other colleagues found
themselves drawn in.   Wardell, Davies, Beaver, Bradstock and
Woolman parents were all amongst our visitors, whilst Esther
Bower's cousin, Editha Jackson, and her friend, Doris Martin, were
quickly absorbed in helpful participation.   During 1959, while
Bradleys were away, Albert Lindley, Headmaster of Ackworth
Friends' School in Yorkshire, on a sabbatical term, stayed for
part of the time in our house and helped in the school.   In 1964
John Woods' Father-in-law, Sidney Brown, just retired from the
Deputy Headship of Bootham School, was actually recruited to the
staff for several months.

(Incidentally, it is perhaps worth mentioning that we had direct
links, through different Kamusinga folk, with almost all the
Quaker schools in England.)

I referred earlier to our good relations with Makerere.   These
were continually being refreshed as tutors from the Education
Department came to supervise the teaching practice of their
students who were spending a term with us.   Professor Eric
Lucas, Head of the Education Department, was for several years on
our Board of Governors, on the nomination, at our invitation, of
Sir Bernard de Bunsen, who also visited us several times.

But our most welcome and most helpful scholastic visitor was Edgar B. Castle, about whom I have already written. As I mentioned, after 20 years as Head of Leighton Park School he became Professor of Education at Hull. In 1960 he visited his friend and ours, Sir Bernard de Bunsen, (himself an Old Leightonian), and was invited to come back to Makerere as resident Visiting Professor. This involved a slightly early retirement from Hull. But he made little resistance to the suggestion, and in the following year he was installed. He became a Governor of Kamusinga, and stayed with us a good number of times, visits which everybody enjoyed. When he wrote "Growing Up in East Africa" he even gave a brief description of Kamusinga, though without mentioning the name. He became very well known in East Africa, particularly as Chairman of the Uganda Education Commission in 1963.

We had visits from government officials, high and low, some of them even from the very senior ranks of the Civil Service. Encouraging visits such as that of Sir Christopher Cox, Senior Educational Adviser to the Colonial Office, may well have helped considerably to convince Kenya Education Department that Kamusinga would make a good job of a Sixth Form.

It was pleasant to exchange visits with people in other schools and colleges. They often contributed to our worship, and sometimes to our entertainment. Boys were fascinated, for instance, to see the model steam railway engine which was displayed by Bertram Bowers, the Headmaster of Maseno School. And one Saturday evening high-light was a conjuring display by Carey Francis, the famous Headmaster of the Alliance High School.

We had fairly regular visits from the British Council representative in Kisumu, who brought films to show us.

We had many visits from people in England and America who were in some way associated with the school or interested in it. Amongst these were George and Mary Whiteman, from Saffron Walden. I was in constant correspondence with George, the Personnel Secretary of the Friends Service Council in London, from the December day in 1954 when we first went to Friends House even until we had finally settled back in England in 1964. It was a great help to be able to show him the place for which he was recruiting staff, so that he would be able both to understand the kinds of persons who would be good potential recruits, and to give such persons a first-hand account of the place. Like many other guests, George and Mary found themselves, on the morning after their arrival, pushed into a classroom, given a piece of chalk, briefly introduced, told to write their names on the blackboard, and then to answer questions arising. The ensuing hour or so provided them with a stimulating experience !

There were two particular kinds of hospitality which were of outstanding interest to the boys, and these were essentially African occasions, in no way involving people of overt public consequence. The first of these was playing host to groups of young ladies from other schools or colleges. And the other was entertaining the boys' own parents.

Neither of these could be taken at all casually, and some upheaval was inevitable. The major problem, of course, was to provide sleeping accommodation for the visitors, since a return home on Saturday evening was hardly possible for any but those from Lugulu. Apart from the distance, account had to be taken of the weather and the state of the roads. The solution had to be the evacuation of a dormitory or, when the parents came, of more than one. The evacuees slept on the floor, either in other dormitories or in classrooms. The arrangement worked. The proceedings during such visits were always very ordered. Formality and propriety were skilfully blended with warm cordiality. The very buildings, so it was said, expressed the spirit of Kamusinga; as one writer in the magazine of 1967 expressed it :-

"The new buildings stand out bowing, as though to say 'Welcome !'
                                or 'Good-bye !' "

(This is a reference to the fact that the gables of some of the buildings have sides which slope outwards from ground level instead of being upright.)

The first group of ladies to pay a week-end visit were the teacher trainees attached to the Girls' School at Kaimosi, in 1958. Perhaps the most remarkable thing about this visit was that the students joined together in square dances, and that the Principal of the Girls' School joined in. Such a thing had never before happened with approval. Later on there were visitors from Lugulu, who joined in mixed volley-ball. More distant visitors came from Butere and Ng'iya, with whose girls contact had already been made by the touring Kamusinga Dramatic Society. The visit of Ng'iya ladies in 1965 is described with some enthusiasm in the magazine for that year. The programme was evidently typical. It included decorous meal-times and perambulations, some dancing 'in western styles', and volley-ball. In the evening there was a debate on the motion "That Co-education is a good thing"; it was carried. Next morning there was 'heavy' photography all over the compound. In a thankyou letter written a few days later one of the ladies suggested "that Kamusinga and Ng'iya should join together and become Kamusi-Ng'iya."

35. – Classrooms

'The buildings stand out bowing, as though to say "Welcome!"'

Dormitories

The first Parents' Week-end attempted took place in July, 1961, and was attended by about 150 parents. As I have mentioned, the school normally had little contact with parents, and it was the Governors who suggested a week-end. But it depended for its undoubted success on the fullest and most enthusiastic co-operation given by the boys. For reasons into which I need not go at this point, the Form 3's were away at the time, so the accommodation problem was alleviated. Some parents were able to stay with relatives near by, but most stayed in the school, arriving on Friday evening. There were separate dormitories for Mothers and Fathers, and most of them had to be gently instructed in the use of all the plumbing arrangements, which were unfamiliar to them. After breakfast and morning prayers the parents were able to inspect the school facilities. The first-year pupils demonstrated experiments in the laboratories, and the tale is told that one old man, who had spent ten minutes watching his son show that air occupies space, came out with the comment that Kamusinga students were serious rivals of the great Russian Scientists. (This was not long after the launch of Sputnik I.)

During the afternoon the annual sports took place, which meant that both entertainment and the opportunity for conversation were available. The trophy was presented to the winning house by Senior Chief Jonathan Baraza, himself a parent, as well as a member of the Board of Governors.

On Saturday evening there was a great feast, attended by all the boys, the staff and their families, and all the parents. Sons sat beside their parents, but staff and their wives and the rest of the school were scattered about the various tables, so that each was a convivial mixed company. After eating was over the choir performed, and of course there were speeches, all of which had to be given in two languages. When a parent spoke the practice was that his or her son stood alongside and interpreted. Few who were present will ever forget the enthusiasm of one mother, and the bashful expression of her son, when she said she had had such a good time that she thought she should go home and have another son, so that she could come to another parents' week-end. (Talking with this same student in 1982, I learned from him that his Mother had also complained that boys were lazy in the holidays, and that we should tell them not to be, - but that he had omitted this from his translation !)

At the service on Sunday morning Benjamin Ngaira, Chairman of the Governors, spoke on the theme "that every person, whether rich or poor, has some important part to play in life." Later in the day those who remained were able to see slides showing the early history of the school, and it was only on Monday morning that the last of the guests departed.

The second Parents' Week-end took place in June, 1963, but this time there was also an official element.   The new Sixth Form buildings were complete, and we had invited the recently appointed first African Director of Education to honour us by making the opening of our new facilities his first public engagement. Unfortunately this was not possible for him, but he sent a very senior colleague, Mr. Kyale Mwendwa, and on 29th June the official opening took place.   The principal speeches, by the Chairman, then Senior Chief Jonathan Baraza, the Guest of Honour and myself were all delivered in Kiswahili, recorded by the K.B.C. and broadcast a few days later on Kisumu radio.

In other respects the week-end was much as before, except that laboratory demonstrations were given this time by the Science Sixth, as well as by more junior classes.   It was something of a novelty, but seemed perfectly natural and unembarrassing, too watch a biologist elucidating details of the human reproductive system to fascinated mothers and sisters.

No. 5 of the magazine reports on a similar event held in 1965, when the school was honoured by the presence of the Hon. Mr. Konchellah, Assistant Minister for Education.   By this time a greater proportion of the boys were drawn from Bungoma District, and I suspect that more parents would have been able to manage the visit.

Finally, I must briefly record a visit which took place late in 1963.   John and Rosamond Peirson had brought with them a broadening of the school's musical experience, both being keen instrumentalists.   They also gathered together a number of musical friends, from as far away as Kericho, for a musical week-end at Kamusinga.   Several members of staff, also instrumentalists, joined in.   The week-end culminated in the performance of a selection of numbers, - arias, recitatives and choruses, from "The Messiah", with orchestral accompaniment.

A special choir was gathered, including both staff and boys.   It was really a very exciting occasion, the first on which a live orchestra had performed at Kamusinga.   How delightful it was to imagine the periwigged countenance of George Frederick Handel peeping through one of the wooden window-frames of the mud-and-thatch church, to eavesdrop on what must surely have been the first time that the "Halleluja Chorus" was heard in such a setting.

37. – Arriving

38. – End of term

2. My African Education. 12. Prefects, Plumbing and Apparel.

This section and those which follow will try to give some idea of
the way in which life at Kamusinga was regulated and how both the
trivialities of daily routine and major eruptions of crisis were
handled.   It is a story in which concord and discord, advances
and set-backs, patience and impatience all played a part.

Intermediate and Secondary Schools in Kenya all conformed to a
similar pattern.   This doubtless derived from the influence and
example of the earliest and most prominent of all the African
Secondary Schools in Kenya, the Alliance High School, where the
way in which daily life was ordered owed much to the English
Public Schools system.   The authority of the Headmaster over
staff and boys was very marked.   Staff were set over boys, and
the boys had their own hierarchy of prefects, led by a Senior
School Prefect, or Head Boy.   Parades took place daily.   The
concepts of command and discipline were constantly in evidence.
There was a well-established code of conduct, with a good many
rules, and scales of punishment which ranged from petty penalties
up to corporal punishment, suspension and, in certain cases,
expulsion.   It was natural that later schools should model
themselves to a greater or lesser extent on this pattern.

Kaimosi Boys' School was no exception, as far as the prefectorial
system went.   But it was so small, and existed, under such
physical handicaps, that by comparison with most schools, let
alone A.H.S., it was a very casual and easy-going community.   The
Senior School Prefect, (S.S.P.) and his Assistant, (A.S.S.P.), the
Food Prefect and Dormitory Prefects were appointed by the Head, in
consultation with the staff.   They organized the 'domestic' life
of the boys, but did not possess any formal disciplinary powers.

At the beginning of 1956, since as yet I knew practically nothing
about the boys, I decided that we would use the three terms of
that year to give three different boys a spell as S.S.P.   The
first was chosen on the recommendation of the departing Head,
Onni Rauha, and the other two in the light of assessments made
during the year.   Each understood that the replacements implied
no reflexion on the performance of those office holders.   And we
said we should make a more permanent appointment when the school
moved to Kamusinga.

Apart from their 'domestic' functions the S.S.P.'s were of great
value to me because of the consultations I had with them, which
enabled me to learn about the school community.   I should add
that in recent conversations with former students I have learnt
that the S.S.P. sometimes exercised more disciplinary and moral
authority than I realized at the time.

During the year we established a School Council, which proved helpful and which became part of the Kamusinga scene. The S.S.P. was ex officio Chairman and the A.S.S.P. Vice-Chairman. There were two elected representatives from each class, from amongst whom the Council elected its own Secretary. The agenda was very free. An article in the magazine for December 1960 describes it as follows : -

"The School Council was started by students with the consent of the Headmaster in 1956. It started with the aim of creating better understanding between members of staff and students, and to deal with some inconveniences which may arise in the school. It is also to promote the interest of students and the development of the school in general. The School Council meets once in four weeks and emergency meetings can be called if there is anything important which should be attended to without delay."

It became the normal practice for the Chairman and Secretary to call upon me after each meeting, to report on it, and to present me with such proposals and requests as the Council might have resolved to put forward. This proved to be a very healthy institution, since it provided both a safety valve for various agitations amongst boys, and a means by which I was kept in touch with grass-roots. Many of the suggestions were helpful and could be adopted. Some of them were financially impossible, and I was able to explain the difficulty to the Chairman and Secretary, who would report back to the Council at its next meeting. I was always at pains to make sure of agreeing each time to at least one of the requests.

At Kamusinga the number of Prefects gradually increased. Each house had two, and occasionally it was found advisable to move senior boys from one dormitory to another, if there were too few suitable candidates in one and a surplus in another. Also, when new dormitories were established their members, and not only their prefects, were usually drawn in about equal numbers from the other dormitories. In this way each dormitory had a more or less similar mixture of boys from all age-groups.

The S.S.P. and A.S.S.P. had no house duties. The A.S.S.P. was normally responsible for the dining-room, and when the school grew in numbers, from 1962, it was found convenient to have two A.S.S.P.'s. Another prefect without house duties was the Water Prefect, who was responsible for general care of all the ablution blocks, and to report to me when taps or drains or cisterns were not functioning properly.

I must digress briefly to refer to the inauguration of our sanitary arrangements, which took place fairly early in the first term of 1957. Water-borne sanitation was a complete novelty to a majority of the boys when they first arrived.

And a system involving drains and man-holes and septic tanks could easily be upset and choked, and even overflow, if traditional African practices were used.

I therefore invested in a large stock of toilet rolls, and assembled the school for instruction in the use of the new facilities. I stressed first that it was essential to use only toilet paper in the toilets, since leaves would cause disaster; and I carefully explained how to pull the chain and let go at the appropriate time. Taking a leaf (sic !) from the book of Makerere experience, as reported by an ex-Makerere colleague, I then prepared to issue to each boy a personal toilet roll.

"This roll," I explained, "is large enough to last you for the rest of this term. I have counted the number of sheets in each roll, so I know. (Laughter) You have no excuse for using forbidden materials."

"Question, sir !" - this, in a resonant voice, from Arthur, (who could always be depended upon for a question).

"Yes, Arthur ?" with a smile, since Arthur was a well-known wit.

"Sir ! I think that some people go to the choo (W.C.) more than once a day, and the paper will not be sufficient until the end of term."

"In that case," I replied, with some presence of mind, "You must make friends with somebody who only goes every second or third day, and arrange things with him."

General laughter, during which the formal presentation of the toilet rolls proceeded, as the boys, in single file, passed by the carton containing them.

As time went by we did indeed have problems with drainage, mainly because the 30-foot pits into which the septic tanks overflowed refused to allow the water to seep away. So we had to learn all about French drains, in which I personally became more expert than I was in Kiswahili.

(A French drain is a long trench, at least 4 feet deep. It has to have a slight fall in it so that it can carry away the overflow from the inefficient soak-pit, to which it is connected by a short pipe. Along its bottom are laid large stones of irregular shape, and upon these are laid layers of banana leaves or cardboard or paper or any kind of waste sheeting, which will prevent the gaps between the stones from being filled in when the trench is back-filled. The water flowing down the drain gradually soaks away, giving some benefit to the land on either side.)

Some sewerage problems were extra difficult because of taboos.
The minor staff claimed they could not work on the overflowing
septic tank unless they first sacrificed a goat. It was
necessary to set a personal example, and then a sufficient number
of boys overcame their own revulsion and helped to clear up the
mess.

Incidentally, our first Water Prefect introduced a new word into
the language. He always referred to the urinals as "shanks"
because that was the name of the manufacturer which appeared on
them. I was told in 1982 that the term still persists !

But to return to the institution of prefects. This persisted
long after I left Kamusinga. But it never operated in such an
authoritarian way as that which is found in many English Public
Schools. At Kamusinga, although I did consult with outgoing
prefects as well as with the staff about the appointment of new
prefects and the choice of S.S.P., I did retain the prerogative of
actual appointment for myself.

My own view of the institution altered considerably after I
returned to England, and when I had the opportunity, which I shall
write about later on, of establishing a new school there I
entirely avoided setting up a prefect system, and I found that
this worked. The purpose of any system must be to cultivate in
pupils a personal sense of responsibility, and I believed that
this was not most likely to be achieved by a system resembling a
chain of command, and no pupil is too young to take
responsibility. In his book, "Growing up in East Africa"
Professor E.B.Castle had this to say :-

(p.240)" . . . . . no disciplinary system will succeed if founded
only on moral admonition and punishment; . . . . a disciplined
community can exist only when it is composed of reasonable
persons; and . . . . personal responsibility can be exercised only
in community life."

(p.243)"I would place the age of responsibility at three years."

As I have written earlier, I am much indebted to the stimulus and
encouragement of Professor Castle from the very beginning of my
teaching career onwards. Happily I do not believe that the
prefect system at Kamusinga did much harm. It could be regarded
as the vehicle through which prefects, as older boys, could carry
out this 'exercise of responsibility in community life'. Yet it
did not stifle the sense of responsibility in other boys. It is
this concept which runs through so many aspects of life at
Kamusinga. And it is the experience of its effect which enabled
the school at a later stage to recover from a period of stress,
when we knew we had strayed painfully from our usual paths.

I must not give the impression that co-ercion was unknown at Kamusinga. It did occur where school assemblies and worship were concerned, as well as in the matter of community work.

Community work was a part of the Kamusinga experience from the very first day. As I have related, no ordinary school work was undertaken during the first week of our existence. There was so much needing to be done in order to make the school compound reasonably habitable, and this was accepted by all. I believe it was even enjoyed, and everybody took pride in what we had accomplished together.

From the very beginning a part of Saturday morning was always reserved for community work. (During the week, dish-washing was organised on a rota basis, one house each week. Classrooms were permanently the responsibility of monitors.) On Saturdays there were a number of duty squads - in the dining-hall, library and labs. Other groups, which came to be organised on a house basis, were assigned to such work as needed to be done from time to time. Some went to the farm or the coffee plantation. On occasions there were very special efforts. For instance, there was no money to pay for the interior decoration of the dormitories and the hall. But since we could just afford to buy wall paint and brushes, these rooms might nevertheless be brightened up. On a given Saturday the inhabitants of a particular dormitory would carry all the beds out into the open air and stack the lockers in the middle. All hands would then proceed to sweep and wash down the walls, and then apply the distemper. The whole process would be completed in an astonishingly short space of time. And everybody was happy, because the colours had been chosen by the inhabitants themselves. I believe that the hall, which was a larger project, was tackled by a team of volunteers who enjoyed the work.

(After two or three years we were able, however, to assign one of the minor staff to painting duties. He was trained on the job, and followed a 'rolling programme' of maintenance. In 1982 he was still engaged upon it, and when we arrived to stay for six days in what had been our house we found it resplendent with new paint in our honour.)

Certain other projects were also carried out on Saturdays by people who were particularly interested in them. There was a group which concentrated on excavating and terracing an area for an open-air theatre. A small group of meteorologists assisted, first in the construction of a weather centre, and then in manning it. A 'forestry club' concentrated on the planting and nurture of new trees. However, the 1960 leavers carried out a corporate tree-planting exercise as a grand farewell gesture, with the idea of providing some kind of wind-break, but also a supply of firewood for the future.

The nurture of a sense of community was a constant pre-occupation, and it could be undertaken in many ways. An early means was the adoption of a school badge. It appears that the name Kimilili derives from a Masai name for the leopard. (A branch of the Masai tribe inhabits Mount Elgon, over-looking Kimilili.) During one of our earliest visits to Makerere we had made friends with the well-known Chagga artist, Sam Ntiro. (The Chagga people occupy the region of Tanganyika nearest to Kilimanjaro.) At my request he designed for us the heraldic leopard badge which is still familiar. We arranged for an English firm to produce shirt badges for us and these did much for morale. The badge also appeared on the school's quarto note-paper. And to add to our panache, (perhaps I should say, to provide it,) Mary made us a flag, which was flown at the head of the tall flag-pole which had been erected. (It was the stem of a tall gum-tree which had been given to us by our neighbour, the farmer Elijah.) From 1964 onwards the leopard was also rampant upon the cover of the magazine.

Shirt badges were an important addition to plain school uniform, because uniform itself was little more than an issue of outer clothing, which schools had to provide out of their boarding funds. Indeed, nothing caused more amusement to Old Boys (and their children !) during our recent visits, when they viewed a series of slides made during their school days, than the sight of themselves in those ungainly garments. For some years they were made by Mr.Makachela, whom we brought with us from Kaimosi. In former days he had trained a number of apprentices, while making uniforms for various Kaimosi institutions. But as time passed and school numbers rose it became impossible for him to meet target dates, and the unit cost became too high. So we had to arrange contracts with a Kitale outfitter. We also broke away from the traditional all-khaki outfit by providing white cotton shirts. When Form 5 was introduced it became necessary to give special consideration to the clothing of these senior students. If they had gone on to Makerere like their predecessors they would have abandoned school uniform and dressed as university students. Fortunately a larger boarding grant was made for them, and we were able to provide them with dark grey trousers, white shirts, a distinctive tie, and blazers with a woven badge. They therefore had a sense both of well-earned seniority and a continuing identification with the rest of the school.

It was a similar consideration which led us to give them a modest amount of privacy and privilege in dormitories. This was achieved by hanging curtains between the main dormitory and the end section, and providing a table and chairs as well as beds and lockers. A combination of distinction and identification was socially much more acceptable than the segregation of Sixth Formers in a separate dormitory would have been.

The community was also helped to grow by extending its horizons, whenever individuals or groups took part in special activities. The first such occasion occurred in Kaimosi days, when Francis Mwashi attended a Scout Jamboree in England, as one of the Kenyan representatives. On his return he shared his experiences with us all and aroused much interest as well as some amazement. I well remember the horror expressed by certain boys when they heard how he had helped with the washing-up after meals in the English homes where he had been a guest. I well remember, too, his explanation that the experience had made him feel particularly welcome and at home. (Francis Mwashi, like the adjudicator in that mock choir competition, is nowadays a highly respected stipendiary magistrate in a court about 20 miles from Kamusinga.)

In 1958 we had absorbing accounts from a group of people who had taken part in an international work camp at Machakos, which stressed to the school the value of such voluntary efforts. (By a strange co-incidence this report was given at the height of that first crisis which threatened our community.)

In 1962 we were invited to nominate two sixth formers to join a group of sixth formers from England and two English schoolmasters in Uganda, under the auspices of Brathay Park, which was the headquarters of an organisation promoting and organising field study expeditions in the United Kingdom and other countries. The reports given by the two on their return were much appreciated, particularly a description of their predicament when they found themselves trapped between two apparently warring tribes. (One of them, Joshuah Angatia, is the present-day M.P. whom I have already mentioned; in 1985 the other, Phillip Mbithi, became Vice-Chancellor of the University of Nairobi, as I mentioned earlier.)

As early as 1957 we sent our first representatives to the Outward Bound School at Loitokitok, on the slopes of Kilimanjaro. And invariably the reports given by these intrepid climbers on their return were graphic and entertaining. It is certain that the experience was significant for each participant, and for two reasons. First, they were faced with a considerable physical challenge; and secondly, this was their first chance to live on equal terms with Asian and European boys.

After each O.B. expedition I received a detailed report on our representative. The staff at O.B. seemed to be pre-occupied, above all, with the concept of leadership, and the main conclusion of each report seemed to be the assessment of each boy's response to the challenge of being placed in charge of a group. I gradually came to the conclusion that this was an unfortunate tendency, since I felt that it was much more important that boys should show responsibility and initiative than that they should necessarily prove themselves good commanders.

I have already referred (P.132) to what I saw as a weakness in a
school ethos dominated by the idea of command-discipline. The
Outward Bound philosophy struck me as not sufficiently free of it.
This was particularly true in colonial days, when relations
between boys of different races were still affected by the
assumption that authority rested with "Europeans", (as all Whites
were called.)

Fortunately the opportunity came to indulge in mountain
expeditions on a different basis, and closer at hand. In January
1961 took place the first Kamusinga group assault on the summit
of Mount Elgon. This was a 5-day expedition, shared by about 20
people, including our daughter Ruth, who was just 9. Everybody
got to the top, - but just as important, everybody had joined in
an effort which was corporate, and the camp-fire party at about
11,000 feet, when a sheep was slaughtered, butchered, roasted and
eaten, and there was much singing, is still a cherished memory for
all who were there. The hardy group who spent the following
night in tents beside the tarn just below the summit have equally
vivid memories of the cold, which was so intense that one person,
it is said, even donned sun-glasses in bed, to try to keep warm !
Even those remaining at a lower altitude of about 12,000 feet
found ice half an inch thick on a sufuria in the morning. Never
did the equatorial night seem so long.

39. – Mount Elgon from Kamusinga (before afforestation)

40. – Form 6, 1963

41. – Kamusinga students, 1958-1963 inclusive

Back row: J. Amisi, P. Shalo, A. Simwenyi, W. Baraza, J. Wasike,
M. Hongo, J. Angatia

Front row: J. Otieno, T. Wandera, S. Lung'aho, I. Isiiye,
M. Oyugi, J. Lavuna

2. My African Education. 13. "The Reign of Indignation" or
   "The Unexpected Holiday".

I have referred earlier to my belief that the spirit of co-
operation between staff and boys, and the sense of responsibility
which we tried to encourage in everybody were reasons why
Kamusinga for a longer time than other schools was able to avoid
the kinds of trouble that were not uncommon. But we did have
such troubles eventually, and I must now give some account of
them.

The problem of discipline, as it is understood in English schools,
hardly arose in African schools. Education was too precious a
blessing for it to be placed in jeopardy by mischief. This was
even more evident in a secondary school such as Kamusinga. In
the first five years I hardly recall an incident more serious than
the practice of using a lantern to facilitate night- time study, -
the punishment for which, in persistent cases, was exclusion from
classes for a day or two. Nobody threw darts in class or failed
to hand in homework punctually. Old Boys who were in the
earlier classes now repeatedly assert that there was only one
school rule. Apparently it was :- "Use your Common Sense". One
distinguished Old Boy asssured me that on one occasion he was
sent to me for reprimand. (I imagine he had been a bit over-
provocative in argument with somebody.) He says he entered my
office with some trepidation and we had a little chat, at the
conclusion of which, so it appears, I dismissed him with the magic
injunction to which I have referred. He claims he has never
forgotten it. Well ! Well !

In 1960 a number of schools in Kenya were restless and there were
so-called 'strikes'. The usual result was that whole classes,
even whole schools, would be closed, and disciplinary action taken,
often in the form of expulsion of the ring-leaders. Strikes were
not a new phenomenon in Kenya schools. An African colleague
related how, as a new boy at Kakamega many years previously, when
it was still an intermediate school, he had hardly arrived as a
new boy on the first day of term when he was instructed by older
boys to pack up and go home. He had no idea why, and was quite
unable to explain to his parents.

Perhaps this illustrates a point made by one of the Old Boys,
himself the Head of a very large school, namely that the right
word should not have been 'strike', but boycott. This is borne
out by some of our own experience. However, the term in use was
'strike', so I shall use it, with that reservation in mind.

The incidence of strikes from 1960 on suggested some sort of
epidemic. This implies an infection rather than a revolutionary
movement, and I recollect no suggestion of co-ordination or
collusion between the students of different schools.

The infection spread, I suppose, through press and radio reports
of particular cases and, I have no doubt, through the grape-vine
of home contacts or meetings at inter-school functions of various
kinds.   And it has to be considered in the context of the general
health of the body politic in Kenya.   This was in rather a
feverish state, although by 1960 it would have been wrong to
suggest that it was diseased, because the State of Emergency had
been ended a year earlier.   What I am suggesting is that the
feeling got about, that if students in a school had some sort of a
grievance it was a good idea to take corporate action to try to
effect its removal.   On the other hand, the problems of each
school had to be treated on their merits, and not by the
application of some rule-of-thumb.   Each had its own peculiar
problem, often not unconnected with personalities, and the
triggers to action were different in each case.

It should not be deduced from my reference to the health of the
body politic that I believe that the constitutional revolution
which was taking place in the country was provoking in students a
spirit of revolution for its own sake.   It was the growing
success   of   the   movement   towards   independence,   not   the
frustrations   placed   in   its   path,   which   led,   at   least   in   my
personal view, to the difficulties which arose in 1962, and which
I shall have to describe and discuss.

There was never any indication that African politicians gave any
encouragement to strikes.   On the contrary, they seemed anxious
for students to avoid getting involved in interruptions to their
proper occupation, which was study.   In early June, 1961, I had
this direct from the lips of Jomo Kenyatta himself, on an occasion
to which I shall refer again.

I am hoping that when this assessment of mine has been read by
one or two Old Boys who are now in very senior government
educational posts they may be able, from the records, to get some
idea of the frequency and nature of strikes in those days, and of
the way in which they were dealt with.

                *   *   *   *   *   *   *   *   *

Leaving out of account the tense situation which arose in May,
1958, which did not result from student problems, the first time
that difficulty arose with a large group of boys was in June,
1961.

I am not at all sure what the real explanation of this incident
is, since it certainly had nothing to do with the explanation
which can be given of the later, 1962, crisis.   It seemed to
begin with complaints about the breakfast porridge (uji) and it
seems to have involved only boys in Form 3.   Two members of
staff tried to cool the situation down, but without success.

Tension increased when there was a show of some sort of civil disobedience. (This was to do with Saturday community work.) When the matter was referred to me I reacted eventually in a somewhat unexpected fashion, although I must admit that the idea was borrowed from the experience of another headmaster who had told me about it.

The third forms and the prefects were assembled, and I addressed myself to the group of boys who were being difficult. After I had spoken to them briefly I gave them a direct order to do what was being required of them. Nobody moved. I then made a solemn statement : -

"This is the first time that I have been directly disobeyed at Kamusinga. It is evident that my authority has disappeared, and that I have failed in my work. I shall therefore have to resign. I am withdrawing myself and the staff from the school and the school will have to carry on without us." Thereupon I led the staff out of the hall and went to my house.

The next development came an hour or so later, when the S.S.P. came to see me. He had presided over a meeting, during which senior boys had argued with the offenders. And he asked me to return to school. It is my rather hazy recollection that further discussions took place, but that the third-formers could not be persuaded to change their attitude. When it finally became apparent that the group were not to be reasoned with I told them that they had all better go home for a while and come to their senses; they would be sent for in due course. Having announced this decision, as I recollect, I cut short further discussion, and as it was late, I went home to bed. Some time later I was disturbed by a gathering of boys in front of the house, so eventually I donned my dressing gown and went to the door. It appeared that the boys were demanding transport to enable them to get home. In order to get rid of them I decided that it would be quite justifiable to loan them the lorry, and to debit the fees account of each of them with a proportion of the hire charge. This proposal was accepted, perhaps a little sheepishly, and in the morning off they went.

But of course it was necessary to forestall any rumours that might begin to spread in the Kakamega and Maragoli areas, where most of the lorry passengers lived. So I jumped in my car and drove to Musingu, near Kakamega, to see the Chairman of the Governors and tell him what had actually happened. On the way I began to feel that relations were beginning to return to normal:- I over-took the lorry, with its load of exiles, and received cheerful waves of greeting as I went by. Of course I waved back, equally cheerfully.

We allowed the exile to last for 3 weeks, after which all returned.

This period included the first of our Parents' Week-ends, which gave us the opportunity to have discussions with some of the parents. The magazine for August 1961 contains a number of references to the exile. An article headed "The Reign of Indignation at Kamusinga" by one of the prefects is worth quoting in full, as it seems to me to contain clues to the root of the problem.

"When we in the Fourth Form came to this School in 1958 we were introduced into a community which, according to my assessment at the time, was mature and acted rationally nearly in every way. As the first Fourth Formers left that year, and have been followed by others every year, it seems they have been taking away that spirit, leaving Kamusinga with an easily excited community.

"It is very difficult to explain to outsiders the causes of recent troubles which have alarmed many. Most misunderstandings, however, seem to rise from the once popular School Council. To many of us in the Fourth Forms, it was or is a representative body of students which debates on matters affecting students at school and sends them as decided, to the Headmaster for his approval, in which case he can grant some requests or otherwise. But to most lower formers the Council is a High Court of America to which even the head must be subject. This is a very unfortunate conviction and it is almost rendering the Council anachronistic.

"It is clear that many students have missed the purpose of the School Council and to put them right would need a brainwave. Yet there are also students who have no illusions about the solution to the misunderstandings; the students would have to accept the Council as it is constituted and reform it through itself if necessary. They must understand too that without this Council they would not find it easy to present their suggestions and requests to the Headmaster and that this position will never make their demands more effectively attended to, nor will it make the Headmaster give them whatever they demand.

"This is not all, the leading trouble-makers, as one of the parents who were here put it, do not make education their chief purpose in being at School; they no longer realize their position as schoolboys and adhere to the proper behaviour of students. The parent went on to say that boys' food should be well cooked but he did not want students to apply their scientific tests to their food."

(I will not identify the writer more closely than to mention that he is now himself a very well-known headmaster !)

Another article, entitled "The Unexpected Holiday" was written by one of the exiles, who was clearly entirely mystified, and could give his parents no reason for his suspension. He seems to have spent most of his time quietly helping his brother to keep shop, and ploughing his conscientious way through "Moby Dick".

In his notes for the term, the President of the Magazine Committee, Alan Davies, wrote : "The 3rd formers left us for 3 weeks but are back now and seem never to have been away". This suitably rounds off the story.

I am still unable to explain with confidence the 1961 incident. Perhaps it lies in the actual composition of the group, of which a complete list appears in the magazine for 1963, in the shape of their School Certificate results. They include a number of strong characters and lively personalities. They were aware of the sort of agitations taking place in other schools. They were very ambitious. And perhaps it was necessary for them to flex their muscles. What I can say is that a large proportion of them have largely fulfilled their ambition and are now very valuable citizens of Kenya. By the way, the list of exiles includes one of those very senior officials in the Ministry of Education to whose comments I look forward !

2. My African Education. 14. "We're on strike, Madam,
please help us."

Of all the tense situations which arose at Kamusinga the events of
February, 1962 were without doubt the most traumatic, and they are
seared into my memory and into my conscience.

I have already written of the scheme to recruit Teachers for East
Africa from the United States and the United Kingdom. Kamusinga
became involved as soon as the first batch of recruits reached
East Africa. In January 1962 we were joined by Joe Timmons, a
teacher of English. Soon afterwards we were in touch with Paul
Hargrave, a bio-chemist, who was under training at Makerere.
There he had met Elfas Webbo, the art student, one of the first
three of our people to go to Makerere. Webbo made Paul feel that
he wanted to come to Kamusinga after Easter, and this it was
possible to arrange.

Meanwhile we welcomed two T.E.A. teachers for their teaching
practice, both of them young American women. They joined us at
the end of January. Even then we had still not received the new
Form 1 boys, because there had been a delay in producing KAPE
results, so that selection took place very late. But the first
Form 5 students were with us, gathered from all but one of the
provinces of Kenya, and H.S.C. work had begun. There were a
number of other new members of staff, including John Woods, (see
note on P.153), James Bukusi and David Velime, (an Old Boy.) So
there was a good deal of settling in to be done.

I believe that Monday, 19th February was the day when things
began to go wrong. On that day the results of the previous
year's Cambridge O.S.C. arrived, and were announced to the school
after lunch. Much disappointment was felt because nobody had
passed in Division 1, although there were 25 in Division 2, 23 in
Division 3, and 3 who gained G.C.E.'s (which meant that they had
passed with credit in a number of subjects but failed in English
Language.) The English Language results were below expectation.

(I must interrupt the narrative here to make the point that these
results very well illustrate the fact that C.S.C. results are very
inadequate assessments of potentiality for the future. It is
illuminating, in reviewing the list of students who got these
'disappointing' results, to consider the occupations and positions
they occupied twenty years later. They include :- A Member of
Parliament who was also an Assistant Minister in the Kenya
Government, two Under-Secretaries and one Senior Assistant
Secretary in the Civil Service, a Principal Collector of Customs,
the Principal of the Kenya Posts and Telecommunications
Corporation Central Training School in Nairobi, a University
Professor, a Departmental Head in an Agricultural College, one
Principal of an Institute, one Headmaster, three Deputy Heads or

Principals, one teacher, one Senior Inspector of Police in charge of a Provincial Special Branch, four senior Income Tax officers, three conducting their own businesses, and two in senior commercial posts.)

Now to return to my narrative. The mood of the community was subdued. But for the first time I had reports that third year forms had been rude and unco-operative in classes taken by student teachers. They challenged the competence of the young ladies and made themselves unpleasant.

On Tuesday afternoon I had to go to Kaimosi, where I spent the night, and in the morning to Kisumu, to collect our audited accounts. I got back on Wednesday afternoon to see much of the annual football match between staff and boys. Everybody seemed to be in a good mood.

Late in the evening the S.S.P. came to my house with the information that the third-formers had all left their dormitories and were sitting outdoors. I went up to school to investigate, and discovered that the whole group were sitting on rough ground in the compound, quite near the main entrance of the school. I approached them and asked quietly what the matter was. Nobody replied. I pointed out that I was willing to discuss anything that they wished to bring to my notice, but that I could not be of much help unless they would talk about it. Still silence. So I left them sitting there and returned to talk with other members of staff. We agreed that the wisest thing was to give them another chance to explain and then to tell them to return to their dormitories, but to make no attempt to co-erce them, and if they did not come in, to leave them alone.

It was a bright, moonlit night, and I well remember going to see them again, without involving any of my colleagues. I strolled around the group, and again invited them to tell me what was wrong. But they continued to sit silently, just as though they were holding a Quaker meeting for worship. The situation had its funny side, and it was not difficult to remain relaxed. After waiting for a reasonable time I decided that there was not much more to be done. So I told them that they could stay there as long as they liked, but that I was going to bed. And off I went.

I told the staff to do likewise and had a brief word with the S.S.P. I told him to go to bed himself, but that he should come and wake me if there were any development at all.

At about daybreak the S.S.P. came down, reporting that at first light the third-formers had returned to their dormitories, collected their belongings, and left the school compound. It was plain that nothing more could be done, since I was certainly not going to chase them, and that the school should simply carry on with the normal routine.

(It was not until 1980 that I learned that my colleague, Richard Wekesa, who lived near where the group was brooding, had helpfully intervened, by taking them to task, telling them that they should either get back to normal or clear off.)

In my opinion, since the third-formers had departed of their own free-will, without any explanation, we could regard them as having left the school.   Whether, and on what terms, they should be re-admitted, if that was their wish, could be considered at leisure, - and it so happened that the Governors were to meet at the school on the Friday.

When the school assembled at 8 o'clock we had the usual short service and I dismissed everybody without making any reference to the third-formers.   A few minutes later somebody told me that the second-formers had not gone into class, but were all sitting under the murembe tree.   Oh dear !

I approached the new group of malcontents, who were a much more juvenile company, on the whole, than the third-formers, because we were gradually having some success in selecting younger entrants to Form 1.   They wore an air of sheepishness and sulkiness combined.

"Well," I said, "What do you think you are doing ?   Why haven't you gone to class ?"

"We are not satisfied," one of them mumbled.

"Oh ?   What are you not satisfied about ?"

"Teachers."

"What about the teachers ?"

"The teaching is not good, and we shall not learn."

"Really !   And are all the teachers not good ?"

"No, some are good."

"Well now, supposing I were to arrange that your classes should be taught by the teachers you think are good, and the other classes had the rest, would that satisfy you ?"

"Yes !" (very brightly)

"And what do you think the other classes would do ?"

At this point they were non-plussed. - I tried a new tack.

"Now, I suppose that what you would really like would be for me to get rid of all the teachers whom you regard as not good and recruit teachers who are good ?"

"Yes !" (brightening again)

"Well, you know, that is easier said than done. From the time I first give notice that a new teacher is required until the time he actually arrives is about six months. So you'll have no teachers for quite a long time."

"Oh !" (crestfallen)

A brief pause. Then, switching to a peremptory tone of voice - "Come on, now, - get to your classes !" and I stalked off to my office, wondering what would happen. Their classrooms were opposite my office, but the only second-formers in view were four or five who had not joined the protest. A little later I was told that the group were holding a baraza, (a confabulation), sitting in the middle of the old football field.

It was while sitting there that they espied my wife, Mary, passing by on her way home after a call on Kathleen Charles.

"Madam," they begged, "please help us !"

"What are you doing there ?" she asked.

"We're on strike, Madam," was the woe-begone reply. "Please advise us what we should do next."

"You'ld better go to school," she said.

"But we don't know what the headmaster will do."

"If I were the headmaster," she said jokingly, "I'ld put you over my knee and spank you," and went cheerily on her way, quite unaware of a staff meeting which was in session at that very moment.

The staff meeting was a full one. Form 5 could study by themselves. Form 4, with their experience as third-formers 8 months earlier fresh in their minds, and with C.O.S.C. looming ahead, were in very quiet and sober mood. Form 1 had only just arrived hardly a fortnight earlier, so were probably rather mazed by events, and simply needed to be given some suitable occupation.

Last year's experience was of little help. We could hardly send home another large group to cool their heels and their heads. It was therefore necessary to take some kind of summary action, - but what ? At this point African members of staff explained that if boys had shown such disrespect to their fathers at home they would have been beaten. If we did not, at this point, take similar action, our own authority would be severely undermined.

The heart-searching was intense, but no alternative was to be found, and with much misgiving it was decided that the advice of African colleagues must be accepted.

By the time the decision had been reached the second-formers had in fact been seen to creep back into their classrooms. I went into each of the classrooms in turn and announced that I intended to cane each boy. There was no protest.

A secluded part of a dormitory was chosen, and I was accompanied by Henry Owuor, my senior African colleague, to act as a witness. A supply of green switches was produced and the boys were called in one at a time, to receive three strokes each. After 47 boys had been punished in this way normal classes resumed, but I returned to my home in a state of physical, emotional and moral exhaustion, from which I did not very quickly recover.

In the succeeding days I had to deal with a certain amount of unpleasantness in the second forms, where the boys who had kept clear of the confrontation, and so not been punished, were exposed to the kind of treatment which is classically meted out to people regarded as blacklegs. There were no more troubles, though a return to the customary easy, happy atmosphere in the school was slow, particularly since the Form 3 problem was still hanging fire.

It was considered wise, in the circumstances, for the two lady students to be transferred to the Catholic Girls' School at Mukumu to continue their teaching practice. There was no question of moving Joe Timmons, who stayed for his full tour and not only became very popular, but also acknowledged as a most successful teacher of English. One reason for the disquiet which had caused the trouble was that it was supposed that boys would not learn proper English from an American !

＊ ＊ ＊ ＊ ＊ ＊ ＊ ＊ ＊

(The preceding account has recently been read by one of the second-form boys of those days. It seems that the rather "laid-back", or relaxed, classroom manner of Joe Timmons in his early days was very different from the manner they were accustomed to in their teachers, and it was a major reason for their disquiet.

Furthermore, they were not happy about the two lady student-teachers, being under the impression that they were just tourists and not serious about their jobs. This was certainly not so; all the TEA teachers in that category were devoting three years of their careers to East Africa, instead of pursuing them at home. This could certainly not be described as "tourism" and it was a serious matter, - which does not imply that it might not be enjoyable.)

When the Governors, including the Provincial Education Officer, met at the school next day I gave a full report. The Governors approved of the drastic action taken with Form 2, although I know that a visiting representative of the American Friends Board of Missions, who was present by invitation, viewed it with disfavour. I sympathised with his feeling.

I then proposed that the third-formers should be regarded as having left the school, and that they should have to make a fresh application for admission. This was agreed, together with a procedure to be followed. A letter was to be sent to each parent through the office of the Chief of his Location. In this letter he was told that his son had left without any consultation, and that if he wished the boy to be re-admitted he should personally bring him to the school on a specified date, when he and the boy would be interviewed by a representative of the Governors and the Headmaster, who would together decide whether to re-admit the boy.

The letter said nothing about the conditions for re-admission, nor did it refer to a very rude round-robin letter which had been sent to the school by the third-formers after they had left.

Senior Chief Jonathan Baraza agreed to represent the Governors. The terms on which a boy would be re-admitted were defined as :- 1. an apology for his behaviour; 2. acceptance of any punishment which might be imposed; and 3. an undertaking to be of good behaviour in the future. It was also accepted that the third-formers would need, like the second-formers, to be punished by caning, but more severely, since their offence was more serious.

The Governors actually congratulated the school on having, for much longer than other schools, avoided a strike.

Most of the boys and their fathers arrived on the evening before the interviews took place. In the morning the fathers were first assembled, so that we could explain the attitude of the governors and the procedure we intended to adopt. Individual interviews then began, and were not completed before nightfall.

Each boy was required to admit that he was personally responsible for his actions, despite the corporate decisions which had been taken by the group; it was stressed that he had not been carried out, but had walked out on his own feet.   He was also required to admit that he was at fault, and to agree to accept any punishment. We also looked for some sign that no recurrence of his misconduct was to be expected.

After all the interviews were over Chief Jonathan and I reviewed the results.   We decided that 11 of the boys had not satisfied us, but that we should give them another fortnight to consider their position.   The remainder would be re-admitted at once. One or two of those whose cases were deferred re-acted in an unpleasant fashion, which did not make things easier for them on their second appearance.   When they had been interviewed again we admitted 6 more, but refused admission to 5.   My own view was that there must be a limit to the tolerance we were prepared to show.   In order to avoid any unnecessary complications I believe that we refunded the fees so far paid by the boys who were not being re-admitted.

The punishment imposed was simple enough, six strokes for each boy.   This time the infliction of the punishment was shared with me by one English and two African colleagues.

This closed the incident and the normal life of the school was resumed.   For some time it was rather subdued, but one was conscious of sadness, not of lingering resentment.   The wound healed over, and I never again found myself with a comparable problem.

    *   *   *   *   *   *   *   *   *

When I ponder in retrospect on these upsets I believe I can understand why they occurred.   At the time of the 1961 suspensions a crucial stage had been reached in the history of Kenya.   Kenyatta, although moved to Maralal, was still in detention, and was able to receive deputations.   And the unwise public utterances of the new Governor, who spoke of Kenyatta as a "leader to darkness and death", only served to augment the already growing demands for his early release.   So everybody in Kenya was on edge, either through frustration or fear, depending on his point of view.   Small wonder, therefore, that in this atmosphere young people, deeply conscious of African aspirations, should allow themselves to step outside the accustomed pattern of their behaviour.

I have already expressed the view that it was the very success of the movement towards national independence which led to the 1962 difficulties.   Independence was approaching very rapidly, and as it did so, the process of "africanisation" of the administration, as well as of commerce and industry, was also accelerating.   It was clear that the career opportunities in prospect for successful secondary school leavers were virtually unlimited.

And it was equally clear that the best careers would go to the
best qualified people.   The pressure to succeed was therefore
enormous.   And the first requirement was a good School
Certificate.   Ironically enough, the best chance of success
appeared to depend upon being taught by "European", and in
particular by English teachers.   What I might call a side-non-
effect   of this was that anti-white prejudice was quite
insignificant.   But the moment the students suspected their
teachers to be inadequate they were on edge.   In a word, they
were afraid for themselves.   Our Kamusinga experience bears out
the argument that fear, and not revolution, was at the root of the
trouble.

One reason why it was relatively so late that this happened is
that the staffing of the school, despite expansion and some
changes, was so very stable, and nothing allays fear so well as
stability.   Government schools, in particular, often fell victim
to the system under which staff were education officers, and
education officers could be drafted, often at short notice, from
one post to another, into and out of schools, into and out of
education offices.   For instance, during my period of service at
Kamusinga there were at least 5 different headmasters at Kakamega
School, - and I have already referred to the half-dozen or so
different P.E.O.'s with whom I had to deal.

School strikes were often publicly condemned, and there was much
talk of discipline.   What was really required was more stability,
more understanding of the pressures upon the young, and a greater
effort to reassure them.   (Curiously enough, in 1980 I had the
feeling that my point was being illustrated by current experience,
as schools with well-established heads flourished and some with
over-frequent changes of headship were inclined to suffer just the
same kind of troubles as we had.)

I still do not know what different action we could have taken in
1962, and I do not know whether we were right.   But I do know
that my conscience still bears a scar.

(Biographical Note.   John Woods.   Pupil at Friends' School,
Saffron Walden.   Degree in History, Dalton Hall (Quaker college),
Manchester University.   Had taught at Wennington School,
(Independent, Quaker led,) and a Grammar School in a London
Borough.)

2. My African Education.   15. From Security Risk to Uhuru.

I have made several references to the impact of contemporary
politics on life at Kamusinga.   It is now time to give a rather
more detailed account, without which the picture would not be
complete.

I am not qualified to write even a synopsis of the history of
Kenya between 1955 and 1964, the years when we were in the
country, years during which we witnessed a total constitutional
revolution.   But certain stages in that history, and aspects of
it, were of particular significance for us.   And the way in which
our community responded at such times was important.   As a
framework to what I have to tell, the following simple table may
help to show how national, school and personal dates were related.

Comparison of Dates.

Political events.   School events.

1954 Kenya under State of Emergency
     since 1952.   Littleton   Aug.1955 Bradleys arrive.
     Constitution.   4 African
     nominated members of Leg.Co.
     B.A.Ohanga Minister for
     Community Development.

                                          May 1956 Building begun
                                          Aug.1956 Yearly Meeting
                                                   at Kamusinga.
                                          Jan.1957 Kamusinga opened
May 1957 First African Elections   with Forms 1,2+3
     for Legislative Council.
     (Multiple vote system and
     about 60% of Africans
     enfranchised.)
     8 African Members denounce
     the constitution, refuse
     office and demand 15 seats.

     Lennox-Boyd Constitution, (to
     lead to Independence in 10 years) Jan.1958 Form 4 added

March 1958 6 more African members
     elected, and 4 out of 12
     "Common Roll" seats.   Building complete.
     Musa Amalemba Minister of   Roads and Playing
     Housing.   Field constructed.
     Trial of 8 members for defam-
     ation of candidates for   May/June Controversy over
     Common Roll seats.   Teacher contracts.

154

July Choir win in Nairobi
Dec.'58 Cambridge O.S.C.
taken for first time.

March '59 New Kenya Group formed. Jan.'59 Numbers rise to 240
Hola Affair.   First 3 students
Emergency ended.   accepted at Makerere.
Sir Patrick Renison Governor.   "Everyman", "Macbeth"
                                   (Bradleys away, June-Jan.)
Jan. 1960 First Lancaster House   First meeting of Board
Constitutional Conference.   of Governors.
(Ian McLeod Colonial Secretary)

Feb.1960 Macmillan's "Wind of Change"
Speech.   "Henry V"
33 African seats in Leg.Co.
20 for minority communities   Promise of funds for
on Common Roll.   Forms 5 and 6.

4 African Ministers
Kenya National Party formed (Muliro)
K A N U formed
K N P becomes K A D U

Feb.1961 General Election   Jan.'61 6 Kamusinga folk
(Kenyatta Election)   join Form 5 in other
K A N U majority, but refuses   schools.
office while Kenyatta detained.
K A D U takes office with   Building for Forms 5
New Kenya Party and others,   and 6.
                                   "The Rivals".

April Kenyatta to Maralal
April 11 Kenyatta Press Conference.June'61 A.B. visits Kenyatta
                                   and reports to school
                              July "Reign of Indignation"
                                   First Parents Weekend
August Kenyatta released and becomes
    (Oct.?) President of K A N U
                                   Jan.'62 Form 5, Kamusinga
Feb.'62 Second Lancaster House   Teachers for E.Africa
Constitutional Conference.   Scheme at Kamusinga.
(Maudling Colonial Secretary) Feb. "Strikes".
K A N U and K A D U Coalition.   "Twelfth Night"
                                   (Bradleys away June-August)
                                   Jan.'63 Form 6,Kamusinga.
May'63 General Election, won by KANU.
Kenyatta Prime Minister.   June 29-30 Parents Week-end.
Malcolm MacDonald Governor.   New Buildings opened.
Oct. Independence Conference. Dec. Higher Cert.1st time

12.12.63.KENYA INDEPENDENT   March'64   Bradleys leave.

155

In December, 1984 Kenya became a Republic, with Jomo Kenyatta as its first President.

I have often stated, both at the time and since, that in our day an ex-patriate teacher committed a political act in arriving on the scene. In those days the mere appearance of an English teacher immediately tarred him, (if that is not too paradoxical a metaphor,) with the colonialist brush. Fortunately the circumstances in which I was recruited meant that my own handicap was probably less than that of teachers in government schools. But it was necessary to be careful. For instance, I have already mentioned how I tried to deal with the use of the word "boy". Fortunately again, there were few occasions, and only the one in 1958 a serious one, when I sensed that my exercise of authority had any other than a professional basis.

A political aspect of our work was noticeable in quite another quarter, namely the settler community in and around Kitale. We often went there, both to shop and to visit our children in the Primary boarding school. When we first met individual settlers the opening question asked was usually: "Where are you farming ?" And when we said we were "running an African school in the Reserve" the response was not very enthusiastic. At one hotel where we occasionally went to stay in 1956, before we had moved to Kamusinga, the wife shrugged her shoulders with the remark : "Oh well, perhaps we shall begin to get some decent house-boys." When Ruth was a pupil in the school we invited an elderly lady teacher to come and spend a day with us. It happened that Henry Owuor and I were touring some of the intermediate schools in our area, to interview possible new entrants, so she came with us for the ride. "I had no idea there were so many schools," she said; "No wonder it's so difficult to get house-boys."

On the other hand, one of the best-built schools near Kamusinga was built at the expense of the neighbouring 'European' settler.

We did, in fact, try to supply a few stepping stones, (nobody could say a bridge,) towards understanding by settlers. Various members of staff invited settler friends to the school, and some of these allowed visits to their farms by groups of boys. Several came to our school plays, and on one occasion the drama critic of the "Kenya Weekly News", which was essentially for the farming community, came to our current production.

He wrote a sensitive and appreciative review, which not only appeared in his paper, but also, later on, in our magazine. (June 1962)

There was always, of course, much political discussion in the
school, but it was never repressed.   Sometimes it expressed
itself in formal debates.   From quite an early stage photographs
of Kenyatta appeared in the dormitories, sometimes alongside
pictures of the Queen.   Evidently such freeedom was not to be
found in all other schools, and in some I believe it was
forbidden.   Some people found it a bit shocking.   As I have
remarked,   I   never   hesitated   to   show   visitors   round   the
dormitories, whoever they were.   Occasionally the P.E.O. brought a
visiting dignitary.   Some time after one such visit, (in 1960, I
think,)   I   got   wind   of   the   fact   that   somebody   had   been
complaining of the unwarranted liberty that reigned at Kamusinga.
I remember going to discuss the matter with our local D.O.
(District Officer), to explain the way we handled politics.   He
saw nothing to object to, and I believe I asked him to inform the
D.C. (District Commissioner) of our conversation, so that the D.C.
could, if necessary, report to Kisumu.

Shortly afterwards I was talking with a new P.E.O. in his office
in Kisumu, when he rather wrathfully informed me that Kamusinga
was guilty of encouraging the Kenyatta cult, and was regarded as a
security risk.   "Is that so ?" I asked, confronting him, almost
literally, eye-ball to eye-ball.   "In that case , please let us go
immediately to the P.C. (Provincial Commissioner) and have it out.
He will doubtless be able to hear the truth from the D.C. Bungoma,
who will have it from the D.O. Kimilili, with whom I have
discussed our activities at Kamusinga."   The confrontation was
soon over, and I heard no more.   Indeed, this particular P.E.O.
was one of the most helpful of very helpful P.E.O.'s.   But the
story illustrates the sort of atmosphere in which we all lived.

The magazine, in the copies which I have, beginning in December,
1960, provides many illustrations of students' political reactions
and thoughts.   Articles include the following, all by students :-

Dec. 1960. Kenya's Economic Strength after Independence.
                African Students in Kenya.   (On school strikes and
                tyrannical headmasters.)
April 1961 Kenyatta's Release.
                Kamusinga Election
                My Country. "Politicians are too self-important.)
Aug.1961   Tribalism comes to Kamusinga. (Already quoted.)
                What to think about. (Women's Liberation.)
                An East-African Federation draws near.
                The Leader of Kenya.
                Multi-racial Kamusinga.
1962   A Paradise that was Kenya.
1963   - no political articles -
1964   A momentous Day in Kenya's History. (12.12.63)
                - a poem.
                My Beloved Country.   A poem.

It is clear that as Independence came in sight pre-occupation with political matters became less tense. So by 1963, - no political articles, - and in 1964 we had poems of celebration. The magazine itself began to have many more contributions of a literary character, including poems and folk-tales.

The most interesting year, from a political point of view, was 1961. The back-lash from the Lennox-Boyd Constitution of 1958 was making itself felt. Kenyatta was no longer incommunicado, and in August he was released. An election had taken place, and the first African Government had taken office, amidst much controversy. Small wonder that a group of boys such as our third years became unsettled, and then involved in the incident I have described, - though on the face of it the incident had nothing to do with politics. Some account of that year at Kamusinga, from a political point of view, will illustrate both the stresses and the way in which they were survived.

The General Election, under a much extended franchise, and with two principal parties, KANU and KADU, in contention, took place early in the year.

We were fortunate in having what the boys laughingly called a "failed M.P." on the staff. This was Guy Barnett, (see note on p.117) who had unsuccessfully fought the Scarborough seat in the British General Election of October, 1959.

With such an adviser on the spot we decided to have a "Mock Election", with all the trappings. But we thought it wise to sanction none of the existing parties, insisting on ad hoc organisations. So we had candidates from the "Kenya Reformation Movement", "Kenya National Congress", "Kenya Democratic Socialist Party", "Kenya Uhuru Party", "Msambwa Political Movement" and "Kenya Democratic Multi-tribal Party". There were two "seats" to be won. There was a week of campaigning, with a "Public Meeting" as the climax. The Chairman was the District Commissioner in person, (real, not pretend), and each candidate made a speech. A deposit of 50 cents had to be paid by each candidate, and this was forfeit if he failed to get 10% of the votes. Polling took place on 20th February under the supervision of Guy Barnett as Returning Officer. The result was announced at 7 p.m.

For these details I am indebted to George Omwono, who wrote an article in the magazine, and it is appropriate to quote his conclusion :- "It was not surprising to find the candidates representing K.R.M. and K.D.M.P won, because they worked harder."

The result of the General Election was that KANU won a majority of the seats, but refused to take office as the Government unless Jomo Kenyatta had first been entirely released, and not merely moved to Maralal and allowed to have what contacts he wished. KADU agreed to form a government, together with a few individuals from smaller minority groups.

This created still further controversy, at the height of which a debate took place at Kamusinga one Saturday night in May. I have already mentioned it; the motion was one of "no confidence in the present Kenya Government." As the debate proceeded feelings became very heated, until finally the authority of the Speaker was flouted and there was pandemonium. I was listening to the debate, as I usually did, sitting unobtrusively in "the body of the house". The Speaker was sitting at a table which was resting on another table, which served as a dais. I made my way through the shouting and gesticulating throng and stood at the Speaker's feet. The hubbub subsided and I sat down on the dais.

"I think we had better have a few minutes silence, don't you ?" I said. So we all sat silently for about five minutes. Everybody was quite accustomed to sitting silent in this way, though never, up to then, in such a situation. I do not remember that I needed to say any more. Tempers cooled, and the boys dispersed rather shame-facedly to their dormitories.

Subsequent comments came from the boys themselves. I believe that during a period of silent worship which was a part of the next day's Sunday service there was a very suitable contribution from somebody, a boy, who expressed the general feeling that the school's record for mutual tolerance had been marred. And some weeks later there appeared in the magazine the article I have already quoted, entitled "Tribalism comes to Kamusinga." Here, again, are some sentences lifted from it :-

"In the first place I shall condemn the African boys who follow their emotions."

" . . . let us be realistic. It is expecting too much from human nature to think that all the Africans in Kenya can obediently and unanimously come into one party."

"We have under tribalism abused the privilege of free speeches and expression in the school."

The impressive thing about these events is not that there existed such a variety of people and opinions in the school, but that when the variety erupted into disorder the community had the capacity to handle its own problems without any imposition of authority.

Before I tell the next story of 1961 a brief digression is justifiable and relevant.

The mixture of tribes was always a matter of pride at Kamusinga. Even if there had been none but Abaluhya boys in the school we should have had people from all parts of the area whose mother tongues differed considerably. But even before we left Kaimosi we already had one Tanganyikan, one Luo, one Kikuyu and one Kalenjin. 1957 saw a considerable influx of Luos, not 'first-choice' entrants, but boys with good KAPE results who were crowded out of schools nearer home.

They became such enthusiasts for Kamusinga that a year later there were applications for admission to our Form 1 from many Luo boys who were high on the KAPE list. After that we found ourselves able to choose our entrants from all districts almost exclusively from amongst boys for whom Kamusinga was first choice. We also admitted the first Turkana boy to go to a secondary school.

With the opening of Form 5 our 'catchment area' was extended, and by 1964 we had students from 6 out of the 7 regions in Kenya. In 1963 the magazine listed the following : - 196 Luhya, 53 Luo, 10 Kikuyu, 8 Teso, 4 Nandi, 3 Kipsigis, 3 Kamba, 3 Sabaot, 1 Nubian, 1 Turkana, 1 Kisii and 1 Meru. In 1964 we admitted the first Pokot boy to advance beyond Form 4, and an Indian boy from Kimilili entered Form 1.

However, the pride taken by members of the school was not merely in such a list, but in the fact that the mixture became an integrated whole. An article in the magazine for July,, 1964, entitled "Harmony Within", begins with the words :-

"Mrembe 'bro'"; "Misawa Omera"; "Chamker Arap . . . "; "Vimwega Kamau"; "Yoge, Otwani"; "Vimseo, Musyoki"; "Mbuya Ore"; "Mat, Etir"; and ends:-

"H A R A M B E E !"

I should explain that each pair of words contains a traditional greeting and a name from a particular area. Thus "Mrembe", corrupted from "Mirembe" and meaning Peace, is the usual greeting all over the Abaluhya area; Arap is a Kalenjin name, Kamau is Kikuyu and Etir Turkana. "HARAMBEE" is the national motto of Kenya, instituted by Jomo Kenyatta. It is the cry used by a team of workers when they are all heaving together on a load, something like "One - two - three - HEAVE ! !

I have no doubt that this "Harmony Within" is a major reason for the warm feelings which Old Boys clearly still have for the school of those days.

During the first half of 1961 Jomo Kenyatta was able, as I have mentioned, to receive visitors at Maralal. He met the press. He met leaders of the African political parties. He met a group of African clergymen from different denominations. He saw some members of the European community, — but not the Governor, who had not withdrawn his description of Kenyatta as the "leader to darkness and death". It was entirely up to Kenyatta to decide whom he would receive. An approach was made to him, asking him if he would receive a visit from a group of six Quakers, 3 African, 2 British and 1 American. He agreed, and this was the first inter-racial group, and the first group from a single denomination, who went to see him.

There were three representatives of East Africa Yearly Meeting, Thomas Lung'aho, Hezekiah Ngoya and Samuel Mwinamu; with them went Fred Reeve, American Secretary of the Mission, Walter Martin, F.S.C. representative in Nairobi, and myself, for the largest Quaker centre outside Kaimosi.

For me the projected visit to Maralal was very exciting. And as representative of Kamusinga I felt under a special obligation. I called together the prefects, and told them confidentially that I was expecting to go. I explained that I had no idea what the procedure would be, or how long the visit would last. But I asked them what they would like me to say to Kenyatta, or to ask him, if the opportunity did occur. So they drew up a list of questions, together with their greetings and assurances of support, and I wrote them all down, to take with me.

The visit took place on 2nd June. We had spent the previous night at Nakuru, and drove the dusty 150 miles to Maralal in the morning. We were warmly welcomed by Kenyatta, who impressed us all by his vigour, and his entirely relaxed manner and frame of mind.

We sat round a large dining-table. Kenyatta sat at the head, and I found myself immediately to his left, with his powerful profile only two feet away. I still have it vividly in mind, particularly his extraordinary eyes. The brown irises were flecked with blue, and there was a complete ring of blue encircling the left iris. I had not seen the like on any of the many Africans I knew.

We began by talking about Quakers whom Kenyatta had known in England, and for whom he had a very warm regard. And from there we proceeded to talk, for almost three hours in all, on a wide range of topics. A full account of these would be irrelevant here, although I am fortunate in possessing a copy of a confidential summary, running to some 14 pages, which was subsequently drawn up by Walter Martin. But in the circumstances I had every opportunity to put forward the greetings and questions from Kamusinga, and to note his replies.

Unfortunately I no longer have those notes but Valter recorded the answer to one of the most important questions, which was whether Kenyatta thought that young people in secondary schools should take any interest in politics. (As I have mentioned, I had been criticised in some quarters for allowing this.) Kenyatta replied that he thought it important for young people to learn all things, including sex and politics, in a healthy atmosphere. Secondary school children should be encouraged to think about, consider and weigh up political questions, just as other aspects of life. They should be on their guard against being moved by slogans.

As Kenyatta outlined these and other views Valter Martin laughed and remarked: "It is almost as if I were listening to Allan Bradley or some other Quaker headmaster expressing his views !" It was indeed very encouraging to discover our agreement.

The only other important point I remember is that Kenyatta felt that political activity, as distinct from thinking, was something to be postponed until later. Meantime, young people's first responsibility was to become well qualified to pull their weight when the time for activity and service came.

Our press release, published a day or two later, concluded with the view of us all that we could think of no good reason why the complete release of Kenyatta should be delayed.

(In passing, I recall that I myself wrote shortly afterwards to the Governor, Sir Patrick Renison, referring to our visit,and urging him to meet Kenyatta for himself, so that he, the Governor, might have a chance to reconsider the unfortunate views he had expressed just after the General Election.)

I reached home late on Saturday night, and on Sunday evening everyone at Kamusinga gathered in the school hall to hear my report. There was complete silence for an hour and a quarter while I spoke, and then there were some probing questions. I only distinctly remember one of these, which came from a Kikuyu boy, right at the end:- "Did you like him ?" I said that I certainly did, and that he had impressed me as a magnanimous and great man. I made it perfectly plain that I thought he should be released at once.

I feel sure that this event was at least as significant for the boys as for me, and it contributed much to the character of Kamusinga.

＊　＊　＊　＊　＊　＊　＊　＊　＊

Two other political experiences, both of a very happy nature, contributed towards my personal education in Kenya.

The General Election in the middle of 1963 was much less troublesome than an earlier one, when there had been several wild incidents in the neighbourhood, and Kamusinga had sheltered from pursuit not only a candidate, but also Clyde Sanger, at that time the East Africa correspondent of the "Manchester Guardian", who is nowadays in Canada, and a radical-minded and rather unconventional young D.O.

The 1963 election was, of course, on the basis of "One Man, One Vote", and we too were on the electoral roll.   So we cast our votes in both the local (regional and district) and the General elections.   But for the latter I was also recruited to serve as an assistant returning officer at a polling station on Mount Elgon.   There were numerous illiterate voters, who needed help in casting their votes.   So I sat behind a screen and each voter brought his or her voting paper to me and told me whether the vote was to go to the "hand", the "cow" or other symbol which represented the party allegiance of each candidate.   Several languages were involved, so I had to know the various words for these symbols.   The voters had all just dipped their finger or thumb, as statutorily required, into a pot containing indelible red ink, and this was still wet when they reached my booth.   I had an old rag, and dried their fingers as they came in.   At the end of the day my own hands were stained all over, and I have a cherished colour-slide of myself, taken when I got home in the evening, with my hands till apparently gory from the strife.

*   *   *   *   *   *   *   *   *

The other occasion was one of magnificence.   Mary and I had received official invitations, which of course we accepted, to be present at the official ceremony and celebration of the coming of Independence on 12th December, 1963.

It was a very muddy, but enormously emotional and happy occasion. On New Year's Eve I wrote our (hopefully) annual circular letter to our many friends and relations, which included the following passages :-

The stadium is about 4 miles from the centre of Nairobi.   We passed the centre soon after 7 on the evening of 11th December and got to our seats at - 9.45 !   It took an hour and three quarters to reach a place to park the car.   Then the way to the entrance lay through a sea of mud,, so that everybody was filthy on arrival.   What a crowd !   Said to be about a quarter of a million.   The stadium, when we got there, was full of many teams of tribal dancers, with drums and whistles and ostrich feathers and sisal skirts and shields and spears and, of course, fly-whisks.   The flood-lighting was good, and we even got some tolerable snapshots on Tri-X film.

On the far side, against the sky, stood two tall spot-lit flag-poles, with the Union Jack at the head of the right-hand one, - the other unadorned.

At about 10.30 came Mzee Kenyatta in his long white Lincoln, driving very slowly round the stadium. He was standing all the way, flourishing his white fly-whisk at the crowds, who cheered him past. Then came some of the distinguished guests, the Duke of Edinburgh the most prominent. Then came some marching by massed bands, followed by a parade of 6 companies of the new army, who marched and handed over colours and Trooped the Colour. It was an impressive display of disciplined drill, which had the crowds clapping with delight whenever the troops halted, presented arms, etc. as one man.

After this there were prayers by 4 or 5 religious leaders, leading up to the climax of the occasion. The spot-lights fell on two men in dark suits, walking together across the stadium from the grandstand.   One silver-haired, almost casual, - Malcolm MacDonald ; the other almost dancing, with the famous fly-whisk flickering about him as he went. It was fairly dark where they stood, as midnight drew near. The bands, also in the gloaming, rolled their drums and all stood for "The Queen". The Union Jack fluttered at the mast-head, almost the only illuminated object; no-one looked anywhere else. The anthem ended; a pause ; - complete hush.   -   And suddenly it was gone, wrapped in darkness, - nothing to be seen ! "Ai !" cried a man behind us, - and then sound was released again. "Rat ! tat ! tat ! tat ! tat ! tat !" sounded the drums in quick time, to lead in the new Kenyan National Anthem   -   but it was scarcely heard as people cheered and ululated and whistled as they watched the new National Flag, black, red, green and white, slowly rise to the head of the second mast. And then - pandemonium ! The fireworks began - what a show ! It is quite obvious that there is no better way to express high spirits, and enjoyment was terrific.   Most successful, perhaps, were the whistling rockets, which piped :- "U - u - hu - ru - u !" as they burst. Before long the Prime Minister and the Governor General and the Duke got away, and people began to swarm on to the arena, which was soon a mass of cheering, whistling, laughing folk of all races, - hoping to get home ! We ourselves arrived at our temporary abode at 3 in the morning of Independence Day itself.

Members of the school had their own chance to see the new Prime Minister, Jomo Kenyatta, when he visited Kimilili in late March, 1964, but we ourselves had left for England about a week earlier. Unfortunately the visit planned for an earlier date had been postponed, so that the plans which Mary had discussed in Kitale with Tom Mboya, to provide refreshments at Kamusinga itself, never materialised.

2. My African Education.   16. The Crucible.

The early development of education in Kenya owed everything to
voluntary bodies, - that is to say, to the various missions.   I
have already mentioned that as late as 1952 about five sixths of
the schools in the country were managed by missions or churches.
The remainder were sponsored by Government, mainly, apart from a
few Intermediate Schools, through District Education Boards.

No apology is needed, therefore, for the vital influence of
religion in Kenyan education.   Without that influence who can say
by how many years the spread of education - and indeed of so
much else - would have been delayed ?

The development of education made itself felt in a number of
stages and a number of fields, and it resulted in quite as many
problems as it did in benefits.

The first stage might be described as the attainment of "religious
literacy", achieved under the authority and sponsorship of
missions.   People learned to read their Bibles and hymn-books, -
which was seen as the first purpose of the ability to read.
(Parts, at least, of the Bible were translated into local languages
as soon as possible.)   Those who achieved literacy in this way
naturally became the first leaders of the indigenous church.

At a second stage literacy came to acquire wider application as
the tool of all kinds of advance, mainly through the schools.
These new literates grew in competence and know-how at many
levels.   The indigenous churches grew, and by the 'fifties were
playing an increasingly significant part in partnership with the
missions.   This part included even a critical approach towards
the relationship between church and mission.   The mission might
well be sensitive about this, as it saw the day coming when the
church would assume guidance over the mission, instead of the
other way round, and would ultimately replace it.

Inside the churches themselves fresh problems began to emerge.
Younger members, who had achieved the wider literacy to which I
have referred, were eager to make their own contribution to church
life.   This, in turn, led to sensitivity on the part of the elders,
who found it difficult to reconcile their own belief in tradition
with the enormous advance in sheer know-how, especially in the
English language, of younger people.   This was accentuated still
further where the very latest generation was concerned.
"Knowledge comes, but wisdom lingers" is a saying which only
suggested half the problem.   The other half was that knowledge
in the young so far outpaced the knowledge of the old that it was
often very difficult for the generations to communicate.

165

One of the most vital elements in the individual's advance in education was the concept of intellectual honesty, a questioning search for truth, – a concept almost unknown to the old. So the young began to have problems that many elders could not experience, such as the 'conflict' between science and religion, the Bible and the laboratory.

Again, within living memory African tribal societies had been organized on accepted lines, which included the apportionment to each age-group of its particular role. Under this scheme it was normal for youth to defer to age, not only because age knew better, by reason of longer experience, but also because it was privy to mysteries which no youth might share. However exuberant he might be, it was a bold youth indeed who attempted to outbid the authority of his father's generation. Yet now it was the youth who was privy to a new kind of mysteries.

The generalisations which I have here advanced were drafted by a trio of Friends, Benjamin Ngaira, Logan Smith, of F.A.M., and myself, in a working paper prepared in 1961 for the Friends' World Committee for Consultation, when it met at Kaimosi. (Sadly, I am now the sole survivor of the trio.) They are certainly true for Friends' Mission and Church, as I believe they are for other missions and churches at that time. I suspect that for us they were intensified, because of the two Quaker traditions which met at Kaimosi and had to seek reconciliation during that period. What might be called the Eastern (and English) tradition always laid much more stress on individual seeking and personal responsibility than the Middle-western tradition, with its pastors and programmed meetings and more fervent discipline.

Historically Kamusinga "occurred" just as all these problems were becoming recognizable. I believe that some people thought that Kamusinga was the cause. But of course it was really a kind of crucible, a vessel in which the inevitable seethings of the age were apparent.

‡ ‡ ‡ ‡ ‡ ‡ ‡ ‡ ‡

I have already given details of some of the ways in which the historical situation affected the story of Kamusinga, and I shall shortly give some more examples. But first I must describe the religious practice which we evolved and adopted as a regular part of our community way of life.

Our practice was a compromise, or perhaps it would be truer to call it a synthesis. On the one hand we had programmed meetings, with hymns and prepared addresses, but including periods of silence. On the other we also had meetings on a basis of silence, usually with a reading, and not excluding the option of a hymn or two.

On week-day mornings, except Wednesdays, we held a short assembly
in the hall, for the leadership of which various people were
responsible, usually for a week at a time.   The treatment varied
as considerably as did the leaders.

On Sunday morning there was a service in the old church, attended
by the whole school and by staff and neighbouring families.   If
we had a visitor I usually conducted it, choosing the hymns and
arranging the programme, and the visitor gave an address.   But
we always included a period of about 10 minutes of silent worship,
when anybody was free to speak, or to lead in spoken prayer.
And both boys and other people present often did, to great effect.
More than one rather dry-bones service which I myself was leading
received a breath of life from some unexpected quarter.   At
harvest time the Young Farmers' Club was responsible for the
service, and I remember an illuminating intervention through which
we were reminded that harvest thanksgivings were an important
part of African society long before the Christian religion was
introduced.   Indeed, the speaker went so far as to say that
Africans took religion more seriously before the missionaries
came.

On Sunday evenings there was another meeting in the school hall.
Apart from the students and myself there were sometimes no more
than a couple of staff present, but more would attend when, for
instance, we had a guest.   This meeting usually included 2 or 3
hymns, suggested impromptu by anybody who called out a number.
(By this time, by the way, we had introduced "Songs of Praise",
which we found, to provide a more satisfying selection of hymns.)
There was usually a reading, and there would be a quarter of an
hour or so quite unprogrammed, during which vocal contributions,
sometimes in the form of prayers, might be offered.   Occasionally
I had something I wanted particularly to speak to students about
on my own.   The form was very free.   On one such evening the
celebrated Carey Francis, of Alliance High School, sat with me
facing the school.   I had explained to him that he would be very
welcome to speak during the period of silence, but that he need
feel under no obligation to do so.   He was rather puzzled by our
procedure, but he did give a short address.   On particular
occasions the meeting would be devoted to a special purpose, as
when I reported to the whole of the Kamusinga community on my
visit to Kenyatta.   (At quite a different level, we sometimes
spent most of the time learning a new hymn-tune or so.   We had
no musical instrument, so it was all done by ear.   We accumulated
quite a respectable 'repertoire'.   I became reasonably good at
giving the pitch and starting the singing; from then on two or
three parts were usually to be heard.)

But it was on Wednesday mornings that we held the meetings which, as far as East Africa Yearly Meeting was concerned, were most peculiar to Kamusinga. And I believe that these times were amongst the most significant of all. We met in the open air beside the old church. The benches were arranged in several rows in a rough semi-circle, with one straight row completing the D shape. A member of staff was usually responsible for introducing the meeting, with a reading, and possibly a short address. But the main feature was half an hour or so of worship based on silence. Sometimes silence was maintained throughout the period; usually it was broken by vocal contributions. These were quite often statements of problems about which people were thinking, and these were often succeeded by attempts to answer the problems. Occasionally there was a flurry of contributions which almost became a debate. But the spirit of the meetings was such that they were capable of resolving tensions. Once in a while there was a visitor who was invited to speak. I remember a morning when Douglas Steere, an eminent Quaker theologian from America, gave an address, after which questions, comments and arguments kept him for quite a long time "on his toes".

But the most abiding memory I have is of sitting in company in absolute peace and quiet, with the warm morning sun on my back, while from about 3 miles away came the sound of a slender, high waterfall, rushing into a gully from the lower slopes of Elgon. And more than one article in the magazine bears witness to the appreciation of Wednesday mornings. Here is one of them in full.

"Before the worship begins we are already assembled here in a sort of ring where all face all, united in a single rhythm of silence.

"The minister announces Quiet Worship which to some of us is just thrust in our way, but to others who have grown familiar with it, it is meaningful and essential. Every head now drops hanging on the chest - concentrating deeply in the unploughed fields of thought. Now and then there is a gentle whisper in every head; the gold sunlight shines steadily; the heat ray creeps silently into the flesh of the backs and the fronts.

"The morning is clear, the ground dewy green. A light breeze springs up at times clappering through dripping clothes on the wires in the east. From time to time the voices of the woodcutters are heard, accompanied by rhythmic sawing. But one does not seem to hear all these noises. It has never been absolutely silent. A thought crops up in the mind, but it withers soon. Maybe it was bad. The Holy Ray stalks the broken hearted. The unconscious mind ponders on and He insistently whispers. He reforms the troubled minds and the souls of the miserable.

At an instant, after a mysterious change within, a person shoots
up to proclaim the 'Light Within, That of God in him, the Seed' -
a thing I have never done for, I must confess, fear holds me fast
by the throat whenever I want to. All the eyes in the gathering
rise up to pin-point him. The proclaimer puts forth his thoughts
with less humour than seriousness. It is done. He resumes his
seat.

"The heads drop again but intrusively the lorry engine starts near
by which roars away in the distance - out on his duties - leaving
us quiet again."
          (The writer was in the third year at the time.)

        ‡   ‡   ‡   ‡   ‡   ‡   ‡   ‡   ‡

The visitors who came to us on Sunday mornings were many, and
in great variety. At least twice a term we liked to have local
African Friends to speak, which often meant that an interpreter
was required. Their addresses, so different in character from
those we could offer, were vivid and memorable. Such visits were
very important, both to the school and to the local Friends'
Meetings, and to relations between the school and the Yearly
Meeting.

Of course by no means all our visitors were Friends. For
instance, we welcomed Heads and Principals from various other
schools and colleges, both mission and government institutions.
One Sunday we were visited by a European settler who was an
enthusiast for Moral Re-armament, together with some African
adherents to M.R.A.

One week-end our guest was the Rev. Stanley Booth-Clibborn, editor
of "Rock", the periodical published by the Christian Council of
Kenya. (Since 1980 he has been Bishop of Manchester.) As we
had a considerable number of Anglican boys in the school, (mainly
Luo boys from the C.M.S. area round Maseno,) we invited him to
hold an Anglican service of Holy Communion in our church on
Sunday morning. I remember that he asked for a loaf of bread
from our table and, I believe, for some Coco-cola, to serve as the
Elements in the sacrament. It was a very happy occasion,
attended by a good number who were not Anglicans.

        ‡   ‡   ‡   ‡   ‡   ‡   ‡   ‡   ‡

In the school there were three other religious activities which
did not involve everybody. These were Friends' membership
classes, the Fishermen's Club and Sunday School teaching.

The membership classes presented a problem, because the ways in
which E.A.Y.M. and London Y.M. approach membership are so
different, and yet it was hoped that I personally would take part.

In a good English meeting enquirers about Quakerism who wished to become members would usually have an opportunity to attend a series of discussion and study groups organized by Elders or Overseers, with the object of making sure that those interested were aware of the history and beliefs and practices of Friends. When an actual application for membership was made Monthly Meeting would appoint two Friends to interview the applicant to discuss these matters, and to satisfy themselves that he/she was in sympathy with them. They would normally report back to the Monthly Meeting with a recommendation for acceptance, and this would be recorded and forthwith take effect.

(In the English Society of Friends the Monthly Meeting is the body in which authority is vested. It consists of all the members of a small group of local meetings, which, when they meet for business purposes, are themselves known as 'Preparative Meetings'.)

In East Africa Y.M. the arrangements were very different. Membership would be granted in two stages, each of them involving a course of instruction, including the learning of a number of prescribed scriptural texts, and culminating in a formal catechism by an Elder or Pastor at a meeting for worship. Having successfully gone through the process the candidate would be recorded as a Book 1 or Book 2 member, as the case might be. There would normally be an interval of about 2 years between the two.

One of the main differences between the two systems lay really in the balance between church authority and personal responsibility. Added to this was the wide difference in doctrine between the evangelical and what I have called the "eastern" branches of Quakerism. The evangelical branch, which founded the Mission, laid much stress on the acceptance of "Jesus as personal Saviour", with the renunciation of Sin, which was itself defined in considerable detail in the Book of Discipline. The Ten Commandments, included in the prescribed texts to be learned by candidates for membership, were also supplemented by the strict banning of alcohol and tobacco and disapproval of polygamy, dancing and, of course, irregular sexual behaviour. The "eastern" tradition, as exemplified in the Book of Discipline of London Y.M., operates through a collection of "Advices and Queries", to provide sound guide-lines without imposing actual rules, the breaking of which would entail forfeiture of membership. This does not mean that members cannot be called to task for short-comings, whether in doctrine or behaviour.

To be asked to conduct membership classes placed me in an embarrassing situation, because whereas the key-note of the E.A.Y.M. teaching could be characterised as acceptance, that to which I was accustomed could be more aptly described as seeking.

In addition to this, the early history of Quakerism had little or
no place in E.A.Y.M. teaching, whereas in London Y.M. it provided,
in some respects, a starting point for the consideration of Quaker
principles and experience. (The lives of George Fox and William
Penn are particularly relevant.) The first of these differences
in emphasis constituted the main problem, and I discussed it with
one or two leading members of E.A.Y.M. I pointed out that it
would be impossible for me personally to conduct classes in the
same way as a Y.M. Pastor. On the other hand, if I presented
Quakerism in the way to which I was accustomed, I might well be
seen as introducing an explosive element into the Y.M. The
members whom I consulted, who had experience of the kind of
Quakerism to be found in England, perfectly understood the
problem. But the answer they gave was clear, namely that I
should conduct the classes on the basis of my own understanding
and belief, and that any "explosive" consequences should not be
shirked. The "crucible" function of Kamusinga, to which I have
referred, was recognized and accepted.

The second difference in emphasis was not so controversial, and
the "safest" approach to the classes was through the early history
of Quakerism. This is the approach adopted by myself and later
leaders of the membership classes. It led on, of course, to
discussions of doctrine and practice, as well as a description of
the way in which church government is conducted at the present
time in London Y.M.

It was essential, however, to make sure that E.A.Y.M. requirements
were met. So candidates were provided with lists of the
prescribed texts and given the responsibility of familiarizing
themselves with them. In due course one of our Sunday mornings
was set aside for receiving candidates into Book 1 or Book 2
membership. The Y.M. Pastor for the area came, and catechised
the candidates as they stood in a row before him, after which
they were recorded as members and the service proceeded, with an
address by the Pastor.

One weakness of the situation is clear. The school meeting was
not constitutionally a unit in the structure of Monthly and
Quarterly Meetings of the Y.M. So reception into membership in
this way did not, at the same time, involve reception into a
Quaker Meeting functioning in the normal local way. So it was
entirely up to the new members.

Their involvement, during the holidays, in their own local
meetings, depended entirely on themselves and the members of the
home meetings.

On the other hand, I must digress to testify that I was personally
never more conscious than at Kamusinga of the inter-relationship
between worship and work.

One might even say that the two infiltrated one another day by day, and it was not really possible to consider them apart.

In a close-knit community with an acknowledged religious background this was not unnatural. Any denominational or inter-denominational boarding school is an environment where such a state of affairs is both natural and desirable, and many such schools, including Friends' schools, exist.I believe, however, that the Kamusinga experience was much more intense than almost all of these.

One reason for this lies, I think, in the age-range of the students. In an English school the youngest pupils might be as young as 11. In an African school at the time when Kamusinga was growing, few boys entered Form 1 much under the age of 16, and a good many were several years older. Educational attainment apart, therefore, practically every boy was at least as mature as the average fifth-former in an English school, - the stage at which English teachers have the rewarding experience of observing an almost abrupt transition to young adulthood. So almost all boys were old enough to take part, on equal terms with the oldest, even with the staff, in the corporate experience of the school in worship. There were, one might say, no "children" requiring a modified approach and practice. So some colleagues, including myself, were occasionally tempted to go too far in the other direction, talking, perhaps, over the heads of everybody !

The second reason for what I would claim as the special quality of the Kamusinga experience is the use we made of worship based on silence. In most denominational schools the form of worship is such that one could describe it as "provided" by whoever holds the pastoral position. In our practice such "provision" was limited in scope, and so responsibility was shared by all. As I have already mentioned, there were very frequent vocal contributions to worship from individual students, both senior and junior. They were very seldom in any way unacceptable, and if they were, it was not at all uncommon for the "correction", if it was needed, to come from a similar source, and not from teachers. Participation in worship was thus recognizably, and not merely theoretically, active, and one person's contribution, whatever his age or status, was as significant as another's.

As far as those new members were concerned, one might claim that although they were not very closely integrated into a local meeting they did, nevertheless, throughout their time at Kamusinga, participate in a genuine corporate worshipping experience. As to myself, after this Kamusinga experience I confess that experience of an English meeting, which was mainly a Sunday affair, with little reference to corporate week-day activity, especially in a meeting drawing members from a rather scattered area, fell rather flat.

The Fishermen's Club was founded at Kaimosi long before the foundation of Kamusinga, and it still had its counterpart in the Teachers' Training College there. It closely resembled a Students' Christian Union and was one of the voluntary societies. It held an evening meeting once a week. The name suggested that the members were "Fishers of Men" and it was evangelical in character. It became affiliated to the Kenya Schools Christian Fellowship and members took part in inter-school gatherings. In later years its title appeared in the school magazine sometimes as the Christian Union and sometimes as the Fishermen's Club. It functioned very much under its own impetus and my own involvement was very slight, particularly since its style was sometimes rather uncomfortable to me. I would have been happier with the style of the Student Christian Movement. But the club did make a very practical contribution to the neighbouring community by providing Sunday School teachers. This greatly flourished, especially after Esther Bower undertook regular classes of preparation for the teachers themselves. I believe this contribution by members of the school was much appreciated by the local meetings. On Easter Sunday in 1964, (just after we left), over a hundred pupils from the Sunday Schools came to Kamusinga for service and group discussions and tea.

‡   ‡   ‡   ‡   ‡   ‡   ‡   ‡   ‡

Religious Education had its place in the regular teaching time-table of all classes. It is my recollection that the syllabus was based on the Agreed Syllabus of an English Education Authority, almost certainly Oldham, since I had brought a copy with me. This was supplemented by an account of the origins and beliefs of Quakerism. This was not included with any proselytising in mind, but because it seemed reasonable that all members of the school, who came from many denominations, should have some idea of the background to Kamusinga. In the junior classes the syllabus was based on scriptural studies, but in higher classes it was broadened to include discussion of practical applications of religious belief, such as the consideration of social problems, and also some account of religions other than Christianity. In Forms 5 and 6 use was made of symposiums produced at Makerere under the editorship of Professor Eric Lucas. The first was entitled "What is Man ?" and the second "What is Freedom ?" and both consisted of essays by members of the Makerere staff on different aspects of the two subjects.

Occasionally I was under pressure to allow School Certificate candidates to take Religious Knowledge as one of their examination subjects, particularly since the success rate in this subject among pupils in other schools seemed so high. I consistently refused, since I held then, as now, that religion is too important to be degraded to the status of an examination subject, and that its study needs larger scope and freedom.

173

I was never conscious of any adverse comment on our teaching and practices from African Friends who knew the school. We had the sons of a good many leading Friends amongst our students, and there was always a preponderance of Friends amongst Governors, whom we kept informed about the school's ways.

We were always at pains to maintain our relations with the Mission at Kaimosi, of which I continued to be a full member until we finally left Kamusinga. Indeed there was a period of several months in 1960 when I agreed to act as Education Secretary of the Mission in the absence of Fred Reeve. The other half of his responsibilities was undertaken by Logan Smith, and we were in close collaboration during that time. (I have referred to the consultative document we produced for the World Committee together with Benjamin Ngaira.) I found myself involved in handling a number of problems which arose in Kaimosi institutions and Chavakali School, and in representing the Mission to the Provincial Education Officer. I was also responsible for reporting on these institutions, as well as on Kamusinga, to E.A.Yearly Meeting at its annual conference.

So despite the geographical separation we were not isolated from the Mission. In fact, for a number of years we had our own radio link. There were always two representatives of the Mission on our Board. It was only occasionally that any difficulty arose. One such was when a very evangelical missionary, with whom I was actually particularly friendly, came to speak at Kamusinga and met with some of the students for discussions. He was quite horrified to find some students asking questions and expressing doubts about parts of the gospel which he felt must be accepted as unquestioned and absolute truth. I remember trying to calm him by explaining that it was our function and duty to encourage students to ask questions and to think for themselves; otherwise they would be much more vulnerable to "worldly" pressures. But he would not be convinced, and it was painful to hear that he had subsequently been heard at Kaimosi to refer to Kamusinga as a "hell-pit". But this was far from typical of the attitude towards Kamusinga of Kaimosi folk. There were many occasions when inter-visitation took place, and personal relations were always satisfactory and enjoyable, however much outlooks differed. In any case, of course, Kaimosi itself was developing, as the status of the Training College and the Girls' School rose. Former Kamusinga students went for training at Kaimosi, and no doubt their presence and attitudes had something to do with some painful controversies which arose there. Whereas at Kamusinga our growth had been unimpeded by local complications, at Kaimosi the College existed cheek by jowl with other institutions, and with the mission management itself, and some tension was inevitable, with the consequent risk of confrontations and disturbance.

I do not recall any time when the school did not enjoy good relations with the Yearly Meeting. I was personally accorded ex officio membership of the Yearly Meeting Board, and was always welcome, indeed often expected, at its meetings.

At the annual conference in August I always presented a report, which it became the custom to present in duplicated form in both English and Kiswahili. I still have copies of several of these.

Before ever the school had left Kaimosi the school was, as it were, planted in the Yearly Meeting. In 1956, (as related by Dandy in his letter !), the conference took place at Kamusinga itself, and it was during the conference that the Provincial Commissioner came and laid the foundation stone of the school, which is still to be seen beside the main entrance to the hall.

(The official opening of the school took place after the school had been installed for some time, and was the occasion for a visit by H..E. the Governor of Kenya, Sir Evelyn Baring, (later Lord Hawick). All due formalities were observed. The Governor was introduced to staff, committee members, the architect and contractors, as well as senior boys. He heard the choir sing, and he unveiled a plaque recording the occasion. It was a distinctly "colonial" occasion, but the school did, after all, owe its existence to colonial funds, and it is not entirely inappropriate to remember this. In 1982 the plaque was still in position.)

Our relations with the Board of Missions in Richmond were always friendly. But after the Board of Governors came into operation, in 1960, and financial considerations virtually ruled out the possibility of recruiting staff from America other than through the T.E.A. project there was no administrative link between Richmond and the school. But we were always included in visits by Friends from America, and there were a number of very pleasant occasions of this kind.

However, at the end of 1959, while we were in England, I had an urgent invitation from George Scherer, at that time the Secretary of the Mission Board, to come to America for a month, to visit a whole series of Friends' schools and colleges and the Mission Board Headquarters in Richmond. My expenses were covered from various sources, including the institutions I visited. I was able to talk about Kamusinga wherever I went, and to show slides of its early history. My reception everywhere could not have been more cordial, and I very much enjoyed making so many contacts in so many places, including New York State, Philadelphia, Baltimore, Greensborough NC and even Atlantic City.

The most on-going contact I had with overseas "Quakery" was through George Whiteman. Not only was I in constant touch about staffing, as I have mentioned, but during our first two leaves we were in Saffron Walden, where he and his wife Mary lived, and were their very close neighbours. Added to this, they became surrogate parents to our children, who were boarders in the Friends' School. We owe them both a great deal. Sadly, George died some years ago, not so very long after his retirement.

In 1961 the World Committee for Consultation met at Kaimosi, but there was also a 2-day gathering at Kamusinga, and though the school was on holiday we had the opportunity to show well-known Friends from many countries what we were trying to do.

2. My African Education. 17. End of Term.

In the middle of March, 1964 we went on leave to England.   I
myself expected to be back at Kamusinga in early June, though
Mary intended to stay on in England longer, to see more of Paul
and Ruth.   But in fact neither of us returned.

In August, 1963 we had agreed, albeit in a situation of some
stress, to continue at Kamusinga after our 1964 leave.   So it was
very embarrassing to have to renege on that undertaking, and
without going back in person to explain.   The reasons were
personal.   They had to do with a combination of problems - the
aging of my parents, school holidays for Ruth and Paul,
frustration of our family life, some financial considerations, and
finally, the fact that Mary had to go into hospital urgently for
surgery.

It was not a comfortable decision.   Peter was a student at
Nairobi University, so that he had to abandon his course after
only one year.   To make matters worse, we could not afford to
travel out ourselves to pack up our belongings, so he got lumbered
with that responsibility, having to rely on help from other people
at Kamusinga, who were thus also burdened.

I had left John Woods as Acting Head during my absence.   The
Governors made the very good decision to confirm him in the post
of Head, and he only left, some years later, when appointed as
Head of the Friends' School, Saffron Walden, of which he is
himself a former pupil.   Since then the Head of Kamusinga has
always been an African.

It was 16 years before we returned to Kenya.

                    *   *   *   *   *   *   *   *   *   *

In August, 1963 I presented my usual brief report to the annual
conference of East Africa Yearly Meeting of Friends.   In the
course of that report I wrote :-

"It is, of course, never easy to judge the effectiveness of a
school.   Examinations give some indication of what we have been
doing, but their importance is limited.   In my opinion, the work
we are doing to-day cannot be properly assessed until, say, 1973,
when we may see something of what the boys have done with the
training they are receiving at the school now."

The first classes to take the School Certificate examination at
Kamusinga had left at the end of 1958.   For their final three
years I had been their headmaster, and they had been subjected to
ideas and policies for which I was mainly responsible.   Leavers
in 1959 and later had been "under my wing" for four years.

Of those who took the exam at the end of 1961 13 stayed on for another 2 years, and were joined by 16 students from other Kenya schools which had no Forms 5 and 6, to take the Higher School Certificate exam at the end of 1963. Once Forms 5 and 6 were established this was the normal pattern. By early 1980 17 years had passed since the report I have quoted, and it was 21 years since those first classes had left.

The original "pioneers" of Kamusinga in 1957 numbered 150 and they were joined by about 60 more in the following year. During our visits in 1980 and 1982 I got to know the present occupations and family circumstances of about 80 of those 210, and I actually talked with most of the 80. In addition, in the autumn of 1985 we had visits from 3 Old Boys, now in most responsible posts, with whom we had very thorough-going conversations about our memories of the school. Jotham Amisi was S.S.P. during the stressful years 1961 and 1962 and "emeritus" S.S.P. in 1963. He is now Principal of the Kenya Posts and Telecommunications Corporation's Central Training School at Mbagathi, Nairobi. Alfred Ndukuyu Kimunguyi has been Head of Kamusinga since 1980. William Wanyonyi Wambwa, at one time Head of Chavakali School, is now Head of the Jamhuri High School in Nairobi, the biggest school in Kenya. (In colonial times it was the Secondary School for Asian boys, and known as the Duke of Gloucester School.)

Until 1980 we had only very occasional news of Old Boys, although several did visit us in our home when they were in England. But since 1980 the many contacts I have mentioned have enabled me to hear what established people in middle life think about their schooling. In writing of the difficulties we experienced in 1961 I listed some of the positions held in later life by boys who were troublesome at the time. Similar lists could be compiled of people in other year-groups who are now in positions of importance. When we talked with former students, or rather, when they talked to us, we were overwhelmed by the appreciation which they expressed. We heard the same thing from everybody. There was, of course, an element of nostalgia. But we also heard, on many sides, how their educational foundations, or so they claimed, had helped them to cope with later studies, employment and responsibilities more successfully than students coming, often with more brilliant academic results, from some other school. And they were even eager to tell us why.

It would be wrong to suggest that there were no disappointments. We heard of a number of former students who had weaknesses, problems, failures. But these do not invalidate the general impression, which was that men feel that they gained something, as students at Kamusinga, that was not, at that time, available elsewhere.

What was it ?

Perhaps it had something to do with the story that the only school rule, supposedly, was : "Use your common sense !" The implications of this were: a. that you should stand on your own feet, and b. that your behaviour should be regulated by your own sense of responsibility and not merely by rules imposed upon you. In illustration of their claim we were told that the drop-out rate at Makerere College amongst students coming, with excellent academic results, from a school with a very tight regime, was very high, whereas Kamusinga folk were able to stay the course. This bears out something which I said in December, 1959, when I gave an address to the Friends' Guild of Teachers at Sidcot School. Discussing the consequences of the acknowledged fact that most of the educational system in Kenya owed its development to missions, I said :-

"Government policy has always admitted, or rather expressly encouraged, the idea that moral teaching must go hand in hand with secular instruction, and that this should be handled by religious bodies.

"The weaknesses of this arrangement are not difficult to see. In some areas there is reaction against the missions in their capacity as managers, because this may be just another means for the exercise of paternalism, which is so liable to provoke resentment. And even if it does not provoke resentment, it may well invite ultimate failure. The traditional missionary outlook implies a certain authoritativeness. The gospel preached has about it a strong element of dogma. The church knows what is right and what is wrong. This has been passed on to the faithful as received truth. And many of the faithful have accepted it and put it into practice with sincerity and steadfast conviction, and sometimes the greatest heroism. If it were not so, there would be no flourishing indigenous churches.

"But the fact remains that many are held by an outward authority and depend on it in order to sustain themselves. The authority is not fully their own. So, in a school, boys may have held before them the highest of Christian ideals, and these ideals may be practised by those in authority in their own lives, and even insisted upon in the school, almost to the point of imposition. Some boys may be happy in this; others may chafe. When they go on to College the old authority is weakened, and new authorities may be discovered, to challenge the old. The old may be discarded, and perhaps none accepted to take its place. And so the school feels that its products have failed, and that College has ruined them. This is no more helpful than saying that the world is wicked.

"A Friends' school must, it seems to me, proceed differently. We too are missionaries; and we too believe we know something of the meaning of the Gospel.

But we cannot propagate it by dogma and authority. We must do what we can to help our students to acknowledge an authority which is inward, and a dependence on a spirit which is inward, so that they may achieve a sense of liberty and responsibility which is not merely a reaction against what is restrictive and dominant. What we try to do is to speak to our students of the moral and religious problems which they are facing, or must face, and to suggest what they involve. 'Some of the answers we think we know for ourselves,' we may say, 'But you must test them for yourselves, and find your own answers. We are here to help you as much as we can. But the most important answers are those which nobody can discover but you.' In such a way, we hope and believe, we are preparing boys for the shocks ahead. We try to avoid attaching moral authority to ourselves, so that if we ourselves are discounted in the times ahead, the standards the boys have acquired are not discarded with us."

I have explained that the title, "My education" can be understood in two possible ways. As far as my African education is concerned, the questions I had to tackle were : "What long-term effect did the school have on its students in those early days ?" and "What did I myself learn from the experience ?"

The fore-going pages relate mainly to the first of those questions. I must now address myself to the second.

Fundamentally, the experience of Kamusinga pressed home the lesson given me in the late 'forties by that little Somerset girl, - the one who told me she wanted to teach - children !

When we first arrived in Kenya there were too many people, and not all of them outside missionary circles, who had some idea that Africans were human beings of a lesser status than Europeans. And the reaction of Africans was consistently to demand to be regarded as human beings, with the same dignity as other human beings. The expression "human being" recurred persistently. I found myself with the thought constantly in my mind: "A human being is a human being is a human being." Doubtless it is a reflexion on me that I needed to be made so conscious of what, after all, is a pretty trite and common-place thought, but it did also have importance for me in a later application.

It was during Kamusinga days that I modified my view of the function of the head of a school. My view was very much in line with thoughts I expressed earlier concerning leadership and responsibility amongst students. Responsibility is an individual, yet a shared function. The incident recounted on page 159 is a good ilustration of the benefit to be gained from the establishment of an ethos based on this principle rather than one based on command and obedience.

I came to define my own responsibility as that of an enabler. Not a director, not an originator, not a creator, but a person whose job it is to ensure that the facilities are available to enable the students to live and study and learn, that staff are available who can help them, and that staff have the backing and encouragement which will enable them to apply the originality and creativeness and other powers with which they are gifted.

This is not to say that it is sufficient for a head to be a good organiser. I have constantly found it vital to exercise my imagination. First of all, I needed to be thinking forward to possible future needs and situations and developments. And in the second place, I had to be alert to perceive unforeseen opportunities, and sometimes to act on them impulsively, even instantly.

I have often found myself telling people that my wife and I went to Kenya to build a school. But that is too structural a description of my function. I much prefer to think of myself, at Kamusinga and also later on, as a "scholastic mid-wife". A mid-wife has no share in creation, but she has knowledge and experience, and so she is the support and helper who works to ensure safe and healthy delivery of the result of other people's creativity. She is the "enabler par excellence".

42. – Kamusinga badge

3. My Comprehensive Education.   1. In Limbo.

In the summer of 1964 I found myself unemployed and without a
home. We foisted ourselves on my parents in North Kent. The
ensuing year was the most unsatisfactory of my whole career.

For 6 or 7 weeks I managed to get a temporary post in a Boys'
Technical School situated not too far from where we were staying.
It provided me with my first culture shock. I was landed with
taking over from the Head a time-table consisting largely of R.E.
classes. There was a terrible syllabus and the boys were even
less interested in it than I was. Coming straight from a
situation where pupils were bursting with curiosity and anxiety to
learn, I found myself quite unable to cope with lads who only
wanted to discuss "Mods and Rockers". I have to confess that I
only lasted out the term for the sake of the money.

After the summer, when Ruth and Paul had returned to school at
Saffron Walden, we were able to have a "bed-sit" in the house of
my cousin Alison Bradley, just off Parliament Hill in Hampstead.
She also found a room for Peter, who had got a place at Sir John
Cass College, (now a part of the City University). I managed to
get a post for the term, teaching Mathematics in a co-educational
Secondary Modern School in Edgware and for the only time in my
life I became a commuter, with a season ticket between Belsize
Park and Edgware. I was form-master to a very pleasant fourth
year form, but also taught a number of other classes. I have to
confess that apart fom my own form I found it difficult to adjust
to an ambience so different from Kamusinga. A large proportion
of the school population had the lively temperament which is not
uncommon in the area north of Golders Green, and although they
were not disruptive, some of them were not tremendously
responsive to my efforts to advance their mathematical skills.

I had begun to apply for headships in several places, as well as
for deputy posts in colleges, but achieved no interviews. I
thought perhaps I had shot my scholastic bolt, and that I should
try to get into educational administration. I had sought the
advice of Gordon Bessey, Director of Education for Cumberland, who
told me that one could not expect to switch one's career in that
way. However, when an administrative post in Cumbria was
advertised, (I think it was a "third tier" post vacated by Michael
Harrison, who was moving to Sheffield as Deputy Director,) I wrote
to Gordon Bessey and applied. He is the kind of man who takes
enormous trouble, and before drawing up his short list for
interviews he went all over the country meeting with all the
candidates who interested him. Out of sheer kindness he invited
me to meet him in London, and we had a long talk.

He repeated his previous advice. I complained that at almost 55 I was getting no interviews for headships. His reply was: "You would get one in Cumberland."

Next day I wrote to him and said I was withdrawing my application to him, and sending one to Northamptonshire, for the headship of a new Grammar School to be opened at Corby, - and please would he be one of my referees ? Not only did he agree, but, as I learned later, he forthwith commended me to the Northamptonshire Director, Mr. George Churchill. A short time afterwards I was invited to Corby for interview, and finished the day as one of 3 candidates put on a short list for further interview some days later in County Hall. At the end of the second interview I was appointed Head of Kingswood Grammar School, Corby, with effect from 1st May, 1965, the school to open in the following September. The first interview had taken place on the day before my 55th birthday, and the very amiable and supportive Chairman of the Governors, Mr. G.A.Hunter, used to send me a birthday card every year from 1966 until he died, a good many years later. - which underlined the fact that my age had been a matter of some concern to governors.

The date when I was to take up the appointment meant that I should need a post for the Spring term. I managed to get one, teaching French in a very large Boys' Comprehensive School in N.W.London. I have never known such a long spring term; it lasted nearly 14 weeks, with only a two days break at half-term. And for me it was torture, pure and simple. I remember the first time I went to take a third-year class; the boys simply broke into the room, running amok, before ever I myself had stepped inside. I cannot claim to have made any useful contribution to that school, which depressed me. However, I dare say the experience was salutary. For the first time, for instance, I found myself faced with the problem of teaching a remedial class - French ! I was partly consoled by finding that when Guy Barnett, my former Kamusinga colleague, who also needed a temporary post, came on the same staff, he too was dismayed by the experience.

One positive thing I learned and admired. The 'pastoral' side of the school was so organized that there was always some senior teacher who had detailed knowledge of a particular boy. I think the system was based on year groups rather than 'houses', but each head of a group was a mine of information and had great influence with the boys. I remember thinking that in that large comprehensive school more was known, and more care taken, about each individual than was commonly found in many a much smaller Grammar School.

What helped me to last out the term was the certainty that I had an exciting prospect before me once it was over. But of course, a temporary teacher in any school does not integrate with a school so well as a person who is there for a positive reason. And in difficult situations, particularly, one needs time to acclimatise. I myself felt like a pretty ineffectual beginner. A humiliating experience, which I did not forget in the next few years.

There was another compensatory side to life during those months. The Friends' Service Council appointed Mary as temporary warden for William Penn House in Balcombe Street, Marylebone. This was a residential post, with quarters for warden and partner, and the responsibility was to cater and play host for day-conferences, mainly of people from various Embassies and High Commissions. These were a part of the top-level "Peace" initiatives of the Society of Friends, and many well-known and less-well-known people of different races and countries attended them.

3. My Comprehensive Education.   2. Kingswood, the new Grammar
School.

The organisation of secondary schools in Corby was to change,
with effect from September, 1965.   I learned about this when I
was appointed to Kingswood.   At that time there was Corby
Grammar School, opened 10 years earlier, and there were 5 County
Secondary Modern Schools, one of them only opened in 1964, and
one Catholic Secondary Modern School.   Corby was still growing
fast, and one Grammar School would soon be unable to accommodate
all the potential "Grammar School pupils", so a new Grammar School
was being built at the opposite end of the town to the "old" one.

But the Education Committee was moving tentatively towards the
idea of comprehensive schools, and decided to try out in Corby an
unusual arrangement.   This was that each Grammar School should
have a catchment area of roughly half the town, plus some of the
rural area.   But there should be no 11+ examination.   Instead,
parents of pupils in the senior year of junior schools would be
able to choose whether their children should go to one of the two
Grammar Schools or one of the Secondary Modern Schools.   It was
made quite clear that the two Grammar Schools would be offering a
Grammar School curriculum, which would not make allowances for
pupils lacking appropriate ability.   Counselling would be
available from the Heads of Junior Schools.   A "13+ transfer"
scheme, for late developers, would operate on the same principle.

I remember being asked, during my interview at Corby, what I
thought of comprehensive education.   I replied that I thought the
Corby scheme was a very interesting approach to it.

In passing I should mention that a new Catholic School, named
after Pope John XXIII, was being built next door to Kingswood, and
that it would take all Catholics over 13 who wished to go there.
In other words, it would be fully comprehensive from the outset.
The first two Catholic year-groups would remain in the existing
school, Our Lady's.   (In later years the two schools merged,
though still on two sites, thus constituting a full-blown 11-18
comprehensive school, known as Our Lady's and Pope John School).

Kingswood was being built with accommodation for an annual intake
of 90, with a Sixth Form block.   The whole of the accommodation
was to be available almost from the opening date.   But since it
was not expected that even 90 entrants would be forthcoming at
the start, it was decided that pupils wishing to transfer to
Kingswood in 1965 after one year at Corby Grammar School should
be able to do so, thus providing us with a second-year group, and
that similar arrangements should apply for 13-year-olds, both
those at Corby Grammar School and those at Secondary Modern
Schools, on the same terms as Form 1 admissions.

So apart from the pupils transferring from Corby Grammar School to our second and third years, nobody depended for admission on success in the old 11+ exam; everybody was there by the (hopefully informed) choice of parents. For 4 years our pupils entered a Grammar School on that basis. I can remember only two occasions when we felt, after a year or more, that we should suggest to parents that they had made a mistake. Indeed, I have often declared that I thought parental choice was at least as accurate as the 11+ exam in determining who should go to Grammar School.

Before I go on to write of the change in the school's function which began to take effect in 1969 I must go back to the beginning of Kingswood.

‡ ‡ ‡ ‡ ‡ ‡ ‡ ‡ ‡

Very early in the New Year of 1965 a new home had to be found. Housing in Corby was plentiful, but the modern designs available would not have accommodated all the family and the possessions we had accumulated. We were fortunate in finding a good family house with a large garden and garage in the little town of Rothwell, only 6 miles from Kingswood, - 10 minutes across country in the car, and we moved into it in April. Nine years later we moved into a bungalow we had built in a part of the garden and we sold the first house and the rest of the garden. We have lived there ever since and have no plans to reside anywhere else, - though nobody can claim to be a Rowellian who is not at least a second generation resident, - preferably fifth generation or more ! But life in Rothwell is really a part of "My Further Education" and an account of its implications belongs in that later section.

‡ ‡ ‡ ‡ ‡ ‡ ‡ ‡ ‡

As far as the school was concerned, the immediate task was the appointment of staff. Apart from myself there was a generous allocation of senior posts. As well as a Deputy Head we were entitled to 4 Heads of Department. In addition we could have 5 other "Full-time equivalents." The Education Committee made sure that we should have a staff fully qualified to lead the school when it was fully developed, and not merely one that was based on present population.

The first appointment was that of Deputy Head, and it went to Miss Mary Bevin, who remained a stalwart pillar of the school until she retired in the early 1980's. She had spent even longer than I working abroad, in her case in India. We then proceeded to appoint the other 4 senior colleagues. Teachers from Corby Grammar School who applied were entitled to first consideration, as the staff there was being slightly reduced owing to the opening of Kingswood. We appointed Bert Perry, from Corby G.S., who had spent several years in Ghana; Tom Kydd, who had spent some years in Afghanistan and Kenya; Richard Lumb, who had taught for some years in Germany; and Geoff Bradley, a Yorkshireman who had been teaching at Thetford. It was bruited abroad in some circles that senior posts at Kingswood only went to people who had worked overseas or who were called Bradley, - or both ! The important point was that all but one of us had been off the English scene for a while, and all six of us were ready to look at it afresh, and even to take fresh measures.

Our first opportunity to do this was towards the end of April, when we were able to meet for an all-day staff meeting. We had the loan of the library at Corby G.S. for the purpose. On 1st May I myself took up temporary quarters in some spare space which was available at Lodge Park School, since Kingswood was still in builders' hands.

During the ensuing months the rest of the staff were appointed. At an early stage I went to County Hall and was introduced to the various officers with whom I should have to deal on particular matters. From then on I knew, for instance, how to go about ordering books, stationery and equipment, and the person I was talking to when I needed to consult about staffing, school meals, transport, and so on. And of course I had to keep in close touch with my future colleagues, whose advice was essential. But it is unnecessary to give details of this process. Much more important were the policies which we were going to adopt.

These policies began with the deliberate affirmation that the first priority was the establishment and maintenance of good personal relationships. My preliminary visit to the Education Office was a modest beginning. Within the embryo school community the tone had to be set immediately. At that first staff meeting I told my colleagues that I proposed to address them all by their first names, and that I should be happy if they did the same to me, so long as it did not make them feel uncomfortable. (In those days this was still a little unusual; nowadays it seems to be normal practice).

This was symbolic of my wish to reject the hierarchic principle and to seek consensus. I intended that everybody should be involved in policy making and to take all colleagues, and, later on, parents, as much as possible into my confidence. (In those days the Governors were less implicated, partly because they were attached to both Grammar Schools, - but the Chairman, the late Mr. G.A.Hunter, took great interest in our work and was most encouraging and helpful.)

It was also in accord with the view of a Head's function at which I had arrived by the time I left Kamusinga, namely that the Head should be an enabler, not a director or commander. Once again I saw myself acting as a "scholastic mid-wife".

* * * * * * * * *

I must re-iterate that it is not my purpose to write the history of a school, except in so far as I am recalling the give and take and development of ideas affecting it and myself.

Having done my best to define my relationship with colleagues, the next thing was to draw parents into consultation. This we were able to do before the end of the summer term, once we had a list of the pupils we were to expect in September. It was helpful to meet the parents before meeting their children. We had a very well-attended meeting in the Junior School which would be supplying the largest group of first-year entrants. I believe the Chairman of the Governors also attended in support. Having introduced myself and as many of my new colleagues as were able to be present I went on to outline the way in which we proposed to organise the classes and the curriculum, and to answer questions. The only point here was that we intended to organise parallel classes, and not streamed ones.

The most controversial question was that of uniform for the new school. I opened the discussion by stating that I did not wish to have a school uniform. There were two principal reasons for my view. First, I had found, especially at Oldham, that we had to spend far too much time arguing about uniform, not only with pupils who were non-conformers, but also with business interests, – and even the Borough Council ! Energy and time were wasted which could far more profitably have been devoted to more important matters. The second reason I saw as purely educational. It had to do with the encouragement in pupils of a sense of responsibility – a recurrent theme at Kingswood, which had many facets. One of these is the exercise of good taste. Good taste is a personal matter, which is stultified by an insistence on uniform. To make all pupils look alike is no way to give them genuine education. But if they can exercise choice, then, if need be, we can discuss with them the choice they have made, and good taste has a chance to emerge. If there is no choice, the ultimate reaction to uniform may be equal and opposite to what is imposed, with perverse manifestations.

Perhaps naturally, the parents said they wanted the pupils to have a uniform. The usual arguments were put forward, especially the one about pupils seeking to out-do one another in clothing, the better-off being at an advantage compared with the less-well-off. This is a very weak one, because uniform can be very expensive, and the better-off can buy new ones more frequently, so that there is as much difference between a smart and a shabby uniform as between a pretentious and a simple dress. But the real reason is that parents in this country, unlike those anywhere else, have become accustomed to being able to shift on to the schools the responsibility for the kind of clothes their children should wear. All they have to say to children is: "That's school uniform; so don't argue with me !"

The upshot of the discussion was a compromise. I said to the parents : "All right, you can have your school uniform, and I will even agree with you what it should be. But I shall not insist on pupils wearing it." And that is what happened. I also designed a simple badge for the school, for use on blazers, ties, sports shirts, letter-heads, etc. One of those early parents was able to get a large version of it made in the apprentices' workshop at the steel works, and it still adorns the front of the school building.

At an early stage, if not at that first meeting, we set up a Parents' Association, with a committee of parents of pupils in each of the year-groups. This grew in size with the school, and there were always two staff representatives on it as well as my Deputy and myself. The Secretary was a parent, but the general feeling was that in those early days I should be the chairman. The committee met at school every term, and when the business was completed, (planning events, etc.) a general discussion followed, during which I mentioned and explained curricular and other developments, and parents freely expressed their views. So the committee became a very useful forum. Fund raising was not the purpose of the Association, though modest funds were raised in due course.

When the school opened the hall was not yet complete, so we had our assembly in the library, in which we could all sit quite comfortably. In due course the hall did become available, and I suggested that we might try an unconventional arrangement. This was agreed, - and I believe the arrangement still survives.

The chairs are arranged in a hollow square. This means that there is no 'front' or 'head' to the assembly, - not even the flat portion of the D-shape such as we used on Wednesday mornings at Kamusinga.

No seats are allocated. When the first bell goes, boys and girls and staff begin to move informally into the hall, and sit wherever they like, - in silence. (This became so habitual that I have sometimes been the first member of staff to appear, perhaps 4 minutes after the bell, and found those present sitting perfectly silently, quite undirected.) A second bell goes, 5 minutes after the first, and proceedings begin.

43. – Assembly at Kingswood

I usually took responsibility for leading assemblies in the first and last weeks of term, and sometimes for a week during the term, if so requested. A senior colleague made sure that each week's assemblies would be led, – usually by a member of staff, but sometimes by pupils. This device was to avoid any feeling of moral pressure by the head.

The form and subject matter of assemblies were varied. There was not by any means always a hymn, or even a formal prayer. But there was always a short final pause before any announcements and the dismissal of the assembly, – which was as informal as the initial gathering.

The rationale behind this form of assembly seems to me of wide significance. Suppose one asks, for instance, what lasting memories of school a person carries into later life. Possibly a particular lesson or course of lessons. Probably the character of particular teachers. Certainly one's relationship with one's peers and older and younger students.

But the morning assembly for worship will inevitably have had a remembered impact, whether for good or ill, – or as an irrelevance. One remembers oft-repeated hymns, possibly also oft-repeated prayers, or even readings; and the fact, though not necessarily the substance, of frequent exhortations; perhaps discomforts, such as having to stand or kneel, or share hymn or service books. Far too many of these recollections tend to be negative. It is therefore important for schools to examine their practice.

My own view is based on my interpretation of the meaning of 'worship', - the appropriate starting point for thinking about a school's statutory "Act of Worship". Understanding of the purpose is helped by consideration of the word itself, which is really corrupted from "worth-ship". "Worth" is "value". It seems to me that a valid, working definition of worship might be: "the contemplation, absorption and pursuit of values."

What values ? No longer can these be solely Christian values, - which are in any case themselves so variously perceived. Schools contain pupils and staffs from numerous faiths, and also many who call themselves agnostic, humanist, or even atheist. Each of these viewpoints represents a legitimate set of human values, and if we are concerned, as we must be, with the full range of human values, we have to take them into account.

The second thing to note about my definition of worship is that it is an activity of a personal kind. Worship is not received, - it is performed. It cannot simply be provided; it must be shared, and in a responsible way. (That is not the same thing as saying it cannot be led.)

In most churches, and in most organized religions, the function of priest is recognized and welcomed. The priest has the responsibility for leading, (conducting) the worship, as well as authority for the presentation and defence of the values, (in this case doctrines), of his church.

But a teacher, head or assistant, is not, except in special circumstances, a priest, and is not entitled, nor should he/she be expected, to assume priestly (sacerdotal) status. A good many heads, in particular, find themselves, or place themselves, in a sacerdotal posture, which may well cramp the practice of worship in their schools.

How can the problem be solved ?

The Kingswood pattern has certain advantages. For instance :-

First, the practice of corporate silence, especially as it came to be taken for granted, and needed no more then the gentlest occasional reminder, had a powerful calming and disciplinary effect at the beginning of the day.

Secondly, the very varied contributions, arising from the assembly, kept most people interested, - especially since, at the first assembly in a particular week, practically nobody knew who was going to stand up at the second bell, or where he/she might be sitting.

Thirdly, one was not conscious of a feeling that for most people assembly was a 'bind'. Indeed I have actually been told on occasion that our practice was enjoyed, particularly by people joining us from other schools.

Fourthly, both the Head and the School were relieved of false sacerdotalism, although the Head in no way abdicated from his proper responsibilities. Indeed, the arrangement went far towards illustrating my contention that "Worship is not received, it is performed. It cannot simply be provided; it must be shared, and in a responsible way."

Perhaps I should add that as the school grew it became inconvenient to assemble everybody at once, particularly given the format we used. When a lower school block was provided the first two year-groups had their own separate assembly. The rest of the school was divided, and only half were present each day. This helped to preserve the atmosphere we wanted to prevail. There are very few occasions when it is necessary or appropriate to assemble the whole school, - perhaps at the beginning and end of term or year, and for special purposes.

One further facet of Kingswood practice held good from the beginning. A 'normal' feature of Grammar Schools, from the time of Dr. Arnold onwards, has been the prefect system. Since the third-year pupils when we opened were likely to be the senior pupils throughout the next 3 or 5 years, it would be burdensome for them to have prefectorial responsibilities for so long. In any case, in accordance with the policy of not creating unnecessary hierarchic systems, my suggestion was accepted, that we should not have prefects. People do not learn to be responsible by having the right to command and the duty to obey. It is necessary for everybody to have as much responsibility as appropriate.

Nevertheless, some representational system is needed, for the exercise of corporate responsibility. This was provided by the School Council, which had a boy and a girl representative from each class. (As the school grew it was found sensible to have Senior and Junior Councils.) The main Council elected its own Chairman and Secretary., and a member of staff was present as observer.

The time came when, because of increased numbers, we had to abandon the traditional 'family service' form of school dinner and to introduce cafeteria service. This entailed staggered admissions to the dining area and the formation of a queue, broken up into year-groups. Only a certain number of people were admitted at a time, depending on the speed of service and consumption. Control of this flow was vested in the School Council representatives of each year-group, not staff. The interesting thing was that the other representatives gradually left queue control to the second-year girls. There is nobody more 'bossy' than an 11- or 12-year-old girl, and their authority was generally accepted. Many a time I have seen hulking fifth-year boys get back in line when told to do so by one of these lasses. After we had 'gone comprehensive' these lasses were often amongst the academically least gifted. But that is the nearest we came to having a prefect system.

3. My Comprehensive Education. 3. Kingswood: Going
                                                 Comprehensive.

Early in 1968 the Education Committee of the former
Northamptonshire County Council, (which did not include the
Borough of Northampton,) decided that Corby Secondary Schools
should all start, in September, 1969, to become Comprehensive.
We thus had about 18 months in which to prepare to receive our
first year-group with a full range of ability.

Although Corby was the first part of the former county area to go
comprehensive, in no way were the Corby schools pioneers in the
field; but each was facing a new experience.   The first
Comprehensive Schools in Coventry had opened not so long after
the war, and these and others were by now well established.   So
we were able to pay visits to some of them and to pick their
brains.   Many of the staff took part in these visits and attended
courses, seminars and lectures, mainly at the University Centre,
Northampton.   Teachers' Centres and In-Service Training (INSET)
provisions were yet to be properly developed.

As the school continued to grow, so the staff expanded.   Already
we had colleagues with Secondary Modern experience, although most
of us were from Grammar Schools.   We were able to recruit a
number of new colleagues with excellent comprehensive experience,
as well as one from a Junior School.   All of these added
significantly to the strength of our team.

A number of basic questions faced us, in particular :-

1. How should we allocate the new entrants to classes ?

2. How should we cater for pupils needing remedial help ?

3. What physical and pastoral arrangements should we make ?

4. What curriculum should we provide ?

Considering the first of these I said to my colleagues :- "It
seems to me that as we are starting a new comprehensive school
we should be wrong to proceed as if we were running a Grammar
and a Modern School side by side, in other words, by 'streaming'
our new pupils.   We must have parallel mixed ability classes.   I
do not know how to teach a mixed ability class.   But we must all
try to find out and to prepare ourselves."   This was accepted.
The eventual time-table was so arranged that if, during the year,
the mathematics or language teachers felt that they should grade
pupils in sets for either of these subjects, they could do so.   In
fact, no sets were used in first-year classes.   Later on I
myself taught German with a mixed ability first-year class and

I was pleased to find that the interest of the less able could be maintained for the year, using techniques and resources which were new to me.

The answer to the second question is implied in the answer to the first. We decided that we would not establish a remedial class, but what might be called a remedial clinic. Pupils could be withdrawn, in small numbers, from some mathematics or English lessons for a specialist teacher to give them remedial help; otherwise they stayed with their classes.

The two parts of the third question are not unrelated. It was important that younger pupils should not feel too confused or overpowered by their new environment. From being the oldest members of a small or medium-size community they would become the youngest and smallest in a much larger community and in a much larger building, with a wide range of unfamiliar facilities such as laboratories and workshops. No longer would they spend most of the day in the same room and with the same teacher.

As far as possible we tried to arrange the first-year time-table so that movement of pupils from one place to another was reduced to a minimum. When the time came to design a Lower School building, to house the first- and second-year classes, we put forward an idea for grouping classrooms around a central area which could be used for two principal purposes. First, it would have common resources available, on which teachers and pupils in any of the classes could draw. And secondly, it would allow two or three classes to be taken together when, for instance, some kind of presentation was given, say, a film, a showing of slides, or a key-note talk, which could just as well be given once to a group of 3 classes as 3 times to individual classes. Both these desirable provisions related to a particular feature of the proposed curriculum. Before I explain this I have to say that the completed building fell short of what was really desirable, partly because of cost, but also because of a certain lack of imagination on the part of the architect responsible for the design. The general effect was gloomy and colourless, but I believe that eventually some brighter decoration improved the situation.

Even so, the provision of a separate Lower School block was convenient for the pastoral arrangements we used. We worked on the basis of year-groups, each headed by a year-master or year-mistress, working closely with a team of form masters/mistresses. As far as possible these groups were associated with the same year-groups for two years. A Head of Lower School exercised, within the unit, all the functions of a Head, which were delegated to him, but always, of course, in collaboration with the Head of the school. The youngest pupils were thus not continually in danger of being swamped by the presence of many older pupils, and they and a group of staff got to know one another well.

The curricular activity to which I referred was called "Inter-Disciplinary Enquiry" (I.D.E.) In mid-1968, at one of the courses at the Northampton University Centre, which was concerned with curricular development and planned by the Curriculum Development department of Goldsmith's College, I heard about I.D.E. from lecturers then at the Teachers' College, Canley, near Coventry. The idea interested me, and the Head of Department at Canley, Peter Mauger, kindly accepted my invitation to come and present it to a special staff meeting.

The object of the scheme was twofold. First, it aimed to stimulate pupils to pursue study and learning on their own intiative. Secondly, it aimed to counter the academic tendency to compartmentalise study.

After the presentation I asked if any colleagues would like us to try it. Half a dozen or so agreed. It was further agreed to try out a pilot scheme with the final first-year Grammar School group who would be entering in September, 1968.

Very briefly, this was :-

A group of 2 or 3 classes were combined, in the care of a team of 3 teachers, preferably from different disciplines. A topic would be chosen, for instance, Water. The pupils would perhaps be shown two or three films concerned with various aspects of water. e.g. water transport, water supplies, the precipitation, distribution and condensation cycle, water power, land erosion, etc. Pupils would then be encouraged to explore, either individually or in small self-organised groups, any aspect of water they liked. They would have been introduced to a supply of books, film-strips, etc. which were there for reference, and staff would be available to advise, and either provide information or, preferably, indicate where it might be found. There would be no specific direction, but staff would check on what was being done, and insist on output in the form of written records, possibly with illustrations or models. The work would be assessed periodically. A particular topic would last half a term, perhaps more.

Time for I.D.E. had to be found by reducing the allocations to traditional subjects. At first this was achieved by leaving out traditional history and geography, and some English lessons. Double periods were used. The scheme was amended later, in the light of experience. But clearly, any of the treatments suggested might extend across subject barriers, and mitigate the tendency of subject teaching towards tunnel vision. This was the Inter-Disciplinary aspect of I.D.E.

Emphasis on Enquiry was even more significant. Each pupil was stimulated and expected, perhaps in association with a couple of others, to exercise personal initiative. One might say, to exercise intellectual responsibility. This was important, because pupils of all capacities need to learn to make their own decisions and plans, and to follow them up, rather than to depend upon teachers telling them what to learn, and seeing that they do so. For the gifted this has obvious importance. I spoke, some years later, with a university graduate who had been in that first group, and asked what she thought of the two years spent doing I.D.E. She told me that it was of great value to her at University, because of the early experience of planning her own work. — But it had equal importance for pupils with modest gifts, because they were encouraged to take initiatives and follow them up at their own pace.

Many parents were accustomed to a formal and structured curriculum. So we took pains to explain that we were not, as some feared, depriving pupils of instruction which they should be getting, but rather providing them with positive opportunities to develop their own ability to learn.

In September 1972 we admitted our fourth comprehensive intake. The first group were now in the fourth year. As they progressed up the school we had continually to plan ahead. So before that date a pattern had been set for the two years, just beginning, which led up to public examinations.

Still looking forward, I was conscious of two important developments that needed to be thought through, planned, and executed. One of these was the new pattern which the Sixth Form would need to take on from September, 1974 onwards. The other was the need to develop the potential of the school as a community resource.

The latest date for me to retire was December, 1974. I did not wish to take the lead in these two desirable developments, which I could in any case not see through to realisation. And perhaps I had already 'shot my bolt'; I certainly contemplated with pleasure the prospect of handing over the leadership of the school. The Sixth Form development, in particular, needed planning well in advance, and a new Head should have a year in which to do this.

So before the end of 1972 I handed in my resignation, to take effect in August; and in February the Education Committee and Governors were able to appoint my successor, Richard de Groot. He was very interested in the idea of the community school, and he had excellent experience with Sixth Form organisation in Bristol. He was half my age, and full of energy, — an excellent appointment. We saw eye to eye on all significant matters, and we collaborated closely over the next 6 months;   he was able to take part in all new appointments.

I handed over my keys and office some time in August and left Kingswood, very happy for the school, for Richard de Groot, - and for myself !

But Kingswood did not leave me, - as I was repeatedly to discover, even years later.

4. My Further Education.   First Session.

When I took up my post at Kingswood I resolved that I would
undertake no activities which were not directly relevant to my
work. Mary, however, was soon invited to involve herself in the
affairs of Rothwell, first with the Townswomen's Guild and then
with the Rothwell Citizens Welfare Committee. As Chairman, for 3
years, of the Welfare Committee, she became well known in the
town. When the election for the Rothwell Urban District Council
fell due in 1970 it was not difficult to persuade her to stand as
an Independent candidate. She was elected, - the first woman
councillor for many years. When I came home from school I
became, "Mrs. Bradley's husband." (In Corby Mary was the Head of
Kingswood's wife.) So through her I began to learn a little
about local government.

I must add that there were personal lessons to be learned even
closer to home. Paul left school in 1965 and spent a year
attending Kettering Technical College, (now Tresham College,)
'topping up' his A levels. Ruth also left Saffron Walden, to
enter the fourth year at Kettering Girls' High School. Peter,
meanwhile, had gone to College at Clifton, Nottingham, to train as
a teacher and was home quite often. So we had a spell of family
life at last. This in itself was another element in my
education. In particular, any man with a 'teen-age daughter soon
and persistently finds that he has a lot to learn. Ruth was at
Kettering High School for 4 years, leaving in 1969 to go up to
New Hall, Cambridge, from which base she continued to contribute
to her parents' education. She read Medicine for a year and then
switched to Social and Political Science. On completion of his
training Peter took up a teaching post in a Nottingham Junior
School. In 1969 he married Pauline Dowson, a fellow student who
had followed up her time at Clifton by a year at Manchester,
training as a Teacher of the Deaf. Paul moved to London in 1966,
where he studied at Kingston and North London Polytechnics,
graduating in Geography in 1970. He then studied Environmental
Planning at the Central Polytechnic, and in due course became a
Planning Officer at Camden. So by the time Mary took up Council
work members of the family were dispersed again, and launched on
their own careers.

In 1971 Secondary Education in Northamptonshire became a burning
issue. I have already remarked that Corby was the first area in
the former County to 'go comprehensive'. By 1971 extension of
this to other areas was being debated. There was, of course, a
strong Grammar School lobby, and a scheme was put forward by two
County Councillors to provide Grammar Schools and Comprehensive
Schools in parallel. It was known as the "Cripps-Soans Plan."

In early July the Education Committee had decided, by a modest
majority, to set up a Working Party to look further into the plan.

On 15th July the County Council approved, by a majority of 49 to 32, of the setting up of the Working Party. This was despite clear declarations by the combined teachers' organisations that they would boycott any such working party, so automatically stultifying the scheme, but at the same time postponing progress on comprehensivisation in the county.

I remind myself that I am concerned with autobiography, and not with the history of institutions, except in so far as their history affected my education or allowed me to make some contribution to them. So I need not recount the steps by which, after a heated press and political (though cross-party) debate and campaign, the Cripps-Soans Plan was eventually rejected. However, I did participate very modestly in the fight against it, and that experience did open the way for me to play a constructive role a couple of years later.

In Corby the campaign was collated by the group of Heads of all kinds of schools who met regularly to consider matters of common interest. At the time I was Hon. Secretary of the group, − and for purposes of the campaign we set up an "Ad Hoc Corby Teachers' Association", of which I was also Secretary. It included representatives from all the unions, assistant teachers as well as heads. I have a copy of the letter which I wrote in June, on behalf of the group, to the Clerk of the County Council, with copies to each member of the County Council and the Education Committee, as well as to the local branches of our professional associations. It was possible to present a completely unanimous front.

Similar meetings, which I was invited to attend, took place at County level. The same unanimous result was achieved. Never before had all the associations spoken with one voice.

To back up the circular letters it was decided that each County Councillor should be lobbied personally. I myself agreed to lobby two of those who had supported the scheme. When I did so I was dismayed by the lack of understanding I found in people who had a determining voice in the future of the children of Northamptonshire. This experience was another factor contributing towards a decision I was to make less than two years later.

‡ ‡ ‡ ‡ ‡ ‡ ‡ ‡ ‡

Before I turn to that decision there is one more helpful Corby development in which I was able to share. It was an on-going extension of the Corby Heads' Association which I have mentioned. This Association was an informal professional get-together of people in post, regardless of Union affiliations. On an occasion when we were discussing troublesome pupils somebody remembered a gathering, years earlier, of Heads and local Magistrates. I was deputed to approach the Chairman of the Bench, Mr. Michael Reynolds, and together we set up the first of what came to be known as "Saturday Morning Conferences." To these were invited not only Heads and Magistrates, but also representative Probation Officers, Police Officers, Social Workers, School Welfare Officers, District Nurses, Health Visitors, and people in voluntary social work. At first annual, these gatherings became more frequent, and other teachers than Heads also became involved. The object was the encouragement of mutual understanding and the strengthening of communication lines in dealing with the young people with whom we were all commonly involved. It is one of the virtues of Corby that such collaboration is welcomed and practised. I have often remarked on the apparent reluctance of people in at least one neighbouring town to make common cause together. Perhaps a New Town is more conscious of the need to create a sense of community than an old one, already set in its traditions and its sectional interests.

$$* \quad * \quad * \quad * \quad * \quad * \quad * \quad * \quad *$$

For several years the re-organisation of Local Government was being considered, and in 1973 it came into being. There were several important effects. First, the old County and the County Borough of Northampton were merged into one new County. Secondly, Northampton and six other towns became the centres of new District Councils, which swallowed up some existing smaller authorities. In Kettering District, for instance, the Urban District Councils of Rothwell, Desborough and Burton Latimer were reduced to the status of Parish Councils, though still called Town Councils, while the Kettering Rural District Council and the Kettering Borough Council, (as a Town Council), ceased to exist. Thirdly, the County Education Committee lost such autonomy as it had previously enjoyed, becoming entirely subordinate to the County Council.But the Kettering Divisional Executive Committee, an annexe of the old Education Committee, was abolished.

To ease the change-over there was an overlap of a year. Existing authorities continued in being until May, 1974, although the new authorities were elected in 1973, the County Council in April and the District Councils in May. (County Council elections were for 4-year terms of office. In 1973 and 1976 District Council Elections were for 3 years, after which they too were for 4 years. So nowadays there is a local election of some sort every other year.)

With retirement imminent I was free to contemplate new activities. Having experienced the lack of understanding of educational issues amongst many members of the County Council I thought that somebody with educational experience might have a useful contribution to make. I wondered if I should stand for election.

Ordinarily a serving teacher, as an employee of the County Council, cannot be a member of it. But my employer was the old County Council, and the Council for which I should be a candidate was the new one, which would not be my employer. My successor had already been appointed, and I was free to stand.

I thought at first of being an Independent candidate. Mary had been invited, when she stood for the Urban District in 1970, to be a Labour candidate, but had stayed independent, largely out of consideration for me, since I felt it right, while I was still a Head, not to wear a political label. However, we soon came to the conclusion that the time for fence-sitting was over, and we were both adopted as Labour candidates, Mary for the District (later Borough) Council of Kettering, on which Rothwell had 4 seats, and I for the new County Council, on which Rothwell had one seat. In April I was elected, with a majority of about 300 over my Conservative opponent, the sitting councillor. In May all 3 Labour candidates, (including Mary,) together with one Independent, won the Rothwell seats on the Kettering Borough Council.

So began for me a life very different from the one to which I had been accustomed, though Mary already had 3 years of busy work on Rothwell Urban District behind her. Not only did I have to learn about the many-sided workings of the Council, but both of us had to learn about life in the Labour Party, of which we became members. It must be said, we were both made very welcome in our respective spheres. I remember remarking, about a year later, that most of the many people with whom I was associating and working had been totally unknown to me twelve months earlier. Yet we still lived in exactly the same place.

The overall result of the County Council election in Northamptonshire surprised everybody. Out of 90 seats 47 were held by Labour, 39 by Conservatives, and 4 by Independents. It was therefore clear that Labour would control the Council, taking every Chairmanship and Deputy-Chairmanship, with a built-in majority on every Committee and Sub-Committee.

The election had been, as usual, on Thursday, and on Sunday afternoon the new Labour Group met at Northampton, in very high spirits. The leadership was elected and information collected concerning the committees on which each member would like to serve. I opted for the Education Committee and, if possible, the Social Services Committee, - failing which I was prepared to serve where required. The Social Services Committee proved to be over-subscribed, so my assignments were the Education Comittee and the General Services Committee.

When I consider how much, as a fairly intelligent and well-informed citizen, I had to learn about the powers, resources, responsibilities and procedures of the County Council, its

Committees and Sub-Committees, not to mention its officers, from top tier to base, I cannot feel surprised that so many citizens are baffled. People have a very vague idea of the scale of operations of County, District and Town Councils. I have sometimes been asked to give talks to local societies, and have illustrated the difference in scale between authorities by mentioning the gross annual expenditure of each council. Up-dated to 1986-87 the figures would be :-

County Council :   £284,100,000
Kettering Borough Council : £13,207,000, (which
                      includes roughly £2,000 for
                      the budget of Rothwell T. C.

Looked at another way, the County Council is the largest employer in the County. So the responsibilities of a County Councillor are indeed weighty.

Although the new council and its committees had no formal executive powers until the spring of 1974 there was much preliminary work to be done. Priorities included the establishment of a committee structure and the appointment of officers, beginning with the Chief Executive and other Chief Officers.

As far as I was concerned I became involved in two preliminaries on the educational scene. One was discussion on the application of the statutory requirement to co-opt non-elected people to the Education Committee, which had to number between one quarter and one third of the total committee membership. The other was reform of the governing and managing bodies of schools.

Before the end of the summer term of 1973, while I was still in post, I was authorized by the Labour Group to negotiate with the teachers' associations the principle on which teachers should be co-opted to the Education Committee. In the old County there had been 4 teachers, nominated by the N.U.T.(2) the A.T.T.I.(1) and Joint Four (1). In the Borough there had been 1 teacher representative.

The 1971 campaign to counter the Cripps-Soans Plan had had the beneficial effect that teachers spoke, for the first time, with one voice. It was important to maintain this. Accordingly, with Mary's support, I gave several tea parties in our house. To each of these were invited representatives of one of the associations or a group of associations. These were : National Union of Teachers, (NUT) Joint Four, [Head Masters and Head Mistresses Associations, now merged in the Secondary Heads Association, (SHA) together with the Assistant Masters and Mistresses Associations, now merged as the Assistant Masters and Mistresses Association, (AMMA)] the National Association of Head Teachers, (NAHT) and the

Association of Teachers in Technical Institutions, (ATTI - now sub-sumed in the National Association of Teachers in Further and Higher Education (NATFHE), and the National Association of Schoolmasters,(N.A.S.) with the National Union of Women Teachers,(NUWT), (now merged as the NAS/UWT.)

To each of these I put the same proposal. This was, that the nomination of teachers for co-option to the Education Committee should be made from a joint conference, and not from individual associations. Sharing available places between associations should be organised between them and not involve the Education Committee. Thereafter each of the teachers co-opted by the Education Committee would be a representative of all teachers in the County, not merely of his/her association. The number of places available was, of course, a matter for the Education Committee to determine, since co-optees were not all teachers.

The proposal proved acceptable to all, and was also duly accepted by the Education Committee. I suggested to my Council colleagues that 7 places should be allocated to teachers; the agreed number was 6. Some years later another place was added. The arrangement worked, and I can remember an occasion, some years later, when a teacher representative expressed a sectional interest, and was rebuked for doing so.

      *   *   *   *   *   *   *   *   *

The government and management of schools was due for overhaul, and in any case, differences in practice in former Borough and County areas had to be removed. I was a member of the small Finance and Development Policy Sub-Committee of the Education Committee which considered the new plan before it went to the Education Committee and so to County Council, so that I was able to take an active part in shaping the new proposals.The principles accepted were :-

Each school should have its own governing body. (The term
     'Managers' for primary schools was discontinued.)
Governing bodies should include :
    Nominees of the Education Committee.
     (Primary schools would also have an equal number of
     'Minor Authority' representatives.)
    Representatives of teachers.
    Representatives of parents.
    People co-opted by the fore-going, to represent local
    interests.
Nobody should serve on more than 5 governing bodies.
It was also hoped that nobody would occupy more than one chair.

In 1973 these provisions were a considerable advance on existing arrangements. For instance, I mentioned that in early days Kingswood shared Governors with the other Grammar School. Later on other combinations replaced this one. In the Kettering area the position was much worse. I had learned something about it as early as 1970, because in that year Mary was appointed to represent Rothwell U.D.C. on the Kettering Divisional Executive, and became a Governor of more than one group of schools. (So she preceded me, not only in Council work, but also in educational administration.)

At the time of re-organisation in 1973 there were, in the area of the Kettering Divisional Executive, two single-sex Grammar Schools, two single-sex and one co-educational Secondary Modern Schools, a co-educational Aided (Church of England) Secondary Modern School, and a Secondary Modern School serving Rothwell and Desborough and some villages. Rothwell, Desborough and Burton Latimer each had two Primary Schools, and there were Primary Schools in several villages. In the town of Kettering there were 13 County Primary Schools and several Special Schools. There were also one Voluntary Controlled and one Voluntary Aided C.E. Schools and 2 Voluntary Aided R.C. Schools.

The two Grammar Schools had a joint Governing Body.
The three Secondary Moderns had another.
The 13 Primary Schools were in 2 groups, each with a single Board.

The most impressive illustration of the change brought about by the new system is to be found in the Governing Bodies of these 13 schools. Under the former regime each group had a governing body of 9 persons. Two individuals were on both bodies. So the Primary Schools of Kettering were 'governed' by 16 individuals. When the new arrangements came into effect the number of individuals involved as Primary School Governors had risen to about 116.

The first stage in the creation of new governing bodies was the appointment of the Education Committee and Minor Authority nominees. It was from these that the Chairman of each board would be chosen, and it would be this group, constitutionally, who would co-opt the representatives proposed by teachers and parents, who would then take part in the further co-options from the community.As the only Labour Councillor from the Kettering area who was on the Education Committee I found myself with the task of taking the initiative at this first stage. There was also only one Kettering Conservative Councillor on the Education Committee, so we had to consult together, as well as with our local party organisations.

The Labour administration of the County Council and the Education Committee had determined that a majority of the Education Committee nominations for each school should be at the disposal of Labour. This was seen by some Conservatives as "bringing politics into governing bodies". Since there had previously been virtually no Labour representative on the Kettering bodies, owing to the de facto dominance of Conservatives, it would have been truer to say that the new scheme "introduced a Labour voice into Governing Bodies." But it is also true that the change was a great one.

The task of nominating Governors for so many schools was a long and wearisome one. As far as the Secondary Schools were concerned, the nominations involved determining who should be Chairman. This meant that Labour would take certain important chairmanships, but not all. Chairmanship was going to be very important in the Kettering area, because Kettering Schools were about to 'go comprehensive'. To add to the problems inherent in this policy it was also intended to move towards mergers of the two boys' schools and the two girls' schools. The Chairman of the Education Committee, Mrs. Dora Oxenham, CBE, wanted me to be Chairman of one of the Grammar Schools. and to find a really good Chairman for the other. I chose the Girls' School, while Colin Tindley, the very capable Chairman, at that time, of the Constituency Labour Party, was assigned to the Boys' School. As he had little educational experience he had Ray Dainty, Vice-Principal of Kettering Technical College, and Mary, who had already been a Governor of the two Grammar Schools for 3 years, to support him. Conservative Chairmen were assigned to the two single-sex Secondary Modern Schools. I also became a Governor of the Girls' Secondary Modern School, as a link between the two Governing Bodies. Ray Dainty performed the same function for two boys' schools.

I wanted to have some contact with Primary Schools, so I joined the Governors of the Junior School in Rothwell and of an Infants' School in Kettering. (I kept clear of the Infants' School and the Secondary School in Rothwell, because Mary was already well established there; in fact she became Chairman at the Infants' School and Vice-Chairman at the Secondary School, which was, of course, also going comprehensive, as Montsaye School.)

Being Chairman of Governors at Kettering High School was probably my most significant on-going responsibility between 1973 and 1977. It was quite different from routine commitee work, in that it made demands on one's tact, patience and understanding. There were no officers or regulations to provide the answers to questions, and there was no possibility of delegating responsibilities. I was fortunate in reaching a good understanding, (which did not preclude suitable differences of opinion,) with the Head, Miss Eileen Lake. Many people were nervous, to put it at its mildest, about the impending changes, and had to be nursed, so to speak, through the tensions which were bound to arise. This applied also to the other Girls' School, with whom we both had to foster positive relationships, at a time when negative attitudes might easily predominate. I have the greatest admiration for the way in which Miss Lake and her colleagues in both schools navigated a course through those difficult years. And I much enjoyed helping to appoint new, forward-looking staff and seeing the new developments taking place.

As I have repeatedly mentioned, it is not my purpose to relate the history of schools. But my participation in the history of Kettering High School during those years stood me and, I hope, others, in good stead when Kettering became the arena, in the mid-80's. for still more tensions, and I found myself deeply involved.

✱　✱　✱　✱　✱　✱　✱　✱　✱

My other formal responsibility was as Chairman of the Accommodation Planning Sub-Committee of the Education Committee. This was concerned with the provision of new buildings and the maintenance of existing ones in use by the Education Committee, as well as of furniture for them. At that time a long process was required before a new building could be occupied. It had to appear one year in a preliminary list of projects approved by the Ministry of Education. The following year it would hopefully appear in a planning programme, and in the year after that in an approved 'Starts' programme. And throughout those years it competed for priority with other projects, the list being continually under review, both by the Committee and the Ministry. A few years later the system was modified, the Committee being informed annually by the Ministry of the total capital expenditure which was sanctioned, details being left to the Local Education Authority. But under both systems approved expenditure was inadequate for the developments required. There was, and still is, a serious back-log of projects. Pressure was constant from many schools, but many also were the delays and disappointments. It was nevertheless very interesting to me to be involved in discussions about sitings and construction, although it was frustrating, for instance, to feel helplessly unable to satisfy the needs of all the surprisingly numerous schools where young children still had to use outside toilets or be taught in cumbersome Victorian buildings. But it is also true that some of the schools most disadvantaged in this way were amongst the happiest and most progressive places to visit.

To be a member of the General Services Committee was a most instructive experience, which I much appreciated. Its responsibilities at that time included the Fire Service, Consumer Protection, Refuse Disposal, (but not collection,) the County Farms and sites for Gypsies. During 1973-74 members were given a thorough-going introduction to all these services. I think we visited every Fire Station in the county, and also a couple of national research and training establishments. We also went to some of the farms and to the laboratories of the Consumer Protection Department. We went, too, to a number of land-fill sites and to the new installation at Brackmills for compacting refuse to be sent as landfill to Bedfordshire. Being on a special sub-committee considering sites for Gypsies I also visited several "Travellers'" groups and possible permanent sites.

These visits had two beneficial spin-off effects. One was that members got to know one another, politics apart. For instance, I myself enjoyed a very friendly relationship with a farmer member, and learned much from him as we travelled around the countryside, whilst he was glad to consult me, particularly about the school in his village. The other effect of the visits, as of my visits to schools and sites for schools, was that I became pretty familiar with the geography of the county as a whole, and I can think of some person or persons I know in each part of it. Since those days I have often caught myself, on return from a journey outside the county, watching for the Northamptonshire sign at the county boundary and thinking: "Here we are, home again." This, despite the fact that from our house it is about 40 miles to the South-Western boundary, and 20 to the North-East.

One of the first things a Councillor needs to learn is to give close attention to as many as possible of the papers which the over-burdened postman drops through the letter-box, and not merely those concerning one's own committees. In November, 1974 I spotted, in the appropriate report, that amongst buildings listed as 'surplus to requirement', and therefore to be sold off, was the old Fire Station at Rothwell. At that very time consideration was being given to the setting up in the town of a Youth Club for young people who might not be attracted or attractive to church-sponsored clubs and uniformed youth organisations. One problem was to find suitable premises. I managed to persuade the County Council to give free tenancy of the building for what became known as the Rothwell Fire Escape Open Youth Club. I was closely associated with it until 1986.

In 1977, when fresh County Council elections were held, the political climate country-wide was very different from that in 1973. The result was a Conservative landslide. Along with all but about 10 of my Labour colleagues, I lost my seat by 300 votes. My first and, as I then expected, only spell as a Councillor was over, and I turned to other activities.

4. My Further Education.   Second Session.

In late August Mary and I took off with our caravan to France.
We spent a month in all, travelling south to the Atlantic coast
north of Bayonne and then traversing the Pyrenees from west to
east, before driving north again through the centre of France.
In the Pyrenees we made several two- or three-day stops, in order
to do some walking.   As we neared the Mediterranean I was in
fact re-visiting an area which I had last seen exactly 50 years
earlier, on leaving school, when I had been on a camping/walking
tour with W.A.Cooper, the most redoubtable walker of the Bootham
staff.   So I was able to see for myself the commercial rape of
Andorra, and compare it with the detailed account I still
possessed of the previous visit, when all was primitive, rustic
and undeveloped.   Walking amongst the duty-free monstrosities of
Las Escaldas I spotted a semi-circular flight of steps leading up
to the entrance to a modest hotel, tucked away, just off the main
street.   It had been the first and only hotel in Andorra, having,
in 1927, just undergone a number of improvements, including the
provision of those steps.   It was closed, but we were able to
attract attention and to be admitted, to talk with the owner, Mr.
Pla, who was delighted to share recollections of W.A.Cooper and
the several occasions when he had brought walking parties to the
hotel.   But in deploring the eclipse of that intimate and
friendly atmosphere it is only fair to add, that away from the
deplorable new development the valleys are still as wild,
grandiose and imposing as ever, as we were able to discover.

Several days later we drove up a rough road to the Chalet-Hotel
des Cortalets, 2000 feet below the summit of le Canigou, the
dominant peak of the eastern Pyrenees.   When I was 17 we rose in
the early hours to be on top for the sun-rise.   We rushed up in
50 minutes, as I recorded.   Mary and I also reached the top, not
at sun-rise, - and in 3 hours !   However, a number of Dutch
students, doubtless unused to such gradients and altitude,
expressed amazement at the prowess of a pair of such senior
citizens.

The Mediterranean coast at Collioure and Port Vendres had also
changed, but was quite recognizable, despite development.

When we reached home again I plunged immediately into life as a
part-time student on a course which had already begun.   This was
a two year two-days-a-week course in Art at Tresham College in
Kettering.   We had instruction and exercises in the fundamentals
of drawing techniques, and progressed, in due course, to activities
using a variety of colour media, as well as venturing into simple
sculpture or modelling.   We also had some introduction to art
history.   Half of the time was spent on a craft, the choice being
between pottery and print-making.   Having a tendency to
rheumatic spasms I decided not to get involved with wet clay, and

opted for print-making. This opened up a whole range of stimulating, if sometimes very frustrating, experiences. We had a taste of everything, from cardboard cuts and lino cuts, through woodcuts to screen-printing, including the use of tone-separated photographs, which interested me greatly, and even etching. The only technique for which facilities were not available was lithography. We were given guidance, experience and encouragement in practising the techniques to which we were introduced.

Apart from practical activity we also collected notes on the history and use of the techniques and had many lively discussions. The group consisted mainly of very talented house-wives, most of whom had emerged from the cares of bringing up children, and a few senior citizens like myself. It was one of the attractions of the course to compare ideas and work with fellow-students, and to join together in producing a common 'opus'. This was an illustrated booklet on William Blake which, of course, we printed ourselves, and which contained at least one contribution from each student. We were fortunate in our teacher, David Imms, himself a distinguished print-maker and painter, who knew just how to stimulate and encourage each of his students, however great or small their talents.

The sad thing for me is that after the course I became increasingly involved in other activities, and failed to make very much of what I had learned. I still cherish the hope that when, for instance, this present spell of writing is completed, I shall once again be able to bring forth from shelves and cupboards the varied materials that have had to be stowed away.

＊　＊　＊　＊　＊　＊　＊　＊　＊

Apart from the visit to Kenya in 1980, which has been mentioned before, and a couple of visits to Jamaica, of which I have still to write, the activities to which I referred were in the political field. Both Mary and I were busy. She was an elected member of both Kettering Borough Council and Rothwell Town Council. I spent four years on the Executive Committee of the Constituency Labour Party. In addition, we jointly functioned, for a while, as Secretary of the Rothwell Branch of the party, which was temporarily in the doldrums.

Mary had been re-elected to both Councils for a further 3-year term. In the Borough Council, as previously in the former Rothwell Urban District Council, she was particularly active on the Housing and Leisure Amenities Committees. She was continually being called upon to deal with housing needs and problems in Rothwell, but was not solely concerned with housing affairs in our own town. It must be said that she took to council work as a natural-born local government politician, acute in perception and cogent, even pungent, in debate, and held in warm respect by officers and fellow-councillors alike. In 1978-79 she was the first woman Chairman of Rothwell Council, so we had quite a social round during that year, including civic balls in various places. Mary's own Civic Ball was a very jolly occasion, which both our sons, Peter and Paul, with their ladies, were able to attend.

My own activities between 1977 and 1981 were of a different character. At the time of the 1974 General Elections I was still sufficiently leisured to be able to work almost full-time in the party office, assisting the agent. In the spring of 1975 I began my 4-year spell on the Executive Committee, and with it, another phase of my education. I became familiar with the quirks and machinations of the various groups in the party. In the spring of 1978 I found myself, rather to my surprise, elected as one of two Vice-Chairmen of the Constituency Party. That year was dominated by two difficult problems.

First, the sitting member, Sir Geoffrey de Freitas, announced that he would not be standing again, so a new Labour candidate had to be selected.

The procedure was long-drawn-out and tense, with three factions, in particular, in contention. Since the Kettering seat, which included Corby, was regarded as safe for Labour, there were many well-known applicants, including Ivor Richards, Tom McNally and, to stir things up in a big way, Robert Maxwell. Other candidates included Bill Homewood, backed by the Iron and Steel Trades Confederation, the dominant Trade Union in Corby, where the threat of closure of the steel-works was a burning issue, and Roy Mayhew, representing local left-wing activists, who was, as a matter of fact, the only one already known to me personally. Both the two last-named had strong support on the Executive Committee and the General Management Committee of the Constituency Party, the body which, when it came to the crunch, would make the selection. Outside the Committee was a group of people forming the third of the factions which I mentioned, namely people who supported Robert Maxwell.

Canvassing was very active. Members of the G.M.C. were treated to visits from applicants, to seek their support. We ourselves had some very frank talks in our own sitting-room with each of those I have mentioned, as well as with a number of others. There were also Branch meetings, at which applicants were invited to present their claims.

The retiring member and his predecessor, who became Lord Mitchison, were both well-to-do, and had helped considerably to keep the constituency party solvent. Some party members were therefore tempted to look for a candidate who would do likewise.

But the wealthiest of the applicants had a controversial public image, and despite an intense campaign, tempting to some, was not even short-listed. Two others, each with ministerial aspirations, were also not favoured. For some years Sir Geoffrey de Freitas had been much pre-occupied with the European and E.E.C. Parliaments, and despite his generosity had become unconvincing as a constituency man. It was felt by many that the constituency needed to free itself from what seemed to some to amount to personal patronage.

The procedures for selection were fraught with acrimony, in which the local, and even the national, press took continuous interest. A mole on our Executive Committee persistently leaked misleading reports concerning the drawing up of the short-list for submission to the G.M.C. The process had to be repeated, to make sure that all technical requirements had been scrupulously met, - but the resulting short-list was not materially different from the first one.

Although six candidates addressed the actual selection meeting, four were quite soon eliminated and the final choice was between Bill Homewood and Roy Mayhew. The outcome was a fairly narrow victory for Bill Homewood.

The sounds of this selection battle did not quickly die away. Hardly was it over when the second problem to which I referred raised its head. A group of rather ineffectual Borough councillors in Kettering, most of whom had been campaigning for Robert Maxwell, together with the rather ambitious leader of the Labour Group on the Borough Council, formed a break-away group, having no difficulty in attracting a great deal of publicity. They were highly critical of what they saw, erroneously, as domination of the Constituency Party by the far left, as well as of the ascendency of Corby interests through the selection of Bill Homewood. They dubbed themselves the "Borough Independent Group".

In May of 1979 they put up a number of candidates in elections for the Borough Council and were successful in defeating some Labour candidates, though their own leader was bettered by two of the three Labour candidates in a 3-seat ward. The confusion they helped to create doubtless contributed considerably to the reduced Labour majority in the parliamentary election held on the same day. But of course, this was the General Election in which Margaret Thatcher came to power, so the trend was clearly national. However, it can be mentioned, in passing, that when the group put up candidates in the County Council elections of 1981 they were obliterated. In the long run ordinary people have many reservations about turncoats.

So it was that in 1978-79 I had plenty of first-hand experience of the vagaries of life in the Labour Party. What I learned enabled me to understand quite well the problems which have received so much attention in more recent years. My attitude at the time was that the party should play it cool and let the break-away group have its brief flowering and then wither, which is what happened. As far as the left-wing faction was concerned, I had conversations with a number of them. I made the point that their demand for what they saw as pure socialist policies for immediate application was ill-timed and futile. During the approach to Independence in Kenya I had seen African politicians maintain relentless pressure and demand for more than the colonial power and 'moderate' opinion regarded as acceptable. 'Moderates', both amongst Africans and Europeans, were increasingly disregarded. The momentum of the times was in favour of those who demanded most, - and success resulted. No such momentum prevailed, from the point of view of the left, in the Britain of the late 'seventies, so their demands had no chance of success at the time. At best they were whistling in the wind; at worst they were an embarrassment and a nuisance. Labour policy for the times needed a significant component of party loyalty and patience.

In passing I would suggest that the parallel problem at national level needed the same. Had the "Gang of Four" exercised more of both it would not have taken so long for the party's equilibrium to become re-established and its prospects to be improved. The "Gang of Four" and their adherents might even themselves have been more influential than they are at present; more of them might still have been M.P.'s. Election results seem to suggest that the electorate is less attracted to the S.D.P., led by turncoats, than to the Liberal Party, which has a long and honourable history of its own.

In the second half of 1978 I found myself in yet another learning situation. Soon after the selection of Bill Homewood a new G.M.C. and Executive Committee were elected. The new Chairman asked me to be Personal Assistant to Bill Homewood. The idea was that although he knew all about the steel industry and a good deal about Corby, he knew too little about the rest of the constituency, Kettering in particular. My remit was therefore to arrange for him to learn more, and also for people to get to know him, since it was generally accepted that he would be the next M.P. for the constituency.

I agreed, and Bill and I had an interesting year. The pleasantest part, for me, was in getting to know and respect and like Bill himself. Our quite different spheres of experience were complementary, and we became very good friends.

As far as local government in the constituency and the county were concerned I was well-informed and well-enough known. I arranged visits to Chief Executive Officers in Corby, Kettering and County Hall, all of whom received us with friendliness and interest, even appreciation. We also met with the County Education Officer, who gave us permission to visit any of the schools, colleges and other institutions in the county. So we did pay visits to a good many of these, to give Bill a general view of educational provision. These visits included appearing before more than one group of very articulate sixth formers.

We also established good relations with the editor of the Evening Telegraph, who added to his kindness by fixing up for Bill to address a Rotary Club lunch. We met with members of the Kettering Civic Society, a prominent pressure group, and the Pensioners' Parliament. We also visited quite a wide range of industrial concerns, such as Weetabix, Alumasc, Wicksteeds Engineering, Timsons Engineering, Cheaneys Footwear in Desborough and Avalon Footwear in Rothwell, as well as several clothing firms in Kettering and Corby. We were also cordially received and given lunch by Commander Saunders-Watson and his family at Rockingham Castle and were shown round the estate as well as the castle. Whenever an idea or an opening occurred I followed it up. I myself learned a great deal, but not as much as Bill, because he has a remarkable memory for what he heard and saw. He seldom made a note or used a note when speaking, yet he always had relevant facts at his finger-tips. This is one of the reasons for the respect in which I hold him.

＊　＊　＊　＊　＊　＊　＊　＊　＊

To complete the account of my own political activity in 1979 I must record that Mary and her fellow Borough councillor from Rothwell had both decided not to stand again in the Borough Council elections. Rothwell had been divided into two wards, each returning two councillors. The Rothwell party could find only one candidate, which was humiliating. So I agreed to stand in one ward, while David Jones stood in the other. I lost decisively, David by only 6 votes. No doubt many of the people who voted for us gave their second vote to one of the Tory candidates. Perhaps if we had stood together in one ward David, at least, would have got in. However, we licked our wounds, and began to think about the County Council elections in 1981.

When 1981 came along we still had no candidate for the County Council. It would have been disgraceful not to contest the seat, so at the last minute I agreed to stand, hoping to be able, if elected, to retire after two years to make way for somebody else. I did win back the seat, with a majority of only 26 over my opponent, who had unseated me in 1977. What happened after that is the theme of the Third Session of my Further Education.

In Parenthesis.   Caribbean Air and Reggae Rhythm.

There is a part of my education which does not fit neatly into
the three sessions of my further education.   This is the Jamaican
theme.

In 1975 Ruth had married Mike McLeod, second son of a Jamaican
father and an Irish mother, and they had gone as teachers to
Jamaica, to which Mike's Father, Allan McLeod, had recently
returned after 21 years' service in the R.A.F.   Allan McLeod
telephoned to invite us to his home for Christmas.   We accepted
with enthusiasm and spent the six weeks up to Boxing Day in
Jamaica.   We were there again in May 1978, June 1979 and
December 1985 to January 1986.   Each time we learned something
fresh, but the most recent of these visits is really outside the
scope of my present theme.

At the time of our first visit Ruth and Mike were teaching at a
secondary school in up-country Mocho, and living in a bungalow on
a sugar estate near May Pen, the administrative centre of the
Parish of Clarendon.   We visited the school and met staff and
pupils.   We found conditions very difficult because of over-
crowding and the irregular attendance of some pupils, amiable and
biddable though they were.   Educational ideas were on the old-
fashioned side and overlaid, even in a state school, by religious
fundamentalism.   Ruth was actually forbidden to include in her
Biology teaching the theory of evolution. Nevertheless, we met
with much friendliness and had the delightful experience of being
present at an old-time Jamaican "Tea Meeting", a community event
which took place in the school.

As both of us were Councillors at the time, Ruth introduced us to
the Chairman and Officers of the Clarendon Parish Council and we
were welcomed warmly to a Council Meeting, and invited to make
brief speeches and to listen to the proceedings.   (It should be
explained that Jamaica is divided into thirteen Parishes, each
with a Council having roughly the same status as a present-day
District Council in England.)

While in the island I took the opportunity to gain some knowledge
of its history.   Least important, perhaps, of our visits was to
the remains of Port Royal, reputed, in the Seventeenth Century, to
be the wickedest city in the world, which was eventually laid low
by an earthquake.   More importantly, we learned   about the
struggles for emancipation from slavery, as well as of the
achievement of independence.   We learned about the National
Heroes, of whom at that time, there were 7, including the rival
party leaders in the era of the approach to independence, Norman
Manley and Alexander Bustamante.   We visited Morant Bay and
stood before the statue of another Hero, Paul Bogle who, like Hero
George William Gordon, had been hanged in 1865 by the nefarious

Governor Eyre.   (The event is starkly and unforgettably commemorated in the Reggae number, "1865 - 96" in the Shade", recorded by the group "Third World".)

At the other end of the island we visited the scenes where William Knibb, a native of our own Kettering, was an untiring leader in the struggle for Emancipation.   A Baptist minister, he fought hard and long, both in the home country and in Jamaica, to that end.   When Emancipation was achieved he established, near the present-day village of Duncans, a settlement for emancipated slaves, and named it Kettering.

We saw the Kettering Baptist Chapel which William Knibb established, and at Falmouth, along the coast, we visited both the William Knibb Memorial Church and the William Knibb Secondary School.   Jamaicans considered naming him amongst the National Heroes, the reason why this was not done being that he was not a native Jamaican.   In Kettering, England, one of the supporters of the Borough coat of arms is a negro holding a broken chain, - a recognition of his work for emancipation.   But it was not until 1982 that his name was linked, (on my proposal, I am pleased to say,) with a prominent new institution in the town.   The William Knibb Centre, in the former Boys' School premises, now houses the headquarters of the Community Youth Service for the area, an annexe to Tresham College, and several other functions, including a play-group.

The most impressive of our other experiences during that first visit to Jamaica was a performance by the National Dance Company in the National Theatre.   Each part of the programme was rooted in the indigenous culture of the island, which owes a great deal to West African culture.   The dances were an explosion of colour, rhythm, energy and emotion.   Perhaps the most memorable was a new ballet called "Ni".   It was based on the exploits of an almost legendary 16th Century woman, Nanny, leader of the Maroons of that day.   She had just recently been designated the first National Heroine.   The atmosphere, both on stage and in the audience, was palpable, and one was keenly aware of a sense of national consciousness and identity.

Our visit in 1978 took us into new areas.   By this time Ruth was teaching in Trench Town, one of the most disadvantaged parts of Kingston, and associated with Bob Marley.   Mike was teaching in a private school in Kingston.   They lived in a rented house at the top of Jack's Hill, on Sunset Drive, 2000 feet above the city, overlooking the city, the harbour, the sea and the distant hills. At night-time the view was bespangled with the city's lights, framed by the great trees which flanked the house.

We visited the Trench Town school and went along when Ruth and a University lecturer took a group of her students on a sea-side field study trip, - a kind of experience which was quite new to the city-bound students, and much appreciated by them. We also met a Jamaican artist friend of Ruth's, Tony Cole, and through him, a number of reggae musicians, including associates of Bob Marley. Of course, these people were Rastafarians, and as we met them and read about their beliefs and practices, we began to understand. Tony, although something of a musician, is himself a wood-carver and maker of furniture. We have two of his carvings, given to us by Ruth, and he has visited us in our home; he came along with me one day to my art class.

By June, 1979 the domestic situation of Ruth and Mike had changed. They still lived on Sunset Drive, but Ruth had produced Miriam, a very bouncing little lady, born the previous October. Ruth was no longer teaching in school, but was very busy with fabric dyeing, mainly batik, and making shirts, dresses, drapes, cushion covers, etc. She had discovered unsuspected talents in herself, and was able to sell everything that she had time to make. She exhibited at craft fairs, and even had a stall next to that of Edna Manley, for many years past the most distinguished of Jamaican artists. While we were there I said, of course, that I wouldn't mind a batik shirt myself. "All right," said Ruth, "You had better make one yourself !" - Another lesson to be learned! I was provided with a length of cotton material, given free access to all her colouring materials and other impedimenta, including her sewing machine. Under discreet supervision, and using a design of my own derived from work I had been doing at Kettering, I actually produced a passable and colourful,and unique, garment.

Meanwhile Mike, still teaching at the same Priory School, had also taken on responsibility for the evening adult education classes on the premises, with Ruth as his part-time Assistant Principal.

The most unusual, and very memorable, experience we had during that 1979 visit was being present at a celebration called "One Love" in the National Stadium. The celebration in question was the Twelfth Anniversary of the visit to Jamaica of the Emperor Haile Selassie of Ethiopia, or Ras Tafari, who, even after his death, is still regarded by Rastafarians as the Deity. The commemoration took the form of a Reggae Festival attended by about 25,000 people. It began at about 5 p.m. and went on until 2 a.m. or beyond. We ourselves arrived at about 5.30, while it was still light, and stayed until about 1.30 in a crowded stand, while the aroma of ganja (marijuana) smoke wafted about us. Rastafarianism is a fundamentally peace-loving and peace-practising religion, and the object of the Festival was to counter the violent confrontations prevalent at the time between rival criminal gangs, especially in Trench Town and West Kingston, as well as between adherents of the two political parties. Almost all the best-known Reggae Groups and Reggae characters were present, and each entertained for half an hour or so. Leading up towards the climax came Peter Tosh, formerly a Wailer, but now with his own group, performing the number for which he is most famous, "Legalize it" (Ganja, of course.) And finally Bob Marley himself took the stage with the Wailers, to perform the theme number, "One Love". He summoned the leaders of the gun-slinging gangs to join him and one another on the platform in the singing. Then, as we were preparing to leave for home, he had the Prime Minister, Michael Manley and the Opposition Leader, Eddie Seaga likewise joining him and one another. As the two linked hands under the flood-lights Bob danced singing around them, in a cloud of ganja smoke. A recent, (June, 1986) TV Caribbean Festival series included short sequences from the "One Love" celebration. For us it was a unique experience.

The 1979 visit was actually the jam in a sandwich formed by visits to different parts of the United States before and after. Suffice it to say that we first had 9 days in California, after a memorable Great Circle flight over Iceland, Greenland and Hudson Bay, Montana and Utah, to Los Angeles. We spent some days with friends at San Luis Obispo, about mid-way between Los Angeles and San Francisco, and then, after a brief stop in Los Angeles, we flew to Miami to stay a couple of nights with other friends, before flying on to Jamaica. After our 3 weeks in the island we flew to Washington for a short visit and then on by train to New York for a couple of nights. Then by Greyhound to visit more friends from Kaimosi days in up-state New York. With them, a few days later, we went 300 miles by car across country to Boston, where we met three more couples we knew in Kenya days and had a very worth-while tour of the city. Then back to New York by train, and so to our flight home.

Two things struck us, as a result of our American visits. First, we found a tremendous difference in the appearance, character and atmosphere of the 5 major cities we saw. Boston was the one we like best, perhaps, we are told, because it is more English than the others. But it was the car-ride from Oxford,NY and Norwich,NY to Boston, and the visit to Boston itself which made the second of the impacts I have mentioned. I found myself suddenly very aware of the early history of the United States, and when we got home I plunged into reading a whole series of historical and biographical books, not even neglecting fiction such as "The Last of the Mohicans". I also thought afresh about the nature of American history, which I had always felt, with old country conceit, to be so recent and young, - which is why, when we have had American visitors in our home, I have always tried to take them to see the 7th Century Saxon Church at Brixworth, only 8 miles from here. I came to realize, the more I read, that there is a vital element in American history which we here can in no way match, - the concept of extending the Frontier. Perhaps we should be less self-satisfied about the "ancientness" of our heritage, which tends to think of age as a virtue without rival.

4. My Further Education. Third Session. Practical.

When all the results of the 1981 County Council Elections were in
it turned out that of the 68 seats, (to which the Boundary
Commission had reduced the total,) 31 were won by Labour, 31 by
Tories, 4 by Liberals and 2 by Independents. So we had a "hung"
council and the Liberals and Independents would determine who
would take on the administration. That could only be decided at
the first meeting of the Council, a week after the election.
Meanwhile it was clear that my wish to give way to somebody else
after two years would be unfulfilled, especially with such a small
majority. More was to follow when the new Labour Group met on
the Sunday afternoon. I was totally unprepared to hear myself
nominated as Secretary of the Group and elected unopposed.
Leader and Deputy Leader, Chairman and Deputy Chairman, Whips and
Policy Committee were also elected. This meant both that I was
installed as a senior member of the Group and that I had the
responsibility of drafting a list of allocations to the various
committees, as far as possible in line with members' wishes.
This done, the Policy Committee considered the appointment of
Committee Chairmen and Deputy Chairmen, supposing we were to form
the administration. It had been agreed between Labour and Tory
Leaders that whichever of them was voted into office as Leader of
the Council would take all these other offices.

Our Group was approached by the Liberals, who proposed that an
understanding should be reached. The Leader, the Chairman and I
met with them and explained that we should be stating our policy
and that it would be up to the Liberals to decide whether to
support it or not, but that we would enter into no kind of
alliance.

So it was not until the first meeting of the Council that the
crucial decision was made. It was quite a tense, dramatic
occasion. First, the Tories and Liberals combined to instal one
of the Independents as Chairman of the Council, with a
Conservative as Vice-Chairman. Then came 10-minute speeches by
Tory and Labour leaders, followed by a speech by the Liberal
leader, at the conclusion of which he supported tha proposal that
the Labour Leader, Jimmy Kane, should be Leader of the Council.

At a further meeting a week later the new Committees were all
formally constituted and their Chairmen and Deputy Chairmen were
appointed. My own appointments were to the Policy and Resources
Committee and the Education Committee, of which I became Deputy
Chairman. My Chairman, a newcomer to local government and a
fairly recent arrival in the county, was Jack Morrish, who was
also Deputy to the Leader, Jimmy Kane. At each of the three
succeeding Annual Meetings of the Council the Liberals could have
replaced a Labour by a Conservative administration, but did not.

I therefore had quite heavy responsibilities throughout the 4-year life of the Council.

I managed to escape, at the end of the first year, from secretaryship of the Group.   I do not think I am unusual in feeling that party meetings are the least appealing part of life as a councillor.   There are people who, for some reason, seem to be no less interested in being awkward amongst colleagues than they are towards political opponents.   I understand from some Tory fellow-councillors that they have much the same experience ! Even more contentious meetings are those of the County Party, a body which has become much more vocal and more pretentious since the County was first administered by Labour in 1973-1977.   Those of its members who are not County Councillors are mostly people who have never held administrative office as Councillors at any level, and who, without that sort of experience or responsibility, take pleasure in doctrinaire nit-picking, and in sniping at those who have to bear the heat and burden of the day.   Their favourite occupation is opposition, and if the Labour Group itself is not in opposition, (as some would have liked,) then it is the Labour administration   which will be assailed, all in the name of pure Labour doctrine.

This kind of political conflict is wearing, frustrating and unproductive.   It was not in tune with how I saw my own responsibilities.   At one point during our period in office I was one of a number of folk who were interviewed informally on behalf of a well-known Birmingham Councillor, (whose name I forget !) to learn what I thought about "Political Accountability in Education". My answer was simple: the reason I sought in the first place to become a Councillor was to pursue precisely the opposite, namely "Educational Accountability in Politics".

This is why, when I found myself referred to, by the head of one large institution, as one of the politicians, I cringed.   It embarrassed me as much as to be classed, in Kenya days, as a missionary.   The "politicking" aspect of politics is dominated by the spirit of confrontation.   Perhaps I entered the field too late in life.   My own responsibility, during 27 years as a headmaster, had often been to resolve tensions and and differences, not to create or exacerbate them.

However, these views at no time tempted me to break away from the Group or the Party.   Had I been tempted to do so, experience of life on a hung council would have deterred me.

The administration of a hung council has its own peculiar difficulties.   The outcome of every debate is undependable when nobody has a working majority.   So the best of policies are constantly at risk.   A small minority, with rather inflated aspirations, (it made no advance in the 1985 election,) is tempted

to seek limelight and to claim rather more credit than is really
its due when policies are adopted of which both it and the
administration approve.   And this situation pervades every
committee, as well as the Council itself.   So that whilst much of
the work of these is a-political, life can be difficult.   It was
not as though the minority at any time led the thinking of the
Council or actually produced policies which were accepted.   Its
members were in the position where all they could do, in effect,
was to decide whether, at a given moment, they supported Labour
or Conservative proposals.   The Conservative proposals were often
incompatible with other policies being pursued, so that if
Liberals vacillated, confusion resulted.

         *   *   *   *   *   *   *   *   *

Now I remind myself that I am not trying, in this scrap-book, to
write the history of institutions, - even of the County Council
during 1981-1985.   I am trying to describe both the extension of
my own education at different stages and such educational
contribution as I myself was able to make at each stage.

As it turned out, I not only had the opportunity to enter an
important area of education about which I knew too little, but
also to take part in an extended consideration of the basic
purposes of education.   At the same time I was constantly
involved at what I might call the "agenda face" of education.
All this required a great deal of "home-work", especially for
committees and other groups of which I was chairman.

My standing duties included the following :-

Chairman of the Further and Higher Education Sub-Committee.
Member of East Midlands Further Education Council (EMFEC).
Education Committee Chairmen's monthly meeting with Chairman and
                              County Education Officer (CEO).
Member, Finance and General Purposes Sub-Committee.
Member, Schools Sub-Committee.
Governor of each of 5 Colleges.
Chairman, Management Panel, Residential Establishments.
Education Committee representative on Management Committee
                              of Newton Field Centre.
Member of Land and Buildings Sub-Committee of Policy
                        and Resources Committee.
Member of Race Relations Sub-Committee of P.& R. Committee.

"Occasional" duties, some lasting 2, or even 3 years.

Member of Working Party on School Curriculum.
Co-ordinator for appointment of Labour Governors of Schools
                              and Colleges.

Chairman, 12 to 15 times a year, as well as a participant,
    where Secondary schools were concerned, of Panels
    for the appointment of Headteachers.
Member of panels for appointment of Deputy County Education
    Officer and senior posts in Colleges and
    Residential Establishments.
Chairman of upwards of 60 meetings, public and sectional,
    concerning the problem of Falling Rolls
    in Kettering Secondary Schools.
Always being available to attend to problems brought to
    my notice either as Deputy Chairman of the
    Education Committee or as Councillor for Rothwell.

On two occasions I attended the Annual Conference of Local
Education Authorities, and also attended some meetings of other
national bodies.   For instance, I represented EMFEC on the
Examinations Policy Committee of the City and Guilds of London
Institute, and once attended the Bi-ennial National Conference of
the Workers Education Association, as well as sometimes attending
WEA District meetings at Cambridge.

Of all these activities I shall make a selection, concentrating on
those bearing most closely on my main theme.

            *   *   *   *   *   *   *   *   *

The monthly meeting of Education Committee Chairmen had been
instituted during the 1977-1981 Conservative administration.
There was also a regular meeting of Service Committee Chairmen,
dating from the same period.   There were six Education Sub-
Committee Chairmen, - Finance and General Purposes (F&GP), Further
and Higher Education (F&HE), Schools, Accommodation Planning,
Community Youth Advisory and Careers Advisory, that is to say, 4
in addition to the Chairman (F&GP) and myself (F&HE).   I imagine
that these two arrangements were originally set up so that in
each case a powerful inner caucus could decide, in camera, what
the huge majority of those days should be required to support.
No doubt this saved a good deal of time.   In our day the function
of the meetings was bound, with a hung council, to be different.
They were private, and discussions were very free and uninhibited.
This was possible because the meetings were technically at the
invitation of the CEO and not a part of the Council's formal
calendar.   In Committee and Sub-Committee meetings discussion
could not always be so free, since all but a very small part of
them were open to the press and the public.   We really
constituted something like a think-tank, which pre-digested
current and imminent issues.   The meetings were private, but the
Deputy CEO did write detailed minutes of the discussions and
conclusions.   And of course no decisions, other than those
formally delegated to the CEO or the Chairman, could be effective
until they had passed through all the normal committee procedures.

A major benefit of the arrangement was that senior officers and senior committee members came to know and understand one another very well. This was not only very helpful, it was also very enjoyable. I myself learned much by becoming more closely familiar with how the management system worked, and in particular from the friendly relationship which I experienced with the CEO, Michael Henley, and his successive Deputies, Keith Wood-Allum, (who left to become Director of Education in Leicestershire,) and Roy Atkinson, and also, without exception, with all their colleagues at every level of management.

‡ ‡ ‡ ‡ ‡ ‡ ‡ ‡ ‡

The functions of the Education Committee are dealt with by its Sub-Committees before matters reach the full Committee itself. Committee members, co-opted as well as elected, have to be allocated to these sub-committees and Chairmen appointed. My own interest had always been in schools and I had my eye on chairmanship of the Schools S-C. However, the other person likely to be Chairman of either the Schools S-C or F&HE was a Union official for the National Association of Teachers in Further and Higher Education (NATFHE). It therefore seemed wiser for him to take Schools and for me to take F&HE. This meant that I had everything to learn; so although I became an active member of the Schools S-C I devoted myself first of all to this unfamiliar field.

The County has 5 Colleges, and before the first meeting of the Sub-Committee I managed to visit each of them and to learn from each Principal how he viewed the work and problems of his institution. I then established a precedent by becoming a Governor of each of the Colleges, so denying myself any role in the governorship of schools. It would have been invidious to be on the Board of only some colleges. By joining all 5 I was in direct contact with each, and each had direct access to me. This was also, of course, most helpful to me when matters oconcerning any of the colleges appeared on the Sub-Committee agenda; I always had first-hand knowledge of such matters, since I very seldom missed a Board meeting. And knowledge was what I needed, having previously had little more than peripheral involvement with Further Education at any level, despite my 2 years as a student at Tresham College.

Each of the colleges has its own distinctive character and atmosphere.

The most distinctive is, of course, the College of Agriculture at Moulton. It is professionally modern, well abreast of advance in agricultural technology and practice. This is strangely coupled with something of an old-world atmosphere, which has a certain charm, but which will, before long, need to adapt to the way in which present-day young people see the world. I enjoyed meeting the staff and student governors and learning more about agriculture and stock-raising. It was instructive to me to listen to the discussions on the Board, which consisted very largely of farmers.

Wellingborough Technical College changed its name during my time as a Governor, becoming "The Wellingborough College". This was very appropriate, since it is now a College of Further Education having a much wider function than technology. There are, for instance, Business, Secretarial and General Studies courses, with many part-time leisure courses in addition. The college has also developed its own unified curriculum, designed for school leavers. It was good to witness the determination and progressiveness with which the college was adapting to its changed industrial environment and looking forward to considerable development, particularly in physical education, previously un-catered for, as premises released from school use were becoming available.

In 1981 the Northampton College of Further Education seemed to be in a fit of depression. I found myself involved with some of its problems, such as its canteen and its shortage of accommodation. Happily it was successful in extending its operations, using temporary accommodation at Wootton Park for some courses, as well as in inaugurating an annexe at Daventry, meeting a long-standing need in that town. The college has a wide selection of courses on offer, including catering, hair-dressing and beauty culture. Its Drama department, which offers a Foundation course preparing students for entry to Drama School, but also for other careers, is particularly successful. The quality of its productions, with actors of 17 or 18 years of age, is without compare in any of the other colleges in the county, as I know, from seeing a number of them. Now (1986) that more accommodation has at last become available the college seems to have fully emerged from its depression.

Tresham College is the product of a merger between Kettering Technical College and Corby Technical College. The name is that of a family with well-known historical associations in the area as a whole, and therefore neutral as between the two neighbouring towns. The two former colleges were often in uneconomical competition with each other, and it made sense to rationalize provision. The joint provision is now fairly comprehensive, both as regards full-time courses up to G.C.E. A level and equivalents, and part-time vocational and non-vocational courses operating both in day-time and evenings. My course in Art is a good example, paralleled by others in tailoring and dress-making. The college has a particularly good record of response to requests from commerce and industry for special courses, including courses in less commonly taught foreign languages. There are a good many foreign students. Special provision has been introduced for handicapped students, including those with mental handicap or impairment of hearing. A programme of General Studies with carefully designed modular options ensures that the college offers school leavers genuine educational opportunities rather than merely a facility for topping up O-levels and A-levels.

All four of these colleges have responded positively to the need which arose, in those early 1980's, for Y.T.S. courses. The new opportunities, needs and problems presented by the inroduction of the Youth Training Scheme were constantly on the agenda of the F&HE Sub-Committee and I had to devote time to studying them. It was a new field of activity for college teachers, who were faced with students of whom many were at best unenthusiastic. There was a demand for training, and in due course this was provided in courses at a special Centre located at Loddington Hall. Loddington had been adapted from its former use as a residential school for "Moderately Educationally Sub-normal" boys, to provide the possibility of one-week residential courses for YTS students during their 13-week "off-the-job" course; so it had the two functions, which I was able to observe at quite close quarters, since Loddington is only 2 miles from Rothwell.

The largest of the colleges in the county is Nene College, which ranks, after Universities and Polytechnics, amongst "Other Major Institutions", to use the official jargon. It was at Nene that I had most to learn, but also at which I was most consistently drawn into participation. Until 1975 Northampton not only had a College of Further Education, but also a College of Art, a Technical College and at College of Education, (opened in 1972 by Mrs. Margaret Thatcher.) In that year the three last-named were merged into one as Nene College, (pronounced Nenn in Northampton and Neen further down-stream !) It has grown steadily since that time, both by increasing student numbers and by the addition of further functions. First amongst these additional functions was the installation of the Leathersellers' Centre, moved from London and well endowed. It is unique in Europe and attracts students world-wide. 1981 saw the addition of the Blackwood Hodge Management Centre, a prestigious establishment which quickly became self-supporting, but which is an integral part of the college. During my time as a Governor and Chairman of F&HE I took part in a good many meetings leading up to the establishment, jointly with the Northampton Health Authority, of a School of Chiropody. (Incidentally, the reaction to the scheme of the profession's national body was both illuminating and depresssing; Molière could have written a comedy about it !)

The major preoccupation of the college throughout the four years was the future of its degree courses. This was and is controlled by the National Advisory Board and the National Advisory Council for Public Sector Higher Education, which was instituted very soon after our administration came into office. I found myself involved in many discussions about the case for conservation and expansion of our operations, which required to be persistently and convincingly presented. Support for the college's case had to be enlisted, not only from the Education Committee, but also from EMFEC. The college had both success and disappointment arising from the various presentations. The Initial Teacher Training programme was tailored, so as to concentrate on teachers for Primary Schools, but the approved number of admissions was gradually increased, which distinguished the college from the many who were being restricted, or even abolished. The college also won approval to train graduates for a Post-Graduate Certificate of Education. Although Her Majesty's Inspectorate made some difficulties about dove-tailing of some components of B.A., B.Sc and B.Ed. courses, numbers for these have been maintained.

The main disappointment, on the other hand, related to an enterprising and well-prepared proposal to offer an international Business Studies degree course in conjunction with the Fachhochschule of Trier in West Germany. students spending a year of their respective courses in one another's institutions. It is still hoped to overcome the reluctance of H.M.I. to approve of the scheme, and contact with Trier is unbroken.

I have mentioned all these matters, not to present a proper account of them, but to indicate the scope of the activities with which I needed to familiarize myself as far as possible. I will only add that I also found myself drafted into chairmanship of Nene's Buildings Committee, so that I became quite well acquainted with the physical provisions and problems of the college, including problems associated with the installation of a large, expensive and delicate new computer.

Asking myself what specifically educational contribution I made to Nene or any of the other colleges, I am hard put to it to establish any claim at all. Perhaps, if I made any contribution at all, it was as an intermediary between the political and the educational spheres, who either had or acquired tolerable understanding of both.

Through chairmanship of F&HE I had one other interesting opportunity to broaden my experience, since I represented the Education Committee, along with the Chairman of the Committee and the CEO, on the Council of the East Midlands Further Education Committee, which had just been formed by the amalgamation of a former Advisory Council and the parallel Examination organisation. Here I came to know senior councillors and officers from the other four counties in the region, namely Leicestershire, Derbyshire, Nottinghamshire and Lincolnshire, as well as gaining a general view of F&HE provision throughout the region. The Council also included representatives of institutions in the 5 counties. I was allocated to the Council's F&GP committee, and also represented it on the Examinations Policy Committee of the City and Guilds Institute, where I came into contact with still further senior people from all over the country.

As Deputy Chairman of the Education Committee it fell to my lot to be chairman of the small Management Panel of Residential Establishments, with each of which I enjoyed becoming pretty familiar, as regards the staff, the activities and the premises.

Knuston Hall is associated with Adult Education, and runs or provides facilities for courses of all kinds, lasting a day, a week-end or a week. It is a former "stately home", very handsome, and with attractive grounds. It has a very friendly and welcoming atmosphere, provides comfort, (continually being enhanced,) and good meals, and is in constant use throughout the year.

Grendon Hall, another former "stately home", caters for the Community Youth Service, but is also used by independent groups, some of them from abroad, as well as by Scouts, Guides, and so on. Other bodies using it for day or week-end conferences are such groups as headteachers, officers, - even Chief Constables ! For young people accommodation is in small dormitories. The Hall provides much comfort and extremely tasty, weight-building catering. The grounds are extensive, including a swimming pool and tennis courts, and are much used for camping.

Almost in Wales, at Longtown, a dozen or so miles north of Abergavenny, the Education Committee has an Outdoor Education Centre which. like the two halls, is in constant use. It is located in a former farm-house, considerably adapted. Schools and other groups use it by the week, and the Centre has staff expert in their specialities. Experience available can include canoeing, rock-climbing, orientiering, pony trekking and ecological, archaeological and other studies. It has classroom and modest laboratory facilities and is well equipped for the activities I have mentioned. Concerning itself with outdoor activities, it does not, of course, aim to provide comfort similar to that at Grendon, - but users eat very well.

I have already referred to Loddington Hall, which was brought back into commission in connection with Y.T.S. I was involved in this from the beginning and helped to appoint all the staff. This meant also that I was able to take part in a good many of the discussions on how this new kind of work should be undertaken. The official opening of the hall in 1984 was performed by the Duke of Gloucester, who was my neighbour at lunch after the ceremony and the Duke's sampling of some of the activities on display.

One of the most frequent duties which fell to me was taking part in the appointment of headteachers of schools. There are roughly 400 schools in the county and it was not uncommon for as many as 40 new Heads to have to be appointed in the course of a year.

When my successor at Kingswood was being appointed, under the old County Council, I regarded the arangements as very inadequate, although the right candidate was chosen. They consisted simply of an interview of short-listed candidates by a panel of Education Comittee members and School Governors, chaired by the Education Committee Chairman and assisted by the County Education Officer. Several of the Committee members had never been in the school before, and neither they nor the officers had previously met the candidates, unless they happened to know them. I had, however, managed to arrange for the candidates to have lunch with the Chairman of Governors and myself, in an effort to reduce the formality. No other members of the appointing panel accepted either an invitation to join us or an invitation to visit the school beforehand.. I regarded this failure as an insult to the school. The appointment of a Head will affect the tone of a school, perhaps for decades, and will therefore have an important influence on thousands of pupils and their parents. (I have already enlarged upon this in an earlier chapter.) How can any individual presume to appoint a Head to a school of which the individual has no first-hand knowledge ?

When I first became an Education Committee member in 1973 I managed to persuade the Chairman and the officers that candidates and panel members should at least have lunch together, preferably in the school, before interviews took place. By the time I was again on the Committee the procedure had been extended far beyond that modest forward step.

Candidates themselves always had an opportunity to visit the school on a day previous to that of the interviews, and to talk with the Head and the staff. On the morning before formal interviews they had a series of mildly structured talks with individual or pairs of officers. When Heads of Special Schools were being appointed specialist Inspectors were always involved at this stage. When Secondary Heads were being appointed candidates also had talks with two experienced Heads serving in other schools.

The appointing panel always consisted of 4 Education Committee members and 3 Governors. It was only rarely, between 1981 and 1985, that neither the Committee Chairman nor I was available to take the chair. The panel, the candidates, the officers and the Head all had lunch together. Panel members were always encouraged to turn up well before lunch, to see something of the school. (The three Governors already knew it well, of course.)

I myself always made a point of visiting a school some days, at least, in advance, so that I could talk with the Head, tour the school and meet the staff.

After lunch the panel met with officers and inspectors, who reported on their morning interviews, and the panel then decided how many to interview, - sometimes all the candidates, sometimes as few as 2 or 3. At the conclusion of the afternoon, whoever was appointed, candidates commonly said how much they appreciated the way in which things had been done.

The appointments involved a good deal of preliminary homework, in order to study the applications themselves, which were often more than a little wordy. Conduct of the formal interviews, which usually lasted half an hour or more, demanded concentration on my part, and discretion in bringing in panel members at appropriate moments. When interviews were over the succeeding discussions, which were assisted by the two officers present, were sometimes very delicate, and required the exercise of a certain diplomacy, particularly in making sure that Governors were satisfied, - but there were also a good many times when it was quite clear who should have the post. This exercise, many times repeated, kept me on my toes, and I like to think that I learned from it. And it had one very pleasant spin-off effect, namely, that I paid purposeful and meaningful visits to schools all over the county. They included schools of similar size and status, great and small, main-stream and special, rural and urban. But the nature of schools is such that it would have been quite impossible to confuse one of them with another.

*   *   *   *   *   *   *   *   *

The most taxing of all my experiences as Deputy Chairman of the Education Committee occurred between 1983 and 1985.

In recent years the effect of a falling birth-rate has been working its way through the school system, reducing the number of pupils in schools, first the Primary Schools and in the mid-80's the Secondary Schools. The tendency has not been uniform. In Rothwell, for instance, as the result of an extensive house-building programme and the immigration of young families, numbers have actually risen, and the two Primary Schools and the Secondary School have been over-crowded, with a consequent need for school building programmes. However, in most of the conurbations of the county numbers have contracted, and so provoked questions about the economic and educational viability of the number of schools being maintained. Early in our period of office we found ourselves dealing with the closing stages of adjustments being made in Corby, where two of the previously existing secondary schools were being absorbed into a third, with a new name.

In Wellingborough the problem was dealt with by forming, out of an existing boys' school and an existing girls' school, a new co-educational school, with the addition of some new buildings. The process involved a great deal of consultation with staff, governors, parents and the general public, and of course strong feelings were aroused. However, that amalgamation was successfully carried through, and the premises of the boys' school were gradually made available to the Wellingborough College.

In 1983 the County Education Officer asked the Committee to face up to two other problems. The first was in Northampton, where numbers were falling in the Middle Schools (9-13 age-range) nearest the centre of the town, although they were rising in some of the schools in the new Eastern District. The second was that rolls were falling, and would for some time continue to fall, in Secondary Schools in Kettering.

Since both problems would need to be tackled in depth, and simultaneously, Jack Morrish undertook to chair the necessary meetings in Northampton, in partnership with the Deputy County Education Officer and other officers, and asked me to chair consultations in Kettering. The problem had first been brought to the attention of Education Committee Chairmen early in 1983; approval for the suggested solution was not reached until the County Council meeting of November, 1984, - and follow-up meetings continued for the rest of my term of office. I was working closely throughout that period with the County Education Officer, the Assistant County Education Officer for Schools, Richard Alcock, the Assistant Education Officer for the Corby and Kettering area, Alan Wilkinson, and a Senior Inspector, Alastair Broadbent. The Education Committee had appointed an all-party Working Party of 8 Committee members, including one teacher representative, which met a good number of times, also under my chairmanship, but including Jack Morrish.

It would be pointless to attempt a blow-by-blow account of the controversy, but it is worth outlining the nature of the problem and the consultative steps that were taken.

Kettering had six Comprehensive Secondary Schools, - 3 co-educational and 2 single-sex County Schools and a co-educational Voluntary Aided Church of England School. It was clear, when year-groups (cohorts) of children passing through Primary Schools were considered, along with statistics of children already born, but not yet of school age, (in other words, the projected number of admissions to secondary schools in the next 11 years,) that the total number would be reduced by about one sixth over that period. As numbers in the schools were already in decline the problem was obviously going to arise of how to keep all six schools viable, from the point of view of breadth of curriculum, both at Sixth Form and middle-school levels.

Should the number of schools be reduced ? If so, how? By amalgamation or amalgamations ? By closure or closures ? At post-16 level, incidentally, the problem was accentuated by the existence of Tresham College, which diverted a good many students from the schools. The Working Party was required to carry out detailed consultations in Kettering, to formulate proposals for dealing with the problem, and to report to the Education Committee, which would, in turn, report to the County Council, where a decision on the matter would have to be made.

Alan Wilkinson had deeply researched the problem and provided a document which set it out in very great detail. Possible solutions were described and the advantages and disadvantages of each were fairly set out; but none of these was designated as the best answer.

The first step in the consultative process took place at the end of June, 1983, when officers and I met the Heads and Chairmen of Governors of the six schools. Copies of a first draft of Alan Wilkinson's document were provided and we outlined the consultative steps we proposed to take as soon as schools re-opened in September. These were :-

In each school we would, on successive evenings, meet governors and staff. These meetings were to be spread over 3 weeks, and followed by a meeting with the Heads and Chairmen of Governors of Primary Schools in Kettering. In the following fortnight there would be a public meeting in each of the six schools, for parents both of pupils in the school and of pupils who might be entering the school in future. An unlimited supply of copies of an up-dated version of the basic document would be available.

Each of the Governors' meetings was attended by myself and either the C.E.O., the A.C.E.O., or the A.E.O., and chaired by the Chairman of Governors. The staff meetings were chaired by myself, accompanied, again, by one or more of the officers. At each of the public meetings I took the chair and was joined by several other members of the Working Party as well as 3 or 4 senior officers. The number attending these meetings ranged from about 250 to about 650; the largest one overflowed into an adjacent hall, but was kept in touch by Closed Circuit TV, enabling people there both to hear, see and participate in the meeting. I also attended a number of other meetings, for instance, with the Teachers' Unions and Tresham College Governors. The C.E.O. and I were also invited to explain the problem to the Policy and Resources Committee of the Kettering Borough Council. The officers concerned had a good many other meetings at professional level, (in this context I was no professional), with Heads and other staff.

Well before the end of all these consultations it was clear that no consensus was going to be achieved, and that feelings in each of the schools were very strongly defensive. Action Groups sprang up and got publicity. At least one of these sought support from the Kettering M.P., Roger Freeman. I therefore asked him for an opportunity to explain to him what was going on, and he came to my house, so that I was able to do just that. He was as anxious as I not to appear to take sides between schools.

The problem was, of course, that each school aroused strong loyalty in almost everybody asociated with it, as well as experiencing the fears that inevitably arise when the future is uncertain. It was complicated also by the unfortunate geographical distribution of the schools, only one of which, the most recently (and still incompletely) built, was in the north of the town, whereas several were virtually clustered in the south.

The reasons why each of the schools was resistant to any change involving itself may be stated briefly as follows :-

The two single-sex schools had each only recently experienced the double trauma of merging two schools and "going comprehensive". The two mergers had involved the four longest-established schools in the town, including the ancient Boys' Grammar School and the Girls' High School. People in both schools realized that one possible solution to the latest problem would have been a merger of the two into one co-educational school. Their main objections to this were two-fold: first, they had already had to cope with too much recent change; and secondly, they argued for preserving the option of single-sex education.

A co-educational school situated only a short distance from the Boys' School, and on the edge of an estate which had grown a great deal in recent years, had been in the doldrums for some time. But the appointment of a new Head, leading a keen staff, was notably re-vitalising the school, with consequent support from parents.

At the southern edge of the town, not very far from the Boys' and Girls' Schools, a new school had been opened in the middle 70's and was by now well established, with a strong neighbourhood flavour. But housing development in the vicinity had been less than expected, and the school was looking to extend its "catchment area".

At the other end of the town a new school had recently been opened and was still in process of growth and development, with a requirement for more accommodation. It had a very strong neighbourhood flavour, and no lack of children growing up within easy distance. As it was the most recently provided of the schools and not yet complete, the staff and parents feared that they might be closely involved in any approved change. People often said that there had not been a case for providing the school. In fact, it would have been truer to say, with hindsight, that the real mistake was to build the additional school in the south of the town.

The Voluntary Aided School, like the Boys' and Girls' Schools, was not a neighbourhood school. Originally a Secondary Modern School, in the middle 70's it had become comprehensive along with the other schools. By 1983 it claimed to have become the most popular school in the town. This was partly because it had taken on something of an academic bias, and was therefore attractive to parents whose children might, in earlier years, have aimed at their children's admission to one of the two Grammar Schools. The school laid great stress on its status as a church school, and it was understood that priority for admission was assigned to regular church-going families. The number of applications rose to a level above the average for the 6 schools, which implied that better than one in six Kettering families were church-goers. (So presumably the Anglican churches in the town have overflowing congregations.) Secure in its Voluntary Aided status, this school was anxious for a reduction in the number of other schools, so that it might have a larger intake, and a better opportunity to satisfy its aspirations.

After the series of school meetings was over, and before the Working Party met to consider its report, there was one more meeting with representatives of the Governors of the 6 schools. The absence of consensus was very apparent, but towards the end of the meeting, Miss Lake, Head of the Girls' School, threw out a challenging question : "Why can somebody not use some imagination in addressing the problem ?"

Some days later, in opening the meeting of the Working Party, I expressed doubt as to the possibility of taking any action which would not create an even more difficult situation. Perhaps we should let the matter rest for a year or two, and see whether parents would "vote with their children's feet", and so indicate what might be best. I had reckoned without Michael Henley, the C.E.O., who explained that he had accepted Miss Lake's challenge, and wished to propose a fresh way of thinking about the issue, calling it "An Alternative Approach". He sketched out what he had in mind, and promised a fully considered presentation of the idea at a W.P. meeting in early December.

The idea assumed the continued existence of all 6 schools, but had three important features : -

First, the schools should share together in the provision of a curriculum which would offer pupils a complete range of options, particularly in the middle-school and Sixth Form years. This would involve much curricular development and the used of up-to-date learning techniques which had so far been under-exploited.

Secondly, the scheme would stimulate both increase and rationalisation of voluntary input into the schools' activities, (other than class-room teaching), by parents and possibly other friends of the schools.

And thirdly, admission numbers would need to be regulated, so that each school had a roughly equal share.

The Working Party agreed, and in the new year the idea was presented at several meetings of Governors, Heads and other teachers in Kettering, and then at two large public meetings, held one after another on one evening in early February.

In the succeeding weeks each of the schools proceeded to explore the possibilities of the Voluntary Input Plan, (V.I.P.) and I chaired meetings at which notes were compared. A working party of Deputy Heads (Curriculum) was established, chaired by Alastair Broadbent, to consider how the curricular idea might be realized.

At the beginning of June the Education Committee's Working Party met to approve its report, which was presented to the Committee in mid-June, and agreed. However, when it reached the County Council in July it ran into opposition and cries of "Not enough consultation". But it was not rejected. Instead, the Education Committee was instructed to carry out further consultations and report to the County Council meeting in November, when a decision would be made.

A further series of 11 public meetings did take place in September, 6 of them in Secondary Schools and 5 in Primary Schools. Jack Morrish chaired 5 of these, since we ran 2 meetings on the same evening, except in one case, where we anticipated more difficulty. None of the meetings held simultaneously was very well attended, but several County Councillors did respond to an encouragement to them to hear first-hand what Kettering people thought. During this round the strongest support for the scheme came from the schools which had been most disturbed when the first series took place. After the Education Committee had again endorsed the scheme it was agreed in the County Council that it should have a trial run of 3 years from September, 1985.

This enabled further progress to be made, including the appointment of a Co-ordinator, who would have parity of status with the Heads, and would be in charge of the new Curriculum

Development Unit (CDU).   In connexion with the CDU a series of
secondments of teachers was arranged, so that particular ideas
could be researched.   Tim Bartlett was appointed in February, to
take up his post on 1st May, but in the meantime he was able to
attend some evening meetings.

I have given only the sketchiest outline of all the discussions in
which I was involved during almost two years.   But here again, I
am not writing the story of an institution.   What I have written
is to illustrate the need I had to learn how to be diplomatic.
For instance, during many of the meetings which I chaired I heard
people in the schools put forward arguments with which I quite
strongly disagreed, but I managed to bridle my tongue and not get
personally involved in challenging those arguments.   I did have
the feeling, in the end, that I had been reasonably successful in
acting as pilot through a pretty stormy passage, with consequent
boost, I suppose, to my ego.   Meanwhile, officers and senior staff
in schools were toiling patiently and unremittingly in the boiler
room, to keep the craft under way.

As I write, early in 1987, the scheme has been in operation for
four terms, and an independent, professional, appraisal of the
work of the first year has been made available to people
involved in it.   Although I am no longer involved I am of course
still interested, and have been able to learn something of the
development which is taking place.

The striking thing is that the curricular advance being undertaken
by Kettering schools, both individually and in collaboration, is
really achieving educational importance in its own right, quite
apart from the issue which provoked it, - namely falling rolls in
the town's schools.   The title "Alternative Approach" originated to
suggest an alternative to the thought that falling rolls should
involve the surgical device of closure or merger.   Early on we
wondered whether another title might be better, but none was
found.   What is now emerging is that the title is far more
significant than most people, (except, I am sure, Michael Henley,)
at first supposed.   The scheme is now concerned with an
alternative approach to the CURRICULUM, not merely to an
administrative problem.   Indeed, supposing, after 3 years,
economic considerations seemed to dictate administrative surgery,
that would be no reason to abandon the educational project.
Further, what is being achieved and learned will be relevant and
applicable, not only in Kettering, but also in other conurbations,
as well within as outside the county.   Incidentally, it re-
inforces the defence of schools when they are menaced by the
concept of Sixth Form or Tertiary Colleges, both of which I regard
as little more than curricular emporia, surely almost devoid of
the wider educational work done in good 11-18 and 13-18 schools.
What I understand by that assertion will, I hope, become apparent
in the next chapter, entitled "Study Period".

Not all my experiences between 1981 and 1985 were strictly such as could be defined as part of my education (in either sense). But since experience has, it is to be hoped, an inherent educational function, some are perhaps worth mentioning.

Throughout the four years there were many occasional problems in the education service to which I was asked to give my attention. Often these had to do with accommodation in schools, and I paid visits or attended meetings at schools in Towcester and Wellingborough, for instance. The Rothwell schools concerned me particularly, of course, as "on my patch", though I was not a governor of any of them. I was always made most welcome in them all and used such influence as I had at Northampton to try to meet their needs.

I have mentioned that I was always ready to give what help I could in meeting any needs arising in Rothwell which had a County Council aspect. At an early stage there was serious highway flooding in one part of the town, - a problem which had existed for decades. I was able to question and prod and gather representatives of appropriate authorities on the spot, - with the result that remedial work was undertaken and the problem solved.The most important of Rothwell's most immediate problems on which I was in a position to act was the need to provide a long-overdue new library and release the historic Market House for other use. Once I had found a way to persuade the County Council that the new building should be the top priority, as far as County Libraries were concerned, I went on to encourage the Rothwell Town Council to consider what the future of the Market House should be. Both the building of the new library and the discussions about the Market House were very protracted. It was not until 31st July, 1986 that the extremely fine new library finally opened on the site of the old Rothwell Grammar School. Meanwhile a Trust had been established to care for the Market House and other historic parts of Rothwell. The Member of Parliament, Mr. Roger Freeman, was most helpful, and at my suggestion the Chief Executive of the County Council and the Estates Manager had both taken part in discussions with the Town Council.

Throughout the four years I was frequently in attendance at the monthly meetings of the Town Council, to report on County matters to the Council and to hear the views of Rothwell Councillors.

The other major long-term problem concerning Rothwell was the need for a by-pass, which seemed bound to be intensified when the new A1/M1 Link Road was built in a few years time. This was much discussed in the Town Council and public meetings and at an exhibition about the Link Road project. In all of these I was involved. But a solution still lies, unfortunately, in the future.

4. My Further Education.   Third Session.   Study Period.

The years 1981 to 1985 provided me with a very welcome but
totally unexpected experience of a purely "two-way-educational"
character.   It was both stimulating and enjoyable, and quite
different from all the other activities of those years.

Early in 1981 the Secretary of State for Education had published
a booklet entitled "The School Curriculum".   At about the same
time the Schools Council published a similar document entitled
"The Practical Curriculum".   In October, through Circular 6/81, he
required that each Local Education Authority should : -

"(a) review its policy for the school curriculum in its area, and
     its arrangements for making that policy known to all
     concerned;

 (b) review the extent to which current provision in the schools
     is consistent with that policy; and

 (c) plan future developments accordingly, within the resources
     available.

    In taking these actions local education authorities should
consult governors of schools, teachers and others concerned."

Different LEA's reacted to 6/81 in different ways.   Some
delegated to their Chief Education Officers the task of drafting a
response, for possible amendment and subsequent endorsement by
members.   Others invited each of the schools for which they were
responsible to send in an account of its practice and thinking, so
that the LEA could then digest and collate these responses in a
single report for the Secretary of State.

In Northamptonshire the matter was tackled in a manner which was
probably unique.   Even several months before Circular 6/81 a
Working Party had been set up, to study the two curriculum
documents published earlier in the year by DES (Department of
Education and Science) and SC.   This W.P. included both officers
and members of the Education Committee.   The officers were the
County E.O., the Deputy C.E.O., the Chief Inspector and the Senior
Inspectors for Secondary and Primary Schools, supplemented, from
time to time, by other officers.   The committee members were the
Chairman and myself, one other Labour Councillor, 3 Conservative
and 1 Independent Councillors and a teacher member of the
committee.   So when 6/81 came along the basis on which a
response could be considered was already in being.   In fact the
Working Party met for two hours or so every month for about 3
years, as well as taking part in a great many seminars and other
consultative gatherings.

In December 1983 Circular 8/83 required LEA's to send in, by the end of April, 1984, a detailed account of how they had proceeded in response to 6/81, both in considering the nature and resourcing of the curriculum and in consulting with "heads and other teachers, governors, parents and other interested parties in the local community." A punctual and circumstantial response was sent to the DES by the C.E.O., with the full support of the W.P.

The labours of the Working Party culminated in the presentation to the County Council, at its final meeting in April, 1985, of a very handsome 68-page booklet, generously and attractively illustrated, with the title:

The School Curriculum
A Framework of Principles
The Northamptonshire View

(to which I shall refer as the "Principles").

The work of those years is significant in three major respects. First, the final product is the fruit of consultations on an unprecedented scale with a very large number of individuals, communities and organisations. Secondly, the document itself embodies stimulating, contemporary and relevant educational thinking. And thirdly, the document will for some time to come provide everybody concerned with guide-lines which can be used to appraise current practice and plan future development in schools.

‡   ‡   ‡   ‡   ‡   ‡   ‡   ‡   ‡

It would be ridiculous for me attempt to summarise the "Principles", a document which is itself something of a distillation of hours of talk and pages, indeed stacks, of written material, - not to mention the contents of many waste-paper-baskets. But as I was personally involved, purely as an individual 'educationist', (I had regressed, by this time, from being an 'educator' !), and not in a restrictive representative capacity, some account of the experience of participation falls quite unquestionably within the terms of reference which I have set for this 'autobiographical scrap-book'.

At the outset we were provided, of course, with copies of the two 1981 booklets, and then we had a series of presentations of thinking about the curriculum as a whole, and the various people and interests which had a bearing upon it. A diagram was exhibited, which showed the curriculum at the centre of a whorl of arrows pointing inwards, which represented the forces and people acting upon it. I was reminded of a thought I had often expressed, namely, that being a head was rather like being at the hub of a wheel, the spokes of which, representing all kinds of interests, people and concerns, all had sharpened points, like a collection of goads, all directed at the head. This image is not a bad one, but I have to confess that it took me a little while to shake myself free of it and accept the one with the curriculum at the centre.

One might see this as another small strand in my education. But once I had adjusted and we all got our teeth into the matter in hand, I was able, like everybody else, to take a relevant part in the discussions and debates which arose out of the documents presented to us. The atmosphere was entirely agreeable, and we all expressed ourselves without inhibition as we helped to forge each section of the final document. We argued about the ideas, and about the sequence of their presentation; we argued about words and sometimes about syntax and style. I enjoyed myself greatly.

I must not give the impression that the work of producing the "Principles" was done by the Working Party alone. The W.P. was the filter through which the work of a great number of people passed before the final product emerged. For instance, our thinking was stimulated by visits to two schools, in particular, which had radically different curricular arrangements, both of them based on tenable ideas, and each of them with features which attracted us and others which did not. But both schools were continually giving serious and detailed consideration to their philosophy and their practice. Furthermore, staff and governors of schools were not the only groups to whom presentations were made and from whom comments were welcomed. These included several gatherings of carefully assorted students, who were invited to give their views of school and the curriculum. These particular gatherings were conducted, rather than chaired, by Michael Henley himself, the C.E.O., who obviously greatly enjoyed them. We also gave a presentation to representatives of the ethnic minorities in the county, who were naturally interested in the county's attitude and practice where they were concerned. Their comments, some of them fairly astringent, stimulated quite lively discussion in the W.P., where it was quite difficult to formulate statements which directed attention to the need for vigilance and understanding without being too specific. The discussions were also made available to a wide range of organisations, and specific seminars were arranged for the Northamptonshire Chamber of Commerce and Industry and for the staff of Nene College.

The final document did, of course, take account of all these discussions, as well as of the further thinking of the W.P. itself. For instance, the 18 Principles originally formulated for Secondary Schools were re-cast, both as to wording and order, and one of them was discarded.

We did, of course, spend time in considering the various components of the curriculum, namely the subjects or groups of subjects on the time-table. We discussed in broad outline how they should be taught, - and in some cases whether their inclusion was necessarily justified. The latter included, for instance, sex education, political education and Latin. The outcome of these discussions found its expression in the final document with all its implications, and it is not my purpose to duplicate that in any way. But there is one aspect of the curriculum to which we devoted much thought, and on which I had personal views which I was able to put forward. This is what is known as "The Hidden Curriculum".

The "Principles" quote, (p.11) the Taylor Report of 1977, - "A New Partnership for our Schools" - as follows :-

"Our preferred concept of the school curriculum effectively comprehends the sum of experiences to which a child is exposed at school."

Not the range of subjects studied, be it noted, but "the sum of experiences."

"The Hidden Curriculum" is a phrase of quite recent vintage, of which I myself only became aware after joining the W.P., but it very well corresponded to many thoughts already in my mind. It so happened, quite apart from the Curriculum W.P., that I had occasion to sort out my ideas for the purpose of addressing, in February, 1983, a Day Conference in Norwich on "The Secondary School Curriculum into the '80's and beyond". This resulted from a chance circumstance, namely that a personal friend of ours, Jane Petzing, formerly a teacher in Rothwell, was the acting Co-ordinator of the Teachers' Centre at Norwich, and was also a personal friend of Richard Denton, the producer of a 9-part BBC TV series entitled "Kingswood, a Comprehensive School", which had been shown in the previous autumn. The other two invited speakers at the seminar were Richard Denton and Brian Tyler, who had succeeded my successor as Head of Kingswood. Practically all teachers had viewed the series, so it was a good peg on which to hang the seminar.

This, of course, is why I remarked that when I left Kingswood in 1973 Kingswood did not leave me. So I must digress briefly to refer to the series itself. A year or two previously Richard Denton had produced for the BBC a series on Radley, a Public School. As a counterpart to this it was decided to do a series about a Comprehensive School in the public sector. In due course Kingswood was selected and Richard Denton and his crew spent well over half a year in the school.

When the series was shown it turned out that Kingswood was very recognizable as the school I knew, very acceptably developed since I retired. Reactions at local, county and national level were, of course, lively. Some of the episodes were as rivetting (or otherwise) as a soap opera. One of them was amongst the best and most moving TV sequences one could wish to see, as the crew accompanied a group of pupils receiving remedial teaching when they went with their teachers for a week on the Welsh coast. A TV programme must inevitably embody a significant element of entertainment value. It is thus not really surprising that the producer's selection of aspects of the school to be presented did not correspond particularly well with some of its aspects which those associated with it would regard as amongst its most significant comprehensive features. There was also too much about staff, (the soap opera syndrome), and too little about the nitty-gritty of pupils' experience. Apart from the moving episode which I have mentioned there was very litle to indicate how a Comprehensive School differed from a Grammar School. The social atmosphere of the school did, however, come across as very different from that found, for instance, in old-style Grammar Schools.

So when I came to address the Norwich gathering of Deputy Heads in the presence of Richard Denton and Brian Tyler I felt that I must try to present a more rounded picture of the Comprehensive School. (But I must stress, in passing, that I had great admiration for Richard Denton's work, and we got on very well together.) In fact, much of what I said need not be repeated, since I have already recorded it on earlier pages in writing about Kingswood. And much of it relates to what, in later years, I came to recognize as the "Hidden Curriculum".

The importance of this was still in my mind when the Working Party met for a whole day in March, together with the members of the Education Committee's Inspectorate, and we discussed, amongst other things, papers prepared by members of the W.P. My own contribution ran to 4 pages and included much which I have already mentioned. However, some of what I wrote is an extension of earlier thinking, provoked by arguments which had taken place. What here follows is part quotation and part summary of that paper.

"There is a phrase which has frequently popped into my mind during the discussions we have been having. It is 'lâ trahison des clercs'. I fear that I cannot remember where it comes from, or what it was originally supposed to mean. But for me it crystallizes the sort of temptation into which I believe we have been falling, judging by the interim report we are now considering.

"To me the phrase suggests the tendency to intellectualize and organize, and to delude ourselves into thinking that by disciplines of this kind we can successfully define a good curriculum."

(Perhaps it might be rendered as "The Academic Fallacy" ?)

"But a curriculum, like a school, is for people, and people are sentient as well as intellectual entities. And if their feelings are wrong, then the operation of their brains may have unfortunate, even disastrous, effects. Conversely, if their feelings are right, these may more than compensate for any lack of intellectual power or achievement.

"This is why the 'hidden curriculum' is of such vital importance, because the 'hidden curriculum' is the heart of a school, which characterizes it as an organism, and not merely an organisation. It is what makes a school 'tick'.

"Nevertheless, it is not something which just 'happens'. It has to be worked on. The character of a community depends on how all the people within it relate to one another, and relationships are things that can indeed be worked upon by the combined operation of brains and sensitivity.

"If our ideas about syllabuses, time-tables, options and so forth are good, we must be careful to ensure that the whole life of the school is 'in tune' with those ideas."

I referred to a diagram taken from the Schools Council Science Project, which had been borrowed by the Northamptonshire booklet on "Guidelines for the Humanities". This diagram displays 9 objectives for pupils studying science. I suggested that some of these were quite interesting if, as well as applying them to the areas of the academic curriculum, you applied them to the school as a community of young people growing up in the company of a smaller group of adults. I took two examples :-

Objective: "'Communicating'. In what direction(s) does communication take place in assemblies ?"

Objective: "'Posing questions and devising experiments to answer them '. Can this be applied, for instance, to rules, routines and other aspects of social order in the school ?"

I continued :

"What if the school society is seen in a different way from the subject areas? Is there an in-built discord ?"

I then mentioned that in 1965 I had found myself as the head of a school which had no pupils, no staff and no parents, ... and, of course, no curriculum.

I went on to say that in starting the school I had been much concerned, not only with the academic aspects of the curriculum, but with what I later knew as the "hidden curriculum". I went on to give a very brief account of the Kingswood story, similar to the longer account on earlier pages. I referred, in particular, to the determination to give personal relations the first importance, to the open-mindedness of the founding staff, to the avoidance of hierarchy both on the staff and amongst pupils, and to the form of school assembly.

I then returned to my view of the head's role, saying : "The way the head sees this can certainly mar a school and its 'hidden curriculum', whereas although the head alone cannot make it, at least he/she can ensure that a good 'hidden curriculum' has a real chance of being established. You cannot achieve a good 'hidden curriculum' by direction, but only by enabling everybody to participate in forming it.

"In a nutshell, it is my view that a head should not be a director, but an enabler. The head should enable the teachers to do their work effectively, enable the pupils to learn what they need to learn, and enable all other members of the school to feel integrated within it, - including, especially, parents and governors.

"The whole purpose of the school is to assist pupils to grow up. This includes the development of knowledge and skill in the various classroom activities they pursue, but also their development as responsible and sensible members of their community.

"There is an old saying: 'Knowledge comes, but wisdom lingers'. This may sound a melancholy thought. It should, in my view, be our purpose to cultivate wisdom at the earliest possible age. In the light of some of our earlier discussions I prefer to re-word the saying :- 'Knowledge comes (and goes), but wisdom lingers on'. And some of our pupils, I fancy, may acquire more wisdom than knowledge. And to me, wisdom is what the 'hidden curriculum' is all about.

"I have sometimes been tempted to declare:- 'Seek ye first the hidden curriculum, and many of your problems will become much less daunting.'

"But perhaps a corollary would sound a little less presumptuous :-
'Unless you have a sound hidden curriculum, the solution to many
of your problems, and the long-term success of much of your work,
will almost certainly elude you.'

"It would certainly be true to say that the 'hidden curriculum' of
the school I have mentionend played a large part in enabling it to
change from a Grammar to a Comprehensive School."

                 ‡   ‡   ‡   ‡   ‡   ‡   ‡   ‡   ‡

One other experience in my last months on the County Council is
worth mentioning briefly.   It had recently become the practice of
the Department of Education and Science to carry out inspections
of the entire educational provision being made by individual
authorities.   Northamptonshire was an early subject, and for some
months a large team of Her Majesty's Inspectors paid visits to
schools and colleges and talked with countless teachers, students,
officers and other people.   By February, 1985 their report was
ready for publication.   Before this actually occurred some senior
people in the county were able to see it, and a group of about
half a dozen, including me, entered the portals of Elizabeth House
to meet the Secretary of State himself, Sir Keith Joseph, with Her
Majesty's Chief Inspector and several exalted civil servants.   We
were amiably received and had an hour's conversation about the
report.   There were some criticisms, but the general view of our
work was favourable and we received hints that it was the best
report of its kind so far.   It was made clear to Sir Keith that
we should be using the report alongside our "Principles", as
bench-marks for the appraisal of our future practice and as
reference documents in In-Service Training (INSET) programmes.

Actual publication took place a few days later, and in late
February the Education Committee had a special meeting, at which
the whole array   of HMI's concerned gave a presentation of the
report, with some discussion afterwards.   I have to confess that
the presentation itself was unimpressive.   It was only too
evident that the pedagogic techniques of most of the HMI's were
very rusty.   There was even one literary lapse in the report
itself.   A few days later I sent a rather cheeky letter to
Elizabeth House.   I quote :-

"In the offices of Northamptonshire County Council I enjoy a
certain notoriety as what, (when, as ever, they are being polite,)
Education Officers call 'a vigilant proof-reader'.

"So when your report came the Chief Executive asked me whether I
had found any spelling mistakes in it.   I had not !

"It was only while you were presenting the report to the Education Committee that I looked with closer attention at the penultimate sentence in paragraph 178 (p.42). Mentors and mentees ?

"There is a verb 'to ment' ? - I ment, thou mentest; we should have mented, etc.? Presumably a mentee, having had a chance to try practising what he/she had been mented to do, would subsequently, like an airman being de-briefed after a mission, be thoroughly de-mented ?

"As befits such an august body as Her Majesty's Inspectorate, this is the most delightfully sophisticated howler I have detected. As you will recollect, Mentor was, in fact, the name of the tutor, (actually Minerva in disguise,) leading young Telemachus, at the behest of his mother, Penelope, in search of the errant Ulysses.

"Sorry, no menting, no mentees !

"But no offence meant."

A few days later I received an ackowledgement in 2½ lines, - which included two more slips !

It is nice that HMI's are so human, and no longer such ogres as they appeared in days long ago. My own experience of them in my earlier days as a head was very agreeable, since they were invariably sympathetic, understanding and helpful. More recently, perhaps because of my own advancing years, I have had the feeling that some of them are less wise and less understanding than their predecessors. Perhaps they are over-worked, and doubtless to-day's educational scene is as kaleidoscopic for them as for everybody else, so that it is hard to keep it in focus.

5. Withdrawal symptoms ?

Approaching what amounted to my second retirement, since I refrained from standing again for election to the County Council, I was sometimes asked : "What will you do with yourself ?"

I said I thought I might have some withdrawal symptoms. In fact, I had virtually none.   It was splendid to be no longer at the beck and call of an engagement diary, and to be able, for instance, to go away from home at almost any time without neglecting any duty.

Yet both Mary and I still have plenty to do.   We have been able to travel, - and this has often been a stimulus to study a bit of history or of a foreign language.   We have been able to give our garden more of the attention it deserves.   Although neither of us is a performer, we have been able to hear more and more music, especially the classical concerts in the splendid new concert-hall in Northampton, where we always meet a good number of friends. I have enjoyed coming to grips with a word processor as I have put this scrap-book together.   And since the word processor doubles as a home computer I am hoping to plunge, shortly, into studying that.   We are both attending some Adult Education classes.   And our three children are all continually educating us whenever they get the chance.   Peter continues as our constant adviser in everything which is in any way practical.   (For some years now he has been an expert audiologist, and Head of Service for the Hearing-Impaired in Devonshire.)   Paul, now a potter, has given us appreciation of his craft.   He married Angelika Sahla and they live in London.   Ruth, of course, has 4 times lured us to Jamaica and once, also, to Haiti.

So, withdrawal symptoms ?   No!

The end of "One Man's Education" ?   Not yet !

Abbreviations used in the text.

A.F.B.M.	American Friends' Board of Missions, Richmond, Ind.
A.S.S.P.	Assistant Senior Prefect.
C.O.S.C.	Cambridge Overseas School Certificate.
D.C.	District Commissioner.
D.O.	District Officer.
D.Y.M.	Dini Ya Msambwa. (see p.52)
E.A.Y.M.	East Africa Yearly Meeting of Friends.
F.A.M.	Friends Africa Mission.
F.S.C.	Friends Service Council, London.
H.S.C.	Higher School Certificate.
K.A.D.U.	Kenya African Democratic Union.
K.A.N.U.	Kenya African National Union.
K.A.P.E.	Kenya African Preliminary Examination.
K.A.S.S.E.	Kenya African Secondary Schools Examination.
Leg.Co.	Legislative Council. (Pre-Independence Parliament)
London Y.M.	London Yearly Meeting. (English Society of Friends).
P.C.	Provincial Commissioner.
P.E.O.	Provincial Education Officer.
S.S.P.	Senior School Prefect.
T.E.A.	Teachers for East Africa. (see p.95.)

Glossary.

banda	a roof without walls, to provide shade or shelter.
baraza	a meeting of "Pow-wow" character.
boma	a corral or enclosure for stock; also used to refer to the administrative area of a Location. In colonial days the Kenya Girls'High School was jokingly called "the heifer boma".
Harambee	Kenya national motto meaning "All together-HEAVE !"
hoteli	African bar, cafe.
jembe	a large hoe, serving also as a spade.
Mzee	Old Man, Elder. A term of respect, can be used rather like "Sir". Also used as Kenyatta's title.
panga	universally used cutting tool, a machete, rather like a Roman broadsword.
The Reserve.	A term used in colonial days to refer to areas "reserved" for Africans, and not available for "European" settlement.
shamba	a farm or garden.
sufuria	a saucepan with a flange but no handle, used for cooking, fetching water, etc. (see fig.17)
ugali	maize-meal cooked to a stiff consistency, staple diet in Kenya, also known as "posho" (corrupted from "portion" or ration issued by employer).
Uhuru	Freedom, Independence.
Uji	Maize breakfast gruel.

INDEX

253

C₂